Must We Defend Nazis?

MUST WE DEFEND NAZIS?

Hate Speech, Pornography, and the New First Amendment

Richard Delgado and Jean Stefancic

New York University Press
New York and London

NEW YORK UNIVERSITY PRESS
New York and London

Library of Congress Cataloging-in-Publication Data
Delgado, Richard.
Must we defend Nazis? : hate speech, pornography, and the new
first amendment / Richard Delgado and Jean Stefancic.
p.   cm.
Includes index.
ISBN 0-8147-1858-2 (alk. paper)
1. Freedom of speech—United States.   2. Hate speech—United
States.   3. Pornography—United States.   I. Stefancic, Jean.
II. Title.
KF4772.D45   1997
342.73'0853—dc20
[347.302853]   96-25368
                        CIP

New York University Press books are printed on acid-free paper,
and their binding materials are chosen for strength and durability.

Manufactured in the United States of America

10 9 8 7 6 5 4 3 2 1

Contents

Preface

Americans, by and large, are a practical, down-to-earth people, with no great love of grand theory. Lawyers, as a group, tend to be, if anything, more so. We love balancing tests, in which courts expressly and openly weigh the competing values in a case and tell us, in a written opinion, why they decided as they did. (If law were not this way, what place would there be for lawyers?) Why then, in a society committed to roll-up-your-sleeves pragmatism, and in a legal system committed to adversary dialectic, do we have one area, and only one, that is just the opposite—where mechanical "tests," holy-sounding trump cards, and ancient shibboleths foreclose argument and the kind of rational decision-making a society needs to organize itself and devise rules that will satisfy as many of its members as possible?

That Procrustean area is the First Amendment, and our purpose in this book is to liberate thinking about speech and expression from its current straitjacket. We aim to show the reader the good news—namely, that the First Amendment is well on its way to being freed, and the midwives of that liberation are struggles over hate speech and pornography. This book, then, is in part about the efforts of reformers to have society and law take account of the harms caused by these two forms of speech. But it is about a larger project as well, namely, clearing away the cobwebs, dust, and debris that surround the First Amendment. Our society *should* free free speech. When it has done so, our law, as well as our communal life, will be more flexible and humane. And a prime instrument by which we organize ourselves—namely, speech—will be a more effective instrument for citizens to talk to one another in an atmosphere of seriousness and mutual respect.

A hundred years ago, law schools (and legal theory) were dominated by a form of thinking that scholars today call "mechanical jurisprudence." The idea was that law was a type of science, like physics or astronomy, and capable of precise answers. Every case had one right disposition, which intelligent judges, aided by lawyers, could arrive at. This science consisted of a body of principles—legal rules—that were contained in the thousands of case reports (written legal decisions) making up what we know as the common law. The purpose of legal education was to teach students how to read these cases and distill the principles they implicitly contained. Once deduced, these rules would form a vast, consistent system which could then be applied to solve particular cases into the future.

That view of law probably actually served some good in the early years of this century. It lent an aura of intellectual respectability to the new departments of law that were beginning to spring up at American colleges and universities. (Previously, lawyers had trained one another by a system of apprenticeship.) And the effort to square cases and make them consistent with each other provided much intellectual exercise for aspiring lawyers and continues to do so even in today's Socratic classroom.

The legal realist movement of the 1920s, however, forever swept aside that form of thinking. Under the banner "The life of the law is not logic, but experience," this indigenous American movement, which included figures such as Felix Cohen, Jerome Frank, and Karl Llewellyn, demolished the dream that law could—or should—ever be this way. They demonstrated that deciding cases by logic alone was conceptually impossible. The social world is a confusing welter of facts and stories; every case has a variety of rules that arguably apply. In this rich, cross-cutting mass of data—facts, rules, and standards—judges decide cases, the realists argued, by reference to social policy, their own common sense, wisdom, reason, intuition, and, above all, experience. Very few cases—only the most simple (the ones that rarely get to court)—fall squarely under a preexisting rule, the beginning law student's dream. Most cases require *judgment*. To think otherwise is at best a simplification, at worst selfdeception.

And so, today, we are all realists. Except in one area—the First Amendment, where argument-closing *formulas* (the speech/act distinction, the prohibition against "content" regulation) and *shibboleths* (let the marketplace of ideas work; the cure for bad speech is more speech) still hold sway and are solemnly intoned by otherwise intelligent people who ought to know better. Not only that, many of them would choose to *act* better—because they would see more clearheadedly some of the harms that speech can cause to defenseless people—if the archaic system of mechanical First Amendment jurisprudence were pruned away.

This book brings good news: the First Amendment's liberation is at hand. The law of free speech is finally modernizing itself, finally taking in nuance, context sensitivity, and consideration of competing values. Passing into history are the days when stale mottos—"the rule of law is otherwise! you lose"—foreclosed consideration of any and all claims for speech limitation.

Part I, "The Opening Salvo," traces the origins of the debate about scathing speech. Two chapters, one each on hate speech and pornography, show early reformers struggling to "name the harm" and get the rest of society, and the legal system, to take it seriously.

Part II, "The Assault on the Citadel," describes the way in which legal realism arrived on the scene, exploding conventional notions, challenging comfortable myths, and demanding that the insistent claims of the reformers be addressed on their own merits. It also shows how faith in a prime tenet of mid-twentieth-century free-speech jurisprudence, the marketplace of ideas, is now reeling under the assault of the postmodernists, communication theorists, and students of narrative theory, all of whom are beginning, at last, to show us how speech actually *works*.

Part III, "Retreat to Policy Analysis," takes a detour into some fascinating rhetoric. Here we examine the fall-back positions adopted by First Amendment absolutists as a first-line defense to emerging legal realism. Sensing, perhaps, that ancient mechanical tests, door-closing doctrines, and special rules for speech are starting to lose their efficacy, many traditional defenders of free-speech purism are shifting ground and arguing that, *even if* the Constitution does not require toleration of vicious hate speech and hard-core pornography, social policy arguments dictate that we should leave these forms of speech alone. In this part we consider paternalistic arguments, offered by some liberals, why minorities and others, if they knew their own best interests, would not clamor for hate-speech rules. It considers, as well, arguments from the other side urging that minorities and women should just "toughen up." We also consider the assertion that America would become a radically different country if our system tolerated hate-speech rules. An examination of other liberal Western democracies that have put in place such rules shows that this is just not so.

Part IV, "From Where I Sit," examines the special case of judges and progressive lawyers, showing why their commitments and professional situation make it especially hard for many of them to see what everyone else sees—that a revolution is coming in First Amendment thought, and that it is a good thing, too.

Is this book—and the modernist turn whose development it traces—bad news for lovers of free expression and debate? Not at all. For one thing, it can hardly serve the defenders of any system of values to pretend that that system is not in need of reform when it is. For another, we argue that mechanical jurisprudence has seemingly paralyzed the thinking of many First Amendment absolutists. Judging from the naive policy arguments they are now putting forward, their muscles have been paralyzed through disuse. Alerting them to the kind of debate they must now enter benefits them as well as society at large. Finally—a point made in this book in different places—the values of free expression and equal dignity (at stake in the two controversies that form our focus) stand in reciprocal relation. The civil rights struggle relies on speech and expression: equality presupposes speech. But speech in any sort of meaningful sense requires equal dignity, equal access, and equal respect on the part of all the speakers in a dialogue: free speech, in other words, presupposes equality. Adjusting the fine balance between these two seemingly incompatible values can only strengthen both.

It is time for our finest minds—and for citizens at large—to understand this double dependency, to realize that the hard work of balancing competing principles must now begin, time to put aside tired maxims and conversation-closing clichés that formerly cluttered First Amendment thinking and case law. It is with the belief that this hard work will prove to be enormously, even exhilaratingly, beneficial for society—not just for marginalized groups struggling against a tide of vicious depiction—that we wrote this book.

Boulder, Colorado

Acknowledgments

This book is the culmination of our experience and thinking over the past two decades about a problem that deeply affects our lives and those of many others. We thank our colleagues who encouraged us along the way: Gary Schwartz, Steve Shiffrin, Kent Greenawalt, Michael Olivas, Pierre Schlag, Andrew Koppelman, and Robert Nagel. Others who have sharpened our arguments—Nadine Strossen, Nat Hentoff, Marjorie Heins, Robert O'Neil, Michael Greve—we thank as well. And to those who tread our path seeking a more respectful, harmonious, and civil society we especially salute: Mari Matsuda, Charles Lawrence, Kimberlé Crenshaw, Robin Barnes, Catharine MacKinnon, and Andrea Dworkin.

Our book grew from articles and lectures presented at various conferences and colloquia at the University of Chicago, Cornell University, Grinnell College, Harvard College, and the law schools of Case Western Reserve, Harvard, Rutgers-Camden, St. Thomas, UCLA, Washington & Lee, Wisconsin, and Yale. We are grateful for these invitations and the comments that pressed us further to refine our arguments.

We thank Bruce Bode, Michael Kramer, Joan Leon, Anne Najem, and Marisa Walsh, members of a First Amendment seminar at the University of Wisconsin, for drafting one of the chapters, as well as Lora Intrator for her heroic editing of it. Lisa Frye, Elizabeth Griffin, Bonnie Kae Grover, Alenka Han, Charles Holley, Peter McAllen, Blaine Lozano Milne, Tim O'Shea, Titus Peterson, Kim Quinn, Linda Ramirez, Markie Rath, Kelly Robinson, Frank Rodriguez, Frank Sledge, and Patricia Templar provided outstanding research assistance. We are grateful to Marge Brunner, Anne Guthrie, Linda Spiegler, and Kay Wilkie, who prepared the manuscript with intelligence and care.

Our editor, Niko Pfund, as always, provided steadfast encouragement, patience, good humor, and thoughtful suggestions.

Our gratitude goes, most of all, to David Yun for assistance with three vital chapters.

The following law reviews graciously granted permission to reprint parts of articles on which this book is based:

Harvard Civil Rights-Civil Liberties Law Review, for "Words That Wound: A Tort Action for Racial Insults, Epithets, and Name-Calling," 17 *Harv. C.R.-C.L. L. Rev.* 133 (1982), and "First Amendment Formalism Is Giving Way to First Amendment Legal Realism," 29 *Harv. C.R.-C.L. L. Rev.* 169 (1994).

Ohio State Law Journal, for "Pornography and Harm to Women: 'No Empirical Evidence?' "*53 Ohio St. L.J.* 1037 (1992).

Northwestern University Law Review, for "Campus Antiracism Rules: Constitutional Narratives in Collision," 85 *Nw. U. L. Rev.* 343 (1991).

Cornell Law Review and Fred B. Rothman Co., for "Images of the Outsider in American Law and Culture: Can Free Expression Remedy Systemic Social Ills?" 77 *Cornell L. Rev.* 1258 (1992).

California Law Review, for "Pressure Valves and Bloodied Chickens: An Analysis of Paternalistic Objections to Hate-Speech Regulation," 82 *Cal. L. Rev.* 871 (1994), and "Hateful Speech, Loving Communities: Why Our Notion of 'A Just Balance' Changes So Slowly," 82 *Cal. L. Rev.* 851 (1994).

Vanderbilt Law Review, for "The Neoconservative Case against Hate-Speech Regulation—Lively, D'Souza, Gates, Carter, and the Toughlove Crowd," 47 *Vand. L. Rev.* 1807 (1994).

Iowa Law Review, for "A Shifting Balance: Freedom of Expression and Hate-Speech Restriction," 78 *Iowa L. Rev.* 737 (1993).

Arizona State Law Journal, for " 'The Speech We Hate': First Amendment Totalism, the ACLU, and the Principle of Dialogic Politics," 27 *Ariz. State L.J.* (1995).

Must We Defend Nazis?

Part I

The Opening Salvo: Naming the Harm

A prime obstacle to reforming hate-speech and pornography law is the insistence by some that these forms of speech are harmless or that tolerating them is "the price we pay" for living in a free society. The following chapters put forward the view that they are not at all harmless, and that free speech doctrine must change to recognize and deal with the harms they cause.

1

1

Words That Wound

How Racist Hate Speech Harms the Victim.
Law's Earliest Responses

Not long ago, in *Contreras v. Crown Zellerbach, Inc.*,[1] the Washington Supreme Court held that a Mexican American's allegations that fellow employees had subjected him to a campaign of racial abuse stated a valid claim against his employer for the tort of outrage. The plaintiff alleged that he had suffered "humiliation and embarrassment by reason of racial jokes, slurs and comments"[2] and that the defendant's agents and employees had wrongfully accused him of stealing the employer's property, thereby preventing him from gaining employment and holding him up to public ridicule. Focusing on the alleged racial abuse, the court declared that "racial epithets which were once part of common usage may not now be looked upon as 'mere insulting language.' "[3]

Eleven months later, the United States Court of Appeals for the Seventh Circuit in *Collin v. Smith*[4] affirmed a federal district court's decision declaring unconstitutional certain ordinances of the village of Skokie, Illinois, which had been drafted to block a demonstration by members of the National Socialist Party of America. The village argued that the demonstration, together with the display of Nazi uniforms and swastikas, would inflict psychological trauma on its many Jewish citizens, some of whom had lived through the Holocaust. The court of appeals acknowledged that "many people would find [the] demonstration extremely mentally and emotionally disturbing."[5] Mentioning *Contreras*, the court also noted that Illinois recognizes the new tort of intentional infliction of severe emotional distress, which might well include the uttering of racial slurs. Nevertheless, the threat of criminal penalties imposed by the ordinance was held impermissibly to abridge the plaintiffs' First Amendment rights.

Should our legal system offer redress for the harm of racist speech? The first case, from a liberal state court, implies that it should—at least if the remedy takes the form of a private action, a tort suit. The second implies it should not, if the remedy takes the form of public condemnation through the criminal law—a view that has been reaffirmed more recently in the *R.A.V.* (Minneapolis cross-burning) case discussed later. Tort law, rooted in ancient Anglo-American tradition, has often served as a testing ground for new social sensibilities, which are later incorporated into our "public law," for example campus conduct codes (see, e.g., chapter 4) or criminal statutes. Tort law thus serves as a kind of social laboratory, testing theories and assessing harms.

What, then, are some of the harms associated with racial insults? And how have courts viewed these harms over the years?

Psychological, Sociological, and Political Effects of Racism

American society remains deeply afflicted by racism. Long before slavery became the mainstay of the plantation society of the antebellum South, Anglo-Saxon attitudes of racial superiority left their stamp on the developing culture of colonial America.[6] Today, over a century after the abolition of slavery, many citizens suffer from discriminatory attitudes and practices infecting our economic system, cultural and political institutions, and the daily interactions of individuals.[7] The idea that color is a badge of inferiority and a justification for the denial of opportunity and equal treatment is deeply ingrained.

The racial insult remains one of the most pervasive channels through which discriminatory attitudes are imparted.[8] Such language injures the dignity and self-regard of the person to whom it is addressed, communicating the message that distinctions of race are ones of merit, dignity, status, and personhood. Not only does the listener learn and internalize the messages contained in racial insults, these messages color our society's institutions and are transmitted to succeeding generations.

The psychological harms of racial stigmatization are often much more severe than those created by other stereotyping actions. Unlike many characteristics upon which stigmatization may be based, membership in a racial minority can be considered neither self-induced, like alcoholism or prostitution, nor alterable. Race-based stigmatization is, therefore, "one of the most fruitful causes of human misery. Poverty can be eliminated— but skin color cannot."[9] The plight of members of racial minorities may be compared with that of persons with physical disfigurements; the point has been made that "[a] rebuff due to one's color puts [the victim] in very much the situation of the very ugly person or one suffering from a loathsome disease. The suffering . . . may be aggravated by a consciousness of incurability and even blameworthiness, a self-reproaching which tends to leave the individual still more aware of his loneliness and unwantedness."[10]

According to psychologist Kenneth Clark, "Human beings . . . whose daily experience tells them that almost nowhere in society are they respected and granted the ordinary dignity and courtesy accorded to others will, as a matter of course, begin to doubt their own worth."[11] Minorities may come to believe the frequent accusations that they are lazy, ignorant, dirty, and superstitious.[12] "The accumulation of negative images . . . present[s] them with one massive and destructive choice: either to hate one's self, as culture so systematically demand[s], or to have no self at all, to be nothing."[13]

It is neither unusual nor abnormal for stigmatized individuals to feel ambivalent about their self-worth and identity.[14] This ambivalence arises from the individual's awareness that others perceive him or her as falling short of societal standards, ones which the individual has adopted. Stigmatized individuals thus often are hypersensitive and anticipate pain at the prospect of contact with "normals."

It is no surprise, then, that racial stigmatization injures its victims' relationships with others. Racial tags deny minority individuals the possibility of neutral behavior in cross-racial contacts, impairing the victims' capacity to form close interracial relationships. Moreover, the psychological responses of self-hatred and self-doubt can affect even the victims' relationships with members of their own group.[15]

The psychological effects of racism may also include mental illness and psychosomatic disease. The affected person may react by seeking escape through alcohol, drugs, or other kinds of anti-social behavior. The rates of narcotic use and admission to public psychiatric hospitals are much higher in minority communities than in society as a whole.

Achievement of high socioeconomic status does not diminish the psychological harms caused by prejudice. People of color who work and live in white-dominated settings have more encounters with race and racism than ones living in a working-class black neighborhood, for example, and the effort to achieve success in business and managerial careers exacts a psychological toll even among exceptionally ambitious and upwardly mobile members of minority groups. Those who succeed often "do not enjoy the full benefits of their professional status within their organizations, because of inconsistent treatment by others resulting in continual psychological stress, strain, and frustration."[16] As a result, the incidence of severe psychological impairment caused by the environmental stress of prejudice and discrimination is not lower among minority group members of high socioeconomic status.[17]

Racial stigmatization may also affect parenting practices among minority group members, thereby perpetuating a tradition of failure. A study of minority mothers found that many denied the real significance of color in their lives, yet were morbidly sensitive to matters of race.[18] Some identified excessively with whites, accepting whiteness as superior. Most had negative expectations concerning life's chances. Such self-conscious, hypersensitive parents, preoccupied with the ambiguity of their own social position, are unlikely to raise confident, achievement-oriented, and emotionally stable children.

In addition to these psychological harms of racial labeling, the stresses of racial abuse may have physical consequences. Scientists suspect that high blood pressure is associated with inhibited, constrained, or restricted anger, and not with genetic factors, and that insults produce elevation in blood pressure. American blacks have higher blood pressure levels and higher morbidity and mortality rates from hypertension, hypertensive disease, and stroke than do white counterparts. Further, there exists a strong correlation between degree of darkness of skin for blacks and level of stress felt, a correlation that may be caused by the greater discrimination experienced by darker-skinned blacks.

In addition to emotional and physical harms, racial stigmatization may damage a victim's pecuniary interests. The person who is timid, withdrawn, bitter, hypertense, or psychotic will almost certainly fare poorly in employment settings. An experiment in which blacks and whites of similar aptitudes and capacities were put into a competitive situation found that the blacks exhibited defeatism, half-hearted competitiveness, and "high expectancies of failure."[19] For many minority group members, equalization of such quantifiable variables as salary and entry level would be an insufficient antidote to defeatist attitudes because the psychological price of attempting to compete is unaffordable; they are "programmed for failure."[20] Additionally, career options for the victims of racism are closed off by institutional racism—the subtle and unconscious racism in schools, hiring decisions, and the other practices which determine the distribution of social benefits and responsibilities.

Unlike most of the actions for which tort law provides redress to the victim, racial labeling and racial insults also directly harm the *perpetrator*. Bigotry harms the individuals who harbor it by reinforcing rigid thinking, thereby dulling their moral and social senses[21] and possibly leading to a "mildly . . . paranoid" mentality.[22] There is little evidence that racial slurs serve as a "safety valve" for anxiety which would otherwise be expressed in violence.[23]

Racism and racial stigmatization harm not only victim and perpetrator but society as a whole. Racism is a breach of the ideal of egalitarianism, that "all men are created equal" and each person is an equal moral agent, an ideal that is a cornerstone of the American moral and legal system. A society in which some members regularly are subjected to degradation because of their race hardly exemplifies this ideal. The legal system's failure to redress the harms of racism and racial insults conveys to all the lesson that egalitarianism is not a fundamental principle and that respect for individuals is of little importance. Moreover, unredressed breaches of the ideal may demoralize all those who prefer to live in a truly equal society, making them unwilling participants in the perpetuation of racism and racial inequality.

To the extent that racism contributes to a class system, society has a paramount interest in controlling or suppressing it. Racism injures the career prospects, social mobility, and interracial contacts of minority group members. This, in turn, impedes assimilation into the economic, social, and political mainstream of society and ensures that the victims of racism are seen and see themselves as outsiders. Indeed, racism can be viewed as a force used by the majority to preserve an economically advantageous position for themselves.[24] But when individuals cannot or choose not to contribute their talents to a social system because they are demoralized or angry, or when they are actively prevented by racist institutions from fully contributing their talents, society as a whole loses.

Finally, racism and racial labeling have an even greater impact on children than on adults. The effects of racial labeling are discernible early in life;[25] at a young age, minority children exhibit self-hatred because of their color, and majority children learn to associate dark skin with undesirability and ugliness.[26] When presented with otherwise identical dolls, a black child preferred the light-skinned one as a friend; she said that the dark-skinned one looked dirty or "not nice."[27] Another child hated her skin color so intensely that she "vigorously lathered her arms and face with soap in an effort to wash away the dirt."[28] She told the experimenter, "This morning I scrubbed and scrubbed and it came almost white."[29] When asked about making a little girl out of clay, a black child said that the group should use the white clay rather than the brown "because it will make a better girl."[30] When asked to describe dolls which had the physical characteristics of black people, young children chose adjectives such as "rough, funny, stupid, silly, smelly, stinky, dirty." Three-fourths of a group of four-year-old black children favored white play companions; over half felt themselves inferior to whites. Some engaged in denial or falsification.[31]

The Harms of Racial Insults

In addition to these more general harms associated with racism and racist treatment, certain specific harms result from racial *insults*. Immediate mental or emotional distress is the most obvious direct harm. Without question, mere words, whether racial or otherwise, can cause mental, emotional, or even physical harm to their target, especially if delivered in front of others or by a person in a position of authority. Racial insults, relying as they do on the unalterable fact of the victim's race and on the history of slavery and race discrimination in this country, have an even greater potential for harm than other insults.

Although the emotional damage caused is variable and depends on many factors, only one of which is the outrageousness of the insult, a racial insult is always a dignitary affront, a direct violation of the victim's right to be treated respectfully. Our moral and legal systems recognize the principle that individuals are entitled to treatment that does not denigrate their humanity through disrespect for their privacy or moral worth. This ideal has a high place in our traditions, finding expression in such principles as universal suffrage, the prohibition against cruel and unusual punishment, the protection of the Fourth Amendment against unreasonable searches, and the abolition of slavery. A racial insult is a serious transgression of this principle because it derogates by race, a characteristic central to one's self-image.

The wrong of this dignitary affront consists of the expression of a judgment that the victim of the racial slur is entitled to less than that to which all other citizens are entitled. Verbal tags provide a convenient means of categorization so that individuals may be treated as members of a class and assumed to share all the negative attitudes imputed to the class.[32] They thus make it easier for their users to justify their own superior position with respect to others. Racial insults also serve to keep the victim compliant. Such dignitary affronts are certainly no less harmful than others recognized by the law. Clearly, a society whose public law recognizes harm in the stigma of separate but equal schooling[33] and the potential offensiveness of the required display of a state motto on automobile license plates,[34] and whose private law sees actionable conduct in an unwanted kiss[35] or the forcible removal of a person's hat,[36] should also recognize the dignitary harm inflicted by a racial insult.

The need for legal redress for victims also is underscored by the intentionality of racial insults. Their intentionality is obvious: what other purpose could the insult serve? There can be little doubt that the dignitary affront of racial insults, except perhaps those that are overheard, is intentional and therefore most reprehensible. Most people today know that certain words are offensive and only calculated to wound. No other use remains for such words as "nigger," "wop," "spic," or "kike."

In addition to the harms of immediate emotional distress and infringement of dignity, racial insults inflict psychological harm upon the victim. Racial slurs may cause long-term emotional pain because they draw upon and intensify the effects of the stigmatization, labeling, and disrespectful treatment that the victim has previously undergone. Social scientists who have studied the effects of racism have found that speech that communicates low regard for an individual because of race "tends to create in the victim those very traits of 'inferiority' that it ascribes to him."[37] Moreover, "even in the absence of more objective forms of discrimination—poor schools, menial jobs, and substandard housing—traditional stereotypes about the low ability and apathy of Negroes and other minorities can operate as 'self-fulfilling prophecies.' "[38] These stereotypes, portraying members of a minority group as stupid, lazy, dirty, or untrustworthy, are often communicated either explicitly or implicitly through racial insults.

Because they constantly hear racist messages, minority children, not surprisingly, come to question their competence, intelligence, and worth. Much of the blame for the formation of these attitudes lies squarely on value-laden words, epithets, and racial names. These are the materials out of which each child "grows his own set of thoughts and feelings about race."[39] If the majority "defines them and their parents as no good, inadequate, dirty, incompetent, and stupid," the child will find it difficult not to accept those judgments.[40]

Minority children possess even fewer means for coping with racial insults than do adults. "A child who finds himself rejected and attacked . . . is not likely to develop dignity and poise. . . . On the contrary he develops defenses. Like a dwarf in a world of menacing giants, he cannot fight on equal terms."[41] The child who is the victim of belittlement can react with only two unsuccessful strategies, hostility or passivity. Aggressive reactions can lead to consequences which reinforce the harm caused by the insults; children who behave aggressively in school are marked by their teachers as troublemakers, adding to the children's alienation and sense of rejection. Seemingly passive reactions have no better results; children who are passive toward their insulters turn the aggressive response on themselves; robbed of confidence and motivation, these children withdraw into moroseness, fantasy, and fear.

But Will a Tort Remedy Do Any Good?

The various and severe harms associated with racial treatment argue for some sort of social sanction. (Indeed, the following section shows that courts are already affording relief, usually by smuggling in recovery under some conventional, already recognized, legal theory such as defamation or the tort of intentional infliction of emotional distress.) But should a new, *freestanding* remedy be devised? And if so, would it do any good?

It is, of course, impossible to predict the degree of deterrence a cause of action in tort would create. However, as one leading authority has observed, "for most people living in racist societies, racial prejudice is merely a special kind of convenient rationalization for rewarding behavior."[42] In other words, in racist societies "most members of the dominant group will exhibit both prejudice and discrimination,"[43] but only in conforming to social norms. Thus, "[W]hen social pressures and rewards for racism are absent, racial bigotry is more likely to be restricted to people for whom prejudice fulfills a psychological 'need.' In such a tolerant milieu prejudiced persons may even refrain from discriminating behavior to escape social disapproval."[44] Increasing the cost of racial insults thus would certainly decrease their frequency. Laws will never prevent violations altogether, but they will deter "whoever is deterrable."[45]

Because most citizens comply with legal rules, and this compliance in turn "reinforce[s] their own sentiments toward conformity,"[46] a tort action for racial insults would discourage such harmful activity through the teaching function of the law. The establishment of a legal norm "creates a public conscience and a standard for expected behavior that check overt signs of prejudice."[47] Legislation aims first at controlling only the acts that express undesired attitudes. But "when expression changes, thoughts too in the long run are likely to fall into line."[48] "Laws . . . restrain the middle range of mortals who need them as a mentor in molding their habits."[49] Thus, "If we create institutional arrangements in which exploitive behaviors are no longer reinforced, we will then succeed in changing attitudes [that underlie these behaviors]."[50] Because racial attitudes of white Americans "typically follow rather than precede actual institutional [or legal] alteration,"[51] a tort for racial slurs is a promising vehicle for the eradication of racism.

Legal Protection from Racial Insults

As we mentioned earlier, the law already does provide a degree of protection from racial insults under such legal theories as assault, battery, intentional infliction of emotional distress, defamation, and various statutory and constitutional causes of action. However, each of these doctrines has limitations which render it a less than reliable means of redress for the victims of racial insults.

Assault and Battery

In *Fisher v. Carrousel Motor Hotel, Inc.,*[52] the plaintiff, an African American mathematician attending a NASA convention in Texas, was accosted by a white restaurant employee while waiting in a cafeteria line. The employee snatched an empty plate from the plaintiff's hand and told him in a loud voice that he could not eat in that cafeteria. The plaintiff did not allege that he was actually touched, or that he feared physical injury, but rather that he was "highly embarrassed and hurt" by the employee's actions in the presence of the plaintiff's associates. Although the jury awarded him $900, the trial judge denied any recovery. The Texas Court of Appeals affirmed, ruling that there had been neither a battery nor an assault and that under Texas law mental anguish without physical injury does not support a claim for battery—this even though the jury had found humiliation, indignity, and wanton disregard of the plaintiff's feelings.

The Texas Supreme Court reversed, finding that the plaintiff could recover because the waiter's seizure of the plate supplied the offensive touching required for a battery. The court further held that because battery is designed to protect dignity as well as physical security, the plaintiff was not required to show physical harm in order to recover damages.

The holding in *Fisher* that the violent snatching of a plate from the plaintiff's hand constituted an offensive touching is not remarkable.[53] But *Fisher* does indicate recognition by the Texas Supreme Court that racial insults and overt acts of discrimination can cause mental suffering and humiliation. At the same time, however, the facts of *Fisher* illustrate the inadequacies of the doctrines of assault and battery in protecting such a plaintiff. If the waiter had not snatched the plate from the plaintiff's hand, but had insulted him before he picked up the plate, or until the plaintiff put it down and left, the mathematician could not have recovered. And because the employee's words did not put the plaintiff in fear of physical injury or touching, the plaintiff could not have recovered in assault. [Ed.—a related cause of action based on the reasonable apprehension of an imminent battery.]

Intentional Infliction of Emotional Distress

Despite the growing acceptance of intentional infliction of emotional distress as an independent tort, the perennial fear of a flood of fraudulent claims continues to mold the doctrine. The *Second Restatement of Torts* [a classic text], for example, limits recovery to "severe emotional distress" caused by "extreme and outrageous conduct."[54] California permits recovery for physical injury to the plaintiff if the injury was foreseeable, but, in the absence of physical harm, requires that the invasion of the plaintiff's mental tranquillity be "extreme and outrageous."[55] Utah requires that the distress be severe, that either the defendant have acted with the purpose of inflicting emotional distress or the distress be reasonably foreseeable, and that the defendant's actions be outrageous and intolerable. In Texas, the emotional distress must be accompanied by physical injury.

Yet, in addition to *Contreras*, courts on several occasions have upheld causes of action or verdicts for black plaintiffs in cases which stemmed in large part from racial insults. Two of these are from California. In the first, *Alcorn v. Anbro Engineering, Inc.*,[56] a black truck driver advised his supervisor that the supervisor had instructed another employee to violate union rules. The supervisor responded, "You goddam 'niggers' are not going to tell me about the rules. I don't want any 'niggers' working for me. I am getting rid of all the 'niggers' . . . you're fired."[57] Alcorn alleged that he had been neither rude nor insubordinate and that the supervisor's conduct was intentional, malicious, and intended to cause humiliation and mental anguish. The court held these allegations sufficient to state a cause of action for "extreme and outrageous" intentional infliction of emotional distress. The court emphasized the employee-employer relationship between the parties, the plaintiff's allegation of particular susceptibility to emotional distress, and developments in social consciousness that render the term "nigger" particularly offensive.

In *Agarwal v. Johnson*,[58] the plaintiff, a native of East India, sued his former employer and two of his former supervisors for repeated harassment. The plaintiff testified that on one occasion a supervisor had said to him, "You black nigger, member of an inferior race, get out and do it."[59] The jury awarded the plaintiff general and punitive damages, and the state supreme court held that the evidence was sufficient to support the verdict for intentional infliction of emotional distress.

Because the question of whether the defendant's conduct is "extreme and outrageous" must be answered on a case-by-case basis, and because the racial insults in these two cases were linked with other reprehensible conduct, it is impossible to know whether the racial slurs were decisive factors in *Alcorn* and *Agarwal*. Courts always have been extremely reluctant to impose liability on the basis of words alone. However, the *Alcorn* court left open the question whether "mere insulting language, without more" could constitute "extreme outrage,"[60] and the *Agarwal* court declared that the plaintiff "presented substantial evidence that [one supervisor's] use of the racial epithet was outrageous."[61]

In *Wiggs v. Courshon*,[62] a recent law graduate and his family became engaged in an argument with a waitress serving them in the restaurant of the hotel in which they were staying on vacation. The waitress said, "You can't talk to me like that, you black son-of-a-bitch. I will kill you." Later, she was overheard shouting repeatedly, "[T]hey are nothing but a bunch of niggers." The case was tried on the theory of assault, although the plaintiff also alleged mental anguish and emotional distress. At the close of the evidence, however, it was apparent that the plaintiffs were never reasonably in fear of physical injury. And under the controlling Florida law, plaintiffs may recover for intentional infliction of emotional distress only when that distress is "severe."

Nevertheless, the court upheld the jury's verdict for the plaintiff on the basis of a dictum in the controlling Florida Supreme Court decision, *Slocum v. Food Fair Stores of Florida, Inc.*[63] In that case, the plaintiff, a customer in a supermarket, asked a clerk the price of an item the clerk was marking. The clerk replied, "If you want to know the price, you'll have to find out the best way you can . . . you stink to me."[64] The plaintiff sought to recover for her ensuing emotional distress and "heart attack and aggravation of pre-existing heart disease."[65] The court held that these allegations did not state a cause of action because the "unwarranted intrusion [into the plaintiff's mental tranquillity] must be calculated to cause 'severe emotional distress' to a person of ordinary sensibilities, in the absence of special knowledge or notice."[66] Nevertheless, the court noted that a "broader rule has been developed" for "offense reasonably suffered by a patron from insult by a servant or employee of a carrier, hotel, theater, . . . [or] telegraph office."[67] It was this dictum on which the *Wiggs* court grounded liability.[68]

Wiggs exemplifies the shortcomings of the doctrine of intentional infliction of emotional distress as a means for redressing racial insults. The jury was eager to find for the plaintiffs, awarding them $25,000 in compensatory and punitive damages. But the judge was forced to ground liability on dicta which had never before been cited in the state and which had not been suggested to the court by either party. Most importantly, had the plaintiff's dispute developed with another customer rather than an employee, no recovery would have been possible. The injury arguably is lesser when the perpetrator is simply another customer, but in *Wiggs* the plaintiffs' humiliation before the other diners would have been just as great, and their vacation just as ruined.

Of course, the plaintiffs did win in *Contreras, Alcorn, Agarwal,* and *Wiggs.* But in at least two cases based substantially on racial insults, the plaintiffs lost because the defendants' actions were not sufficiently culpable. In *Irving v. J. L. Marsh, Inc.,* [69] the plaintiff, a black architecture student, returned certain merchandise he had purchased to the defendant's store. In order to obtain a refund, he was required to sign a slip on the top of which defendant's employee had written, "Arrogant Nigger refuses exchange—says he doesn't like products." The court held that this conduct was not "sufficiently severe" for the plaintiff to recover. Similarly, in *Bradshaw v. Swagerty,* [70] the plaintiff, a young black man, had been invited to the office of the defendant, a lawyer, to discuss accounts allegedly owed the defendant's client by the plaintiff and his brother. The conversation became heated, and the plaintiff alleged that the defendant called him "nigger," a claim that the defendant apparently did not deny. The court held that such epithets are " 'mere insults' of the kind which must be tolerated in our roughened society" and affirmed summary judgment for the defendant.

The *Irving* court appeared sympathetic to the plaintiff, noting that "[w]hile the derogatory and highly offensive character of defendant's actions is not condoned by this court, the law, in its present state, does not permit recovery for the humiliation plaintiff was forced to endure." [71] The court's reluctance to redress the plaintiff's injuries is symptomatic of the inadequacy of the tort for intentional infliction of emotional distress in such cases. One authoritative legal text holds that "[t]he liability clearly does not extend to mere insults, indignities, threats, annoyances, petty oppressions, or other trivialities. . . . There must still be freedom to express an unflattering opinion, and some safety valve must be left through which irascible tempers may blow off relatively harmless steam." [72] What courts have thus far failed to recognize is that racial insults are in no way comparable to statements such as, "You are a God damned woman and a God damned liar," which the authority gives as an example of a "mere insult." [73] Racial insults are different qualitatively because they conjure up the entire history of racial discrimination in this country. No one would argue that slavery can be characterized as a "petty oppression" or lynch mobs as "mere annoyances," but thus far courts generally have not recognized the gravity of racial insults within the rubric of the tort of intentional infliction of emotional distress. Only an independent tort for racial insults could fully take into account the unique, powerfully evocative nature of racial insults and the insidious harms they inflict.

Defamation

In two of the cases mentioned earlier—*Irving* and *Bradshaw*—the plaintiffs also pleaded a cause of action in defamation, and both lost on that claim. In neither case did the plaintiff allege special damages, and thus both the *Irving*[74] and *Bradshaw*[75] courts ruled that the words alleged did not fit into any of the recognized categories for which relief is available. The *Bradshaw* court, however, did note that "[t]he term 'nigger' is one of insult, abuse and belittlement harking back to slavery days. Its use is resented, and rightly so. It nevertheless is not within any category recognized as slanderous *per se*."[76] Yet, interestingly, in at least three older cases, white plaintiffs were permitted to sue for defamation against defendants who falsely charged that the plaintiffs were black.[77]

It should not be surprising that defamation has failed to protect the victims of racial insults. Defamation is "an invasion of the interest in reputation and good name."[78] In contrast, the maker of a racial insult invades the victim's interest in emotional tranquillity. A third party who learned that a person was the victim of a racial insult, but did not know the victim, would probably conclude that the victim is a member of a particular racial minority. But if this conclusion is true, the victim cannot recover because no falsehood has occurred. And whether or not the conclusion is true, it is not desirable that the law view membership in a racial minority as damaging to a person's reputation, even if some members of society consider it so.

Constitutional and Statutory Provisions

Victims of racial insults who have sued state officials under the Federal Civil Rights Act (section 1983)[79] have achieved mixed results. In *Harris v. Harvey*,[80] for example, a black police officer sued a white judge for a "racially motivated campaign to discredit and damage"[81] the police officer and have him relieved of his job. As part of his campaign, the judge had referred to the officer as a "black bastard." In affirming the jury's award of $260,000 in compensatory and punitive damages and the trial court's award of attorney's fees, the Seventh Circuit Court of Appeals held that "such an intentional tort inspired by racial animus and perpetrated under color of state law constitutes a denial of equal protection."[82] The court also ruled that the judge's use of the power and prestige of his office brought his acts under color of law even though the judge's campaign did not fall within the scope of his judicial duties (and thus the defense of judicial immunity was unavailable).

In contrast, in *Johnson v. Hacket*[83] a district court ruled that the complaint failed to state a federal claim under the same section (1983). The plaintiff alleged that on a certain evening two uniformed police officers on patrol threatened to fight a group of blacks and said that they would return later that evening. The officers did return, one asking, "Where are the night fighters?" the other asking, "What's a dead nigger anyway?" The next day, with the two officers again in uniform and on patrol, one of the officers called the plaintiff a "Chinese nigger." The plaintiff responded with a similar expression, but without racial overtones. A third officer then asked the two officers if they had provoked the expression. After they replied that they had not, the third officer arrested the plaintiff for disorderly conduct.

The court held that there had been no infringement of the right to freedom from unlawful arrest and that the plaintiff's other alleged right, the "right to dignity," was not constitutionally protected. The court also reached the highly questionable conclusion that the two police officers had not acted under color of law because they were not authorized to call anyone insulting names. Reasoning that "the purely personal nature of the offer [to fight] is emphasized by the allegation that, before the challenge was issued, [the officer] removed his gun belt, laying aside, as it were, the symbol or 'pretense' of police authority,"[84] the court concluded, "It is the nature of the act performed, not the clothing of the actor or even the status of being on duty, or off duty, which determines whether the officer has acted under color of law."[85]

The requirements of section 1983 — that the right infringed be granted by the federal constitution or laws and that the official be acting under color of law — present formidable hurdles for victims of racial insults. The campaign of racial vilification in *Harris* was so extreme and unlikely to be repeated that one must conclude that the outcome in *Johnson*, not *Harris*, will emerge as the usual result.

If this is the case, it will stand in sharp contrast to other areas in which the law increasingly is recognizing that the use of racial language by government officials is intolerable. The United States Supreme Court has found constitutional error in a contempt citation issued against a black witness who refused to answer questions until the examining attorney addressed her as "Miss Hamilton" rather than "Mary."[86] And the Minnesota Supreme Court has held:

We cannot regard use of the term "nigger" in reference to a black youth as anything but discrimination against that youth based on his race.... When a racial epithet is used to refer to a [black] person ... an adverse distinction is implied between that person and other persons not of his race. The use of the term "nigger" has no place in the civil treatment of a citizen by a public official. We hold that use of this term by police officers coupled with all of the other uncontradicted acts described herein constituted discrimination because of race.[87]

Similarly, courts and administrative bodies have imposed duties to avoid racial language on prison officials, police officers, and school boards. In 1980 the San Francisco Civil Service Commission enacted a policy under which city officials and employees could be demoted, suspended, or dismissed for uttering racial slurs while on duty.[88] And in at least one case a jury has found government discrimination especially intolerable. In *Haddix v. Port of Seattle*,[89] a case brought under a state antidiscrimination statute against a government agency for four years of abusive treatment at the hands of a white foreman, the jury awarded the plaintiff $200,000, rather than the $145,000 the plaintiff had requested. One juror reported, "We set the sum of $200,000 as a statement that race discrimination is wrong, and that the port is a public corporation and should be in the forefront of fighting discrimination."[90]

Some plaintiffs also have prevailed under state anti-discrimination statutes. For example, in *Imperial Diner, Inc., v. State Human Rights Appeal Board*,[91] a restaurant owner had told a waitress that she thought she was something special, "Just like all the other f——ing Jewish broads around here."[92] The owner repeatedly refused to apologize. The New York Court of Appeals affirmed the State Division of Human Rights ruling that the petitioner discriminated against the waitress by reviling her religion in a matter related to her working conditions and enforced the Division's award of $500 to the waitress for "shock, humiliation, and outrage."[93]

Victims of racial slurs, however, have been less successful in recovering against private persons and entities under state and federal laws. An attempt to invoke two federal provisions to obtain relief failed in *Howard v. National Cash Register Co.*[94] Fellow employees had used the word "nigger" and other race-related language in the plaintiff's presence. Although Title VII of the Act forbids an employer "to limit . . . his employees . . . in any way which would deprive or tend to deprive any individual of employment opportunities or otherwise adversely affect his status as employee, because of such individual's race,"[95] the court found that the invective did not constitute employment discrimination. And in *Irving,* the court held that the plaintiff could not recover under an Illinois constitutional provision prohibiting "communications that portray criminality, depravity or lack of virtue in, or that incite violence, hatred, abuse or hostility toward, a person or group of persons by reason of or by reference to religious, racial, ethnic, national or regional affiliation,"[96] because that provision does not expressly grant a private right of action.

Although many courts recite, as did the Minnesota Supreme Court, that the use of a racial insult against a member of a minority group is race discrimination, apparently none has found discrimination solely on the basis of a single such insult. Courts appear unwilling to impose the liability and opprobrium that follow a finding of violation of federal and state anti-discrimination laws on such slender grounds. Recovery often is stymied further by the requirement, incorporated in many of these statutes, that there be some relationship between the parties, such as a contractual or employment relationship. And, of course, it is reasonable to assume that there is a substantial amount of variation in the protection afforded by state anti-discrimination laws. Such problems would be eliminated by an independent tort for racial insults because it would protect all victims from racial insults regardless of the jurisdiction or relationship between the parties.

Objections to a Tort for Racial Insults

Recognition of a tort for racial insults undoubtedly will face all the objections voiced whenever courts choose to protect a previously unrecognized interest—the difficulty of measuring and apportioning damages, the potential for fraudulent claims, and the prospect of a flood of litigation. Yet this need not be. The now-recognized torts of invasion of privacy, intentional infliction of emotional distress, and compensation for prenatal injuries illustrate new causes of action that were fashioned to cope with substantial injuries that did not fit into an existing category. As Dean Prosser has observed, "[T]hat the claim is novel will not of itself operate as a bar to the remedy."[97]

The Difficulty of Measuring Damages. One objection usually raised to torts that protect emotional well-being is that the intangible and highly subjective nature of the interests invaded makes damages difficult to measure and prove. This objection has been rejected as applied to the tort of invasion of privacy, however, and is rapidly being surmounted in the case of intentional infliction of emotional distress. Behavior that injures a person's interest in psychological well-being is now generally actionable despite any difficulty in measuring damages.

Moreover, a tort for racial insults contains at least one indisputable element of harm, the affront to dignity. The intangible quality of novel interests should not, by itself, preclude valuing them for purposes of compensation.[98] Juries can always assign a value to such interests and their infringement. Alternatively, legislatures can set nominal damages to be recovered for the affront to dignity.

Of course, the law does not compensate for every inconvenience, bumped elbow, jostled shoulder, or offended ear; against many of life's minor misfortunes a "toughening of the mental hide" is the best remedy.[99] Not every reference to a person's race or color is insulting, nor is every insult addressed to a minority person a racial one. The emerging cause of action we suggest is limited to language intended to demean by reference to race, which is understood as demeaning by reference to race, and which a reasonable person would recognize as a racial insult. The psychological or emotional harm alleged in such cases can be proved in the same manner—including through expert witnesses—as in other torts that protect psychological well-being.

The Difficulty of Apportioning Damages. A second potential objection to a tort for racial insults is the difficulty of apportioning damages. A defendant could argue that his or her own contribution to the injury was small compared to the overall effect of racism on the plaintiff or that the racial insult could have caused no damage because minority group members are or should be inured to such treatment. Further, the defendant could point to the circumstance that the "eggshell skull" rule,[100] which holds that a wrongdoer is liable for damages attributable to the plaintiff's peculiar susceptibility even if this susceptibility was not apparent to the wrong-doer, is not followed in intentional infliction of emotional distress cases.

The counterarguments, however, are more persuasive. That a defendant takes advantage of a plaintiff already harmed by earlier victimization makes the act more, not less, reprehensible; a contrary rule would imply that racial minorities are "fair game" for further abuse merely because they have been the object of similar abuse in the past. Further, because a person's race is usually obvious, the maker of a racial insult is exploiting an apparent susceptibility rather than causing an unforeseeable injury, as in the eggshell skull cases. Such an exploitation creates liability even under the doctrine of intentional infliction of emotional distress, which recognizes that the "extreme and outrageous" character of the defendant's conduct may be supplied by the defendant's knowledge that the plaintiff is peculiarly susceptible to emotional distress.[101]

Surprisingly, only two courts seem to have addressed the problem of apportioning damages in cases of the sort we are considering. In *Alcorn*, the court declared in a footnote, "[W]e cannot accept defendant's contention that plaintiff, as a truck driver, must have become accustomed to such abusive language. Plaintiff's own susceptibility to racial slurs and other discriminatory conduct is a question for the trier of fact . . . [Ed., usually, the jury]".[102] In *Contreras*, the court quoted this language with approval, adding, "It is for the trier of fact to determine, taking into account changing social conditions and plaintiff's own susceptibility, whether the particular conduct was sufficient to constitute extreme outrage."[103] That this issue has arisen in so few cases may suggest that once the liability of the defendants in racial insult cases is proved, courts will not deny or reduce recovery merely because of the problem of apportioning damages.

Fraudulent Claims and a Flood of Litigation. Because a tort for racial insults, like other torts that protect psychological well-being, would present complex problems of proof of causation and of damages, it will face the objection that it would encourage fraudulent claims and a flood of litigation. In some jurisdictions, these fears are reflected in a rule that denies relief to plaintiffs who suffer no physical harm. Apparently, these jurisdictions believe that physical injuries are less easily feigned. Whatever its value in other contexts, this limitation is unnecessary in actions for racial insults. If racial invective is aimed at a victim, an infringement of the plaintiff's dignity, at the least, has occurred. Moreover, even if occasional plaintiffs win recoveries based on nonexistent damages, there is no reason to assume that these results would be erroneous more often than is the case in other types of civil litigation. At any rate, both correct and erroneous results would deter future offenses and thus protect the rights of others who cannot or will not seek redress.[104]

The specter of a flood of litigation was also raised, and ultimately rejected,[105] in connection with the torts of invasion of privacy and intentional infliction of emotional distress. Empirical studies show that the volume of litigation in response to judicial recognition of new torts has not been overwhelming. Moreover, the inconvenience and expense of a lawsuit will adequately deter frivolous or fraudulent claims. It is the role of courts to redress wrongs even at the risk of an increase in judicial business. A "flood of litigation," therefore, would suggest that the courts were performing their function of placing the cost of the harm on the perpetrator.

Objections Based on the First Amendment

It is surprising, especially after *Collin*, that the question whether racial insults are protected by the First Amendment has seemingly not arisen in any tort case stemming from a racial insult. Until it does, the extent to which free speech considerations would shape such suits must remain an open question.

Under First Amendment doctrine, regulation of expressive activities is scrutinized more closely when directed at the content of speech rather than merely at its time, place, or manner.[106] Because racial insults differ from ordinary, nonactionable insults precisely because they use racial terms for the purpose of demeaning the victim, a tort for racial insults will almost surely be seen as a regulation of content and thus be subject to exacting scrutiny. But regardless of the standard applied, courts ultimately must balance the government's interest against that of the utterer.[107]

The Government Interests. The primary government interest served by a tort action for racial insults is amelioration of the harms of racism and racial insults discussed earlier. Not only the victim of a racial insult but also his or her children, future generations, and our entire society are harmed by it and the tradition of racism which it furthers.

The government also has an interest in regulating the use of words harmful in themselves. In *Chaplinsky v. New Hampshire*,[108] the United States Supreme Court declared that words which "by their very utterance inflict injury or tend to incite an immediate breach of the peace" are not protected by the First Amendment.[109] Racial insults, and even some of the words which might be used in a racial insult, inflict injury by their very utterance. Words such as "nigger" and "spic" are badges of degradation; they have no other connotation.

The Supreme Court also has recognized that the government may restrict speech directed at a captive or unwilling audience. These cases have concerned speech both inside[110] and outside[111] the home. However, in *Cohen v. California*[112] the court overturned a conviction for wearing a jacket with the words "Fuck the Draft" written on it. In meeting the state's argument that the message was thrust upon unwilling listeners, the court pointed out that viewers could simply avert their eyes.

Racial insults are easily distinguishable from the inscription in *Cohen*. One cannot avert one's ears from an insult. More importantly, a racial insult is directed at a particular victim; it is analogous to the statement "fuck you," not the statement "Fuck the Draft." Finally, a racial insult, unlike the slogan in *Cohen*, is not political speech; its perpetrator intends not to discover truth or advocate social action but to injure the victim.

The Free Speech Interests. Examination of the free-speech values served by a racial insult is best undertaken within the framework of the categories outlined by Professor Emerson in his foundational article, *Toward a General Theory of the First Amendment*.[113] Four categories of value are set forth: individual self-fulfillment; ascertainment of the truth; securing participation by the members of society in social and political decision-making; and maintaining a balance between stability and change.

Individual Self-Fulfillment. The idea of individual self-fulfillment to be furthered through free expression is based on the rights of individuals to develop their full potentials as members of the human community. But bigotry, and its attendant expression, stifles rather than furthers the moral and social growth of the individual who harbors it. In addition, a racial insult is only in small part an expression of self: it is primarily an attempt to injure through the use of words. No one would argue that self-fulfillment should never be limited by consideration of the effects of one's means of expression on other members of society. Although one may dress in Nazi uniforms and demonstrate before the city hall in Skokie, Illinois, one may not paint swastikas on one's neighbors' doors.

Ascertainment of the Truth. According to Professor Emerson, "[t]hrough the acquisition of new knowledge, the toleration of new ideas, the testing of opinion in open competition, the discipline of rethinking its assumptions, a society will be better able to reach common decisions that will meet the needs and aspirations of its members."[114] This function of free speech, to achieve the best decisions on matters of interest to all, has been highly influential in First Amendment thinking. Indeed, one theory of the First Amendment holds that its protections extend only to speech that can be characterized as "political."[115] In this respect, most racial insults are distinguishable from the expressions found protected in *Collin*. The plaintiff in *Collin*, the National Socialist Party of America, was a political party whose race-related beliefs were only a part of a set of ideals. But few racial insults are intended to inform or convince the listener. They invite no discourse, and no speech in response can cure the inflicted harm.

Racial insults may usefully be analogized to obscenity. Although the government may regulate this form of speech, it may not prohibit expression of the view that obscenity should be protected or that, for example, adultery may be proper behavior.[116] Similarly, protecting members of racial minorities from injury through racial insults, and society itself from the accumulated harms of racism, is very different from prohibiting espousal of the view that race discrimination is proper.

The reasons the Supreme Court articulated in explaining why obscenity may be regulated are also instructive in analyzing racial insults. In *Paris Adult Theatre I v. Slaton*,[117] the court pointed to the "at least . . . arguable correlation between obscene material and crime"[118] and the " 'right of the Nation and of the States to maintain a decent society.' "[119] Racial insults, through the racism and race discrimination they further, are severely at odds with the goals of antidiscrimination law and the commands of the anti-slavery Thirteenth Amendment. A prohibition of such insults would surely further the government's interest in maintaining a "decent society."

Participation in Decision-Making. In a democracy, all members must be permitted to voice their opinions so that the government's authority is derived in fact "from the consent of the governed."[120] Racial insults do not further this goal. On the contrary, they constitute badges and incidents of slavery and contribute to a stratified society in which political power is possessed by some and denied to others.

The Balance between Stability and Change. Some of the many evils of the suppression of expression also are effects of racism and racial insults. Professor Emerson mentioned the following arguments, among others, under the rubric of maintaining the balance between stability and change: suppression of discussion substitutes force for logic; suppression of speech promotes institutional rigidity and inability to respond to changing circumstances; free expression leads those who lose public controversies to accept the result because they have had an opportunity to convert others to their opinion; and freedom of expression prevents violent upheavals by alerting the government to valid grievances.[121] But racism furthers all the evils caused by the suppression of speech. It dulls the moral and social senses of its perpetrators, while disabling victims from fully participating in society and leaving unprejudiced members of society vicariously demoralized. Bigotry and systems of discrimination continue to exist for no reason other than that the prejudiced are in positions of power or authority. Institutions infected by these ills will be peopled by like-minded individuals and thus will be slow to respond to changing circumstances. Furthermore, racism excludes minorities from participating in the contemplation of public issues because their concerns are discounted by the majority and because they have been beaten down by repeated victimization. And it is painfully clear that this exclusion, not only from political discussion but also from the abundance of our country's wealth, is capable of leading to violent outbreaks.

Elements of the Cause of Action

In order to prevail in an action for a racial insult, the plaintiff should be required to prove that

Language was addressed to him or her by the defendant that was intended to demean through reference to race; that the plaintiff understood as intended to demean through reference to race; and that a reasonable person would recognize as a racial insult.

Thus, it would be expected that an epithet such as "You damn nigger" would almost always be found actionable, as it is highly insulting and highly racial. However, an insult such as "You incompetent fool," directed at a black person by a white, even in a context which made it highly

insulting, would not be actionable in itself because it lacks a racial component. "Boy," directed at a young black male, might be actionable, depending on the speaker's intent, the hearer's understanding, and whether
a reasonable person would consider it a racial insult in the particular
setting. "Hey, nigger," spoken affectionately between black persons and
used as a greeting, would not be actionable.[122] An insult such as "You
honkey," directed at a white person, could be actionable under this formulation of the cause of action, but only in the relatively unusual situations
where the plaintiff would suffer harm from such an insult.[123]

The plaintiff may be able to show aggravating circumstances, such as
abuse of a position of power or authority or knowledge of the victim's
susceptibility to racial insults, which may render punitive damages appropriate. The common law defenses of privilege and mistake may be appli-
cable, and retraction of the insult may mitigate damages.

As we have seen, an independent tort for racial slurs would protect the
interests of personality and equal citizenship that are part of our highest
political traditions and moral values, thereby affirming the right of all
citizens to lead their lives free from attacks on their dignity and psychological integrity. It is an avenue of redress that deserves explicit judicial
recognition.

2

Pornography and Harm to Women

How Even Social Scientists Have Sometimes Failed to See the Need for Relief

As has happened with racist speech and insult, reformers have been advocating curbs on hard-core pornography. The impetus comes primarily from two camps: religious fundamentalists who argue against pornography on moral grounds, and many radical feminists who are concerned over the way it injures and degrades women. In this chapter, we shall be concerned with responses to the feminist attack on pornography, although some of what we say may hold true as well with the fundamentalist one.

As with media and face-to-face racism (see chapters 1, 4, 5, and 9), pornography has begun to be named and attacked by reformers, including many feminists. Examining how this campaign has fared discloses mechanisms our society deploys to slow the advance of a movement once it is well under way and legal hurdles to regulation begin to seem surmountable. Most members of society's elite groups today profess to find pornography distasteful; they only disagree on whether it should be regulated. One of our findings, however, is that pornography is a tacitly recognized good (not an evil) which the dominant group depends on to achieve certain ends and naturally is reluctant to relinquish. To see how this is so requires a brief look at the social depiction of women in general, and at the history of pornography in particular.

There is no necessity to the notions that women are more passive than men, more domestic, less venturesome, or that they should have primary responsibility for the care and nurture of children.[1] Our ideas about women and women's roles are constructed. Contingent rather than necessary, their maintenance is a product of reinforcement and conditioning.[2] The tools of this construction are both verbal and visual—words, images, pictures, and stories. For the sake of brevity, we denote this collection of representation "narratives."

History of Female Depiction in General

In the early years of this nation, women were needed to perform domestic and farm labor on the frontier and in newly developed areas of the West and prairie regions. Accordingly, images of women in the literature of the day depicted them as pious, God-fearing, resourceful, able to make fires, mend clothing, fend off Indian raiders, raise children, and help their husbands in the fields from morning to night. Not particularly sexual (at least in the image), the woman of this era derived her main satisfaction from work, raising children and standing by her man. Dime novels of the period depicted frontier heroines such as Hurricane Nell, Bess the Trapper, and Mountain Kate, rugged women who rode, roped, toted guns, and confronted grizzlies while, of course, constantly maintaining a proper feminine demeanor. Their ultimate reward was that sought by all members of their sex: an idyllic and fruitful marriage.

Later, the nation's attention shifted from survival to consolidation and economic development. The independent, resourceful image of westward expansion receded, replaced by a much more confined, ladylike one. Women's magazines of the period advised their readers to use caution in exercising because their frail constitutions could bear only moderate exercise; women's "fibres are thin and weak," "[t]heir feeble arms cannot support severe and long-continued labor."[3] Even women writers of this time had to conform to popular taste, upholding virginity, thrift, and similar virtues. Male industrialists and developers were firmly in charge. Independent, venturesome women would have been threatening—large numbers of women workers were not yet needed in the workplace. Popular images reflected these needs and conditions.

The late nineteenth century saw the first waves of feminism. Leaders and novelists such as Kate Chopin urged that women could be independent, had intellects, needs, and a sensuous nature of their own. Most readers were taken aback. Chopin was seen as a radical. The early suffragists were derided and ignored. For example, the 1848 Seneca Falls Convention Declaration was belittled in newspaper articles as "a most interesting document" because of its "amusing" assertion of women's "equality."[4] The public preferred women to be dreamy, frail, innocent, and romantic, a preference that played itself out both in literature and the scripts of the early film period. D. W. Griffith, for example, in *Birth of a Nation, Intolerance,* and other films showed Lillian Gish playing the role of the innocent and virginal child-woman who relies on men for protection.

With World War II, a contrasting image surfaced—the strong, independent woman. Wartime propaganda featured workers such as "Rosie the Riveter," who labored in the factory while her husband or male friend fought overseas. Those women who did not work in the factories were portrayed as cheerfully shouldering additional household responsibilities while waiting faithfully for the man's return.

Immediately following the war, women's image changed again. Women withdrew from the workplace and provided the "baby boom" that stabilized the nation's numbers and compensated for the low birth rate during the war. Films, magazine advertisements, television programs, and stories now depicted women happily engaged in domestic tasks and roles.

With the return of feminism in the late 1960s and early 1970s, images modestly broadened to incorporate the new vistas the civil rights movement had opened for women and minorities. But even then, publications promoted submissive roles. For example, confession magazines often presented accounts of rapes or rape-fantasies in which the female victim was to blame, the rape functioning "as a positive catalyst for the heroine in her never-ending quest for a new boyfriend or an improved relationship with a husband."[5] Even well-known women authors followed well-trod tracks. Lois Gold's *Such Good Friends*[6] and Erica Jong's *Fear of Flying*[7] were permutations of old narratives: the woman strays, explores adventure and sex, then returns to husband or old lover at the end.

As we shall see with ethnic minorities of color (see chapter 5), the dominant stereotypes of women in any era are either limiting or demeaning, yet rarely perceived as such at the time. Rather, they are seen as natural, inevitable, "the way things are." Moreover, the images change to accommodate society's need for labor, sex, reproduction, independence or its opposite. The nation needs workers, Indian-fighters, breeders, or temptresses, and the creative community obligingly responds. All this image-creation takes place largely at an unconscious level; rarely, if ever, does there seem to be anything like a conscious conspiracy.

Pornography and the Debate over Regulation

Pornography, a particular form of female depiction, responds to many of the same forces as female depiction generally, but often with a reverse twist. For example, during westward expansion, the dominant image of women was relatively traditional—defender of home and hearth. Yet, because there were not enough women to go around, music, burlesque halls, and vaudeville flourished, featuring "bawdy women" who spoke and sang of sexual themes, engaged in low humor, and made rude observations on forbidden subjects.[8] They took the existing image of Eve, the sexual woman, and portrayed it as socially forceful, lusty, natural. They depicted women courting men, enjoying conquests, and making fun of it all. Anti-prudes and naughty, they mocked society's reigning view of women as demure and submissive.

Early pornography and erotica were largely the province of wealthy gentlemen. By today's standards it was relatively tame and refined; those who collected it often pretended it was something else, described their interest in it in scientific, delicate, or euphemistic terms. Some portrayed their interest as "hygienic"—as that of controlling, studying, or understanding prostitution and other forms of social "vice." By 1800, the Industrial Revolution was well underway, however, and with it middle-class ideas and conventions gained ascendancy. Sexual morality became more limiting as religious fervor coupled with economic pressure to force women back into subordinate positions. The pornography of this time lacked the subtlety, finesse, or literary merit of earlier periods. A dominant theme became the factory girl who left home, succumbed to the temptations of her new environment but, sadder and wiser, lived to tell all. There were also risqué novels with amorous ladies seducing Civil War heroes.

By the end of the nineteenth century, early feminists and social reformers were inveighing against prostitution, pornography, and the demon rum. These "social purists" believed that enabling women to take their places along with men in the workplace and government would bring about a more virtuous, temperate society. Soon, however, Freud, Krafft-Ebing, and Havelock Ellis would begin writing about the naturalness of sex and the eroticization of much of life. The anti-pornography strain of the reform movement would begin to lose momentum.

By the time of the feminist revival, pornography in the United States was well established. Even by 1902, privately screened films with graphic scenes of adult sexuality were available. Running between ten and twelve minutes without sound or color, these "stag films" generally avoided dealing with female sexual pleasure. The encounter was impersonal; the woman almost did not exist. With the advent of the women's movement of the 1960s and 1970s, however, pornography took on a sharper edge. Photographs and films became more explicit, and a substantial portion—as high as one-third—included force by the male against the female. By the 1980s, pornography had become a big business with distributors, theater chains, and technological advances such as home videos, subscription television, dial-a-porn, and computer sex subscription services widely available.

Like female depiction generally, pornography thus responds to forces emanating from broader society. Pornographers create and respond to a market that in turn wants women passive, active, or abused and repressed. Always at the extreme end of a continuum of female depiction, pornography marks transitions from one construct of woman to the next. During times of change it teaches women what may be done to them, shows men what may be done, and adds new content to the social construct of women.

The Controversy over Pornography's Regulation

Proposals to ban pornography can be traced to the early temperance movement, when reformers inveighed against its evils along with those of prostitution, venereal disease, and alcohol. Beginning in the late 1960s, the American feminist movement gave the campaign against pornography a secular, feminist cast. Instead of portraying pornography as harmful principally to men (the usual consumers) or to society at large (for example, through its impact on public morality), the new critics charged that pornography harms women.[9]

In 1983, many of these issues came to a head when Catharine MacKinnon and Andrea Dworkin helped introduce the nation's first anti-pornography civil rights ordinance in Minneapolis.[10] Enacted by the city council but vetoed by the mayor, the ordinance would have made trafficking in, and coercing persons into, pornography civil harms.

Women who opposed the ordinance formed FACT (Feminist Anti-Censorship Task Force),[11] an organization that successfully opposed a similar ordinance that the city of Indianapolis enacted a few years later. Just as anti-pornography activists were criticized for aligning themselves with the religious right, MacKinnon and others charged that their liberal sisters in FACT were in league with right-wing libertarians and the pornography industry, and were collaborating with male power. Members of FACT responded that MacKinnon's ordinance violated freedom of choice, reinforced the double standard, and rested on a dubious causal link. MacKinnon replied that pornography objectifies women, expropriates their sexuality for men's use, and teaches sex roles in which women are subordinate, degraded, or subject to physical abuse. A number of American cities and the U.S. Congress have enacted or considered enacting anti-pornography regulations, some along the lines proposed by MacKinnon and Dworkin. Recently, the Supreme Court of Canada upheld a Canadian anti-pornography statute, a decision widely viewed as a vindication of MacKinnon's position.[12]

"No Empirical Evidence": Why We Fail to Find Anything (Seriously) Wrong with Pornography

History teaches that dominant depictions of women in any era are not seen as particularly injurious at that time. The images teach those in the culture the role of women and how they may act toward them. They enable us, in short, to construct the idea of woman, one that serves varying purposes at different times. Once the images are in place, they guide what we see.

Pornography, a particular type of negative depiction, flourishes when the needs and expectations of the dominant group with respect to women are not being met in some respect. When, as now, we are in such a period, a predictable sequence occurs: women protest the images; researchers profess to search for evidence of its harmful nature—and find no such empirical evidence. These events occur, we believe, because the broad system of female depiction renders most of the harms ordinary and normal, part of the way things are. Society reserves the terms "shocking," "brutal," and "misogynist" for treatment that deviates from the norm— that falls outside the range the narratives mark out. Thus, a male researcher may genuinely and sincerely look for violence following the showing of an anti-woman movie or television program and find none— neglecting to notice the joke, putdown, comment, leer, offer of a drink, and pressured sex that go on daily.

Narrative theorists and outsider scholars have been writing of the way in which setting and experience shape perception. An example of this mechanism occurred at the sentencing of Mike Tyson. In his statement before the court, Tyson exclaimed, "I didn't hurt nobody. Nobody has a black eye or broken ribs."[13] His statement reveals a common misperception: the act constitutes rape only if the victim suffers physical injuries as a result of the encounter, neglecting that sex without consent is inherently forceful and constitutes rape. A man may envision a seduction in which he is being commanding, she coy. However, a woman may experience the same encounter as a degrading violation of her will.[14] Our engrained ideas of womanhood and male-female relations determine what will strike us as abnormal as well as what we might count as evidence against pornography. The very images under study become internalized; we then use them to judge their own real-world efficacy.

Translation: How to Avoid Hearing What the Feminists Are Saying

One mechanism we encountered by which opponents of pornography's regulation were able to avoid the feminists' attack is *translation*. MacKinnon and others maintain that most forms of pornography degrade and injure women and thus ought to be controlled. Many opponents of this position say they are unable to verify that claim. For example, one well-regarded constitutional scholar rejected the MacKinnon-Dworkin proposal because the scientific case for a link between exposure to pornography and commission of later anti-social acts is not established.[15] The studies, relied on by a recent Attorney General's Commission, he reasoned, show only correlation, not causation.[16] The few controlled experiments that do seem to indicate such a connection can be explained by observer effects or the artificiality of the laboratory setting.[17]

Like many in the anti-regulation camp, the scholar fails to understand that for many feminists pornography is a per se harm, namely that of being derogatorily constructed as passive, hypersexual, masochistic, a sexual plaything, and so on.[18] This harm occurs irrespective of what happens later; there is no need to show copycat offenses the next day. But this injury becomes invisible if one translates the feminists' claim into a causal one to be investigated in the usual way—by conducting interviews, looking at crime statistics, exposing laboratory subjects to particular stimuli. The error consists in treating a novel claim, with roots in postmodernism and the social construction of reality, as an ordinary empirical one.

"No Empirical Evidence": How Not to Find Documentation by Searching for the Wrong Thing

The case against other forms of pornography, however, is based on its tendency to encourage anti-woman acts. For example, many feminists believe that glorified depiction of sexual violence teaches men that this behavior is acceptable because, in reality, the victims enjoy it.[19] Yet, researchers and others fail to find the connection that feminists believe must be there. We believe this failure occurs for two reasons: (1) researchers fail to take account of certain types of evidence that, if counted, would tend to corroborate the feminist claim; and (2) when researchers do find instances of crime incontrovertibly linked to pornography, they deem them abnormal and idiosyncratic.

Looking for the Wrong Thing

One reason why some fail to associate later-committed acts with pornography is that many such acts strike the observer as ordinary and unremarkable.[20] How many of us would find the following events significant enough to record as evidence of sexual oppression: aggressive flirting, conspicuous leering, remarks on a woman's appearance, unwanted requests for a date? Incidents such as these may well be highly correlated with the consumption of pornography, yet our system of female depiction renders them ordinary and invisible, blinding us to the large amount of daily "low-grade" hassling that goes on. The images define what is normal and ordinary; what is ordinary cannot be a harm. Therefore, pornography, if it only results in the ordinary, cannot harm women. Pornography functions like a thermostat, setting our threshold at a high level. Once it is set, we fail to notice or consider important much that goes on around us.

Denial and Dismissal: What Happens When We See Evidence We Cannot Ignore

Sometimes, however, pornography is followed by an event, a "copycat rape" for example, that appears incontestably induced by it. Because we are not accustomed to thinking that images have causal efficacy, we often respond by deeming the perpetrator deranged.[21] Mere imagery should not have that effect, we say to ourselves. So, by a sort of backward reasoning, we dismiss events that might substantiate pornography's efficacy as idiosyncratic, the product of individual pathology, despite evidence to the contrary.

A Third Method: Deprecation

A third approach to minimizing the case against pornography is simple deprecation. If one begins with the premise that pornography is a relatively harmless form of expression, individuals arguing against it must be intolerant and puritanical, bent on depriving men of innocent pleasure, women of free expression of their sexuality.[22] This criticism gains superficial plausibility because some feminists do in fact preach against the evils of patriarchy and speak unkindly of some men's sexual intentions.[23]

But is all opposition to pornography intolerant and puritanical? Only if one assumes that sex is always voluntarily entered into, a manifestation of freely expressed love and eroticism carried out by two equal partners of similar standing and ability to choose. Some feminists question those assumptions. For them, men-women relations are carried out against a background of radical inequality.[24] What many men consider innocent courtship often looks dangerously like coercion, dangerously like rape. The first camp seems anti-male, anti-sex, and puritanical to the second; to the first camp, the second seems only interested in maintaining current power relations.[25]

Why Legal Reform Is So Difficult: A Theory of Cultural Resistance

As we mentioned earlier, resistance to regulation of pornography illustrates a more general pattern of reaction to transformative thought. These patterns of resistance take certain recurring forms almost irrespective of the cause championed. They reappear because resistance stems not so much from the nature of the movement as from that of the actors called on to position themselves with respect to it.

One significant brake on social change lies in our customary tools of thought. These tools have been devised with particular purposes in mind—those of "normal science."[26] Most lawyers, for example, use indexes, digests, and other research tools to locate authority for the case at hand. They make legal research easier; one case leads to another until one finds what one believes one wants. The headings and categories track the main ideas of Western capitalist law. The solutions they enable take the form of incremental refinements and adjustments within that system. If one relies on them, one is unlikely to hit upon a startlingly new solution to a social problem, or even to realize that the case presents an opportunity for doing so. The structure of categories channels legal thought and effort into safe, familiar directions.

Sometimes, however, a client or attorney will recognize that a new problem exists, or a new approach is needed for an old one. Someone wishes to persuade society or the courts that women should be admitted to the bar, that Japanese Americans ought not be interned unless they are security risks, and so on. A study of some of the most notorious cases in American legal history, however, shows that even eminent judges often cannot be made to see the danger in such cases. An argument that women have rights, that Indians should not be relocated, that blacks should not be treated as property, heard for the first time, will frequently strike the judge as unsound. The argument falls outside the dominant narrative. Only years later, after consciousness has progressed and society has adopted a new narrative, do we see what we wrote earlier as monstrous, an embarrassment.

In time, society will begin to understand that the reformers were right after all; the environment requires attention, women are men's equals, and so on. Now the situation is in flux; everyone realizes change is in the wind. At this point, two mechanisms often appear on the scene to confine change to manageable proportions. Anti-essentialist arguments are raised to challenge any radical reformer's standing.[27] How do we know you speak for all women? If the reformers nevertheless persevere, additional mechanisms may come into play—perseveration and refusal to see evidence of any need for reform. The former occurs if the problem calling for reform is widespread; the latter, if it concerns injustice only for a small group. Perseveration consists of society's refusal to see its predicament as serious; instead we opt for what worked before. The current wave of neoconservatism can be seen as a response to large-scale challenges facing American society; the solution—return to the virtues of a former golden era, as an effort to avoid the need for basic reform. Insistence on adherence to time-honored, absolutist interpretations of the First Amendment may be another.

Finally, members of the empowered group may simply announce to the disaffected one that they do not see their problem, that they have looked for evidence of harm but cannot find it. Later generations may well marvel, "How could they have been so blind?" But paradigms change slowly. In the meantime, one may describe oneself as a cautious and principled social scientist interested only in the truth. And one's opponent, by a neat reversal, becomes an intolerant zealot willing to trample on the liberties of others without good cause.

What We Can Do

All these mechanisms are deeply inscribed in cultural practice; every reform movement evokes them. Perhaps most insidious is the one discussed in this chapter, for once one declares invisible the problem the reformers agitate about, any need to deal with it dissolves. The combined weight of the mechanisms suggests that legal reform will often be agonizingly slow, frustrating, and incomplete. Nevertheless, there are a few measures we can take if we desire to provide for orderly change.

First, we may act decisively in the cases of social evil we do see, treating them in effect as proxies for those that we do not. With pornography, for example, we might enact laws prohibiting the worst forms of violent (e.g., "snuff") films, saving treatment of the more general problem for another time. We should be alert to the way current practice may appear different in history's light. For example, we now see many earlier stereotypes of women and minorities as demeaning. Yet, at the time, artists and consumers did not see them that way. We should bear in mind that our own treatment of women's imagery may in time come to seem similarly inexcusable.

To avoid ensnarement by the mechanisms we have discussed, we should empower outsider speakers and listen closely to their message. Their reality, although surely not the only one, may well prove to be the one a later era adopts. We should pay attention even to the most alienated, extreme-seeming elements of a social reform movement. The message of more moderate factions may well appear to us more attractive, sensible, and true. Yet what we know about narrative theory puts us on notice: during times of change and paradigm shift, it is precisely the familiar that holds the greatest danger.

Understanding how the dialectic of resistance and reform works can enable us, perhaps, to avoid the worst forms of narrow-mindedness, the most devastating of history's judgments. A modest hope, certainly. But if we are right, it may be all our predicament as situated actors, limited by our own range of experience and empathy, admits.

Sidewalk Sister

Down the soft dirt path I walk
into the park's massed greenery.
Thumbnail daisies in young new grass
trace bridal chains of welcome.

This world of plants has long dominion.
My world as wife exposed,
laid bare by lawyers and accountants,
dissolves its union.

Coming back toward home
I see your picture on the sidewalk
gazing up at me, shadowed
seductive eyes, hands
cupping lovely breasts.
You wanted everyone to see.

I pass, and then
go back. Lift you up
and look again. Innocent
your beauty. I crumple you into a ball
and toss you into the bushes.

I did it to protect us,
my sidewalk sister.

Part II

The Assault on the Citadel: Legal Realism Shakes Up Orthodoxy

Building on the notions of harm developed in part I, in this part we put forward three key critiques of the First Amendment orthodoxy that, until now, have tolerated these harms—legal *realism* (mentioned in the Preface), *indeterminacy* (the discovery that every speech-related problem can also be seen in other terms), and the notion that the celebrated First Amendment *marketplace of ideas* is unavailing in certain situations.

3

First Amendment Formalism Is Giving Way to First Amendment Legal Realism

In the last few years observers have noticed a sharp upsurge in intellectual activity surrounding the role of speech and expression. Reformers have been demonstrating how hate speech and pornography injure minorities and women. Postmodernists have been pointing out how every speech controversy can be approached in at least two ways. (See chapter 4.) At the same time, defenders of tradition such as the ACLU and other free-speech absolutists have been writing books and articles defending an unfettered First Amendment,[1] to which yet other observers such as Jack Balkin reply: they are caught up in "ideological drift"—failure to notice how an instrument that once promoted dissent and other causes dear to liberals is now wielded chiefly by white supremacists, pornographers, and other dubious allies.

Is this debate merely about who possesses the correct vision—about who is the *real* defender of the right and the true? No. We think there is another, far more intellectually intriguing explanation for the rifts and tugs-of-war over issues such as pornography and hate speech that are testing the limits of First Amendment orthodoxy. In this other vision, the skirmishes are not so much questions of standing one's ground, as some of the old-timers see it, or even of refining that ground slightly, as some want to make it appear. Rather, the ground itself is shifting. The prevailing First Amendment paradigm is undergoing a slow, inexorable transformation. We are witnessing the arrival, nearly seventy years after its appearance in other areas of law, of *First Amendment legal realism*.[2] The old, formalist view of speech as a near-perfect instrument for testing ideas and promoting social progress is passing into history. Replacing it is a much more nuanced, skeptical, and realistic view of what speech can do, one that looks to self- and class interest, linguistic science, politics, and other tools of the realist approach to understand how expression functions in our political system. We are losing our innocence about the First Amendment, but we will all be wiser, not to mention more humane, when that process is complete.

The Transition

Early in American history, we thought the First Amendment was the crowning jewel of our jurisprudence. As recently as 1970, scholars described our system of free expression in sweeping, exalted terms.[3] But shortly thereafter some writers began expressing doubts about whether First Amendment doctrine was capable of delivering on its lofty promises.[4] In the last few years, under the impetus of challenges from critical race, feminist, and other writers, the trickle of doubts has turned into a flood.[5]

The transition to the new paradigm is far from complete. Those who write in the new tradition still expend much energy defending themselves from charges that they are Satanic, forgetful of history, deluded, in league with fascism, etc.[6] It is impossible to predict what the new understanding of the First Amendment will look like when fully mature, just as the early Realists, seventy years ago, scarcely could have predicted how their movement would lead the way to clinical legal education, perspectivism, critical legal studies, and elite law reviews. With these cautions, we offer here the themes and outlines of a new conception of the First Amendment. We make no claim to be comprehensive; the list may be personal to us.

The New First Amendment Legal Realism

First, the paradigm includes an awareness of the First Amendment's limitations. Early in our republic, we made grandiose claims for what the system of free expression could do.[7] But recently, scholars have shown that our much-vaunted marketplace of ideas works best in connection with questions that are narrowly limited in scope. Is this parking space safer to leave the car in than another? Does a heavy object fall faster than a light one in a vacuum? Would a voucher school-finance scheme adversely affect the poor? (See chapter 5.) With such clearly bounded disputes, free speech can often help us avoid error and arrive at a consensus. But with systemic social problems like racism and sexism, the marketplace of ideas is much less effective. These broad-scale ills are embedded in the reigning paradigm, the set of meanings and conventions by which we construct and interpret reality. Someone who speaks out against the racism of his or her day is seen as extreme, political, or incoherent. Speech, it turns out, is least effective where we need it most.

A second theme of First Amendment legal realism is the role of free expression in legitimating the status quo.[8] If, as a starting point, we posit a perfect marketplace of ideas, then, according to the old paradigm, the current distribution of social power and resources must be roughly what fairness and justice would dictate. Our more energetic European ideas, for example, competed with others and won: it was a fair fight. But, of course, it was not fair: communication is expensive, so the poor are often excluded; the dominant paradigm renders certain ideas unsayable or incomprehensible; and our system of ideas and images constructs certain people so that they have little credibility in the eyes of listeners.

This leads to a third component of the new approach, namely that language and expression can sometimes serve as instruments of positive harm. Incessant depiction of a group as lazy, stupid, and hypersexual—or ornamental for that matter—constructs social reality so that members of that group are always one-down.[9] Thereafter, even the most scrupulously neutral laws and rules will not save them from falling further and further behind as private actions compound their disadvantage. (See chapter 5.) Affirmative action becomes necessary, which in turn reinforces the view that members of these groups are naturally inferior (because they need special help). Pornography and hate speech are the two most visible fronts on which the fight to make the legal order recognize and prevent these harms is waged, often against great resistance. But when powerful groups find a particular type of speech offensive and likely to render them one-down, they blithely pass a law to curtail it. We rarely notice these "exceptions" and special doctrines, however, because they are time-honored and second nature. Of course there would be an exception for state secrets, plagiarism, false advertising, and dozens of other types of speech, we say. But one to protect eighteen-year-old black undergraduates at dominantly white institutions? Oh no, we say, the First Amendment must be a seamless web.[10]

Emerging First Amendment realism leads us to notice how even labeling something a First Amendment problem channels and predetermines analysis. Why, feminists and civil rights activists ask, should I be a mere compelling state interest in your jurisprudence, and not you one in my equality-based analysis? We are belatedly realizing that treating hate speech as a First Amendment problem may make as little sense as treating murder under the commerce clause.

We are beginning to scrutinize such sweeping generalizations as the following: speech is minorities' best friend; suppressing racism only causes it to explode in more virulent forms later; talking back is the best solution to bigotry and sexism; and tolerating face-to-face insults is necessary to a university's role as a bastion of free speech and inquiry.[11] (See chapters 6 and 7.) We are beginning to ask the "Who benefits?" question and to raise the possibility that scoundrels and bigots can easily hide under the mantle of the First Amendment.[12] We are questioning whether the continuum of high-value (viz., normal) and low-value speech may not be all there is. Could there be no-value speech, or negative-value speech, which not only could but should be restricted?[13]

We are beginning to flip stock arguments. Until now, the following argument has been determinative: the First Amendment condemns that; therefore it is wrong. We are raising the possibility that the correct argument may sometimes be: the First Amendment condemns that, therefore the First Amendment (or the way we understand it) is wrong.[14] Although it is often said that free speech is the best protector of equality, perhaps equality is a precondition of effective speech, at least in the grand, dialogic sense.[15] We can now take statements such as "The campus ought to be a bastion of free speech," and render them as "The campus ought to be a bastion of equal, respectful treatment."[16] Or, finally, from the old saw "The cure is more speech," why not "The cure is more equality?"

We are beginning to realize that even judges who set out to be scrupulously fair may not be able easily to balance values in cases, such as those concerning hate speech, when free speech and another value (say community) come into conflict. Speech-community is in reality a dyad, not two separate things that a judge can balance, like Jones's right to build a fence and Smith's right to have more sun in his living room. (See chapter 9.)

Birth Pains

On the level of ideas, then, the ground is inexorably shifting. First Amendment formalism is giving way to First Amendment realism. The internal struggles we see waging within formerly absolutist organizations like the ACLU (with some chapters breaking away and supporting speech codes, for example, or officers conceding that it is time for the organization to take seriously the possibility that hate speech can set back equality) reveal the anxiety and ferment that presage a paradigm shift. It is all there—the ad hominem arguments,[17] the effort to have it both ways, accusations of straying from holy truth,[18] a sense of beleaguerment,[19] an increase of the decibel level, a resort to paternalistic arguments[20] ("if those minorities knew their own best interest, they would . . . "), and the strategic retreat[21] ("how about the narrowest possible speech code?").

What will the new paradigm mean for civil rights and civil liberties activism and scholarship? Will we not lose a valuable tool for convincing judges to be equitable and to protect human values? The answer today is the same as it would have been if we had put the question to Cohen, Frank, or any of the early legal realist scholars seventy years ago. They might have replied that misplaced faith in law as a science could not possibly benefit minorities and the oppressed; that understanding how law really works is a first step to marshaling that discipline in the service of causes one holds dear; that safety does not lie in pleasant fictions. For similar reasons, those championing equality and human values have nothing to fear from the new paradigm.

In any event, it is too late to turn back. First Amendment realism has arrived. The last outpost of formalist thought and faith has fallen. Unless the absolutist camp—including the ACLU—adjusts its thinking to take account of the view now emerging, its program, counsels, and pronouncements will seem more and more the futile products of a backwater of legal thought.

4

Campus Anti-Racism Rules: Constitutional Narratives in Collusion

Or, Why There Are Always Two Ways of Looking at a Speech Controversy

Over the past few years, more than two hundred university and college campuses have experienced racial unrest serious or graphic enough to be reported in the press. Most observers believe the increase in racial tension on the nation's campuses is real, and not just the product of better reporting or record keeping.[1]

In response, a number of campuses have enacted student conduct rules prohibiting slurs and disparaging remarks directed against persons on account of their ethnicity, religion, or sexual orientation. A University of Wisconsin rule, for example, prohibited remarks that are directed to an individual; demean due to one's membership in a racial, religious, or sexual group; are intended to demean; and interfere with the victim's ability to take part in education or instruction.

This chapter deals with some of the thorny issues such rules raise, including how we characterize the problem. As will be seen, it may be framed in two ways—as a First or Fourteenth Amendment problem— that are equally valid but lead to drastically different consequences. Yet no a priori reason exists for declaring the problem "essentially" one of free speech or protection of equality. We also take a look at examples of campus racism and various universities' responses to it. Since our society has had relatively little experience with regulating group-disparaging speech, we review efforts of other Western nations in dealing with it, a subject we return to in chapter 8. We also examine the teachings of social science on racism and its control, and apply case law and theories of free speech and equal protection to the problem of campus racism.

These "subnarratives" highlight the inadequacy of conventional analysis in dealing with issues, like campus anti-racism rules, that straddle fault lines in our system of values. None of the conventional approaches discussed in the early sections of this chapter even begins to close the gap between liberty and equality that campus anti-racism rules open. Yet our dilemma may yield to a postmodern insight: regulation of the speech by which a dominant group constructs a stigma-picture of a subordinate group may be carried out without offending core values of the First Amendment, and may be necessary for full effectuation of the Fourteenth.

Framing the Issue

Persons tend to react to the problem of racial insults in one of two ways. On hearing that a university has enacted rules forbidding certain forms of speech, some will frame the issue as a First Amendment problem: the rules limit speech, and the Constitution forbids doing that without a very good reason.[2] If one takes anti-regulation as one's starting point, several consequences follow. First, the burden shifts to the other side to show that the interest in protecting members of the campus community from insults and name calling is compelling enough to overcome the presumption in favor of free speech.[3] There must be no less onerous way of accomplishing that objective.[4] Moreover, some will worry whether the enforcer of the regulation will become a censor, imposing narrow-minded restraints on campus discussion.[5] Some will also be concerned about slippery slopes and line-drawing problems: if a campus restricts this type of expression, might the temptation arise to do the same with classroom speech or political satire in the campus newspaper?[6]

Others, however, will frame the problem as one of protection of equality. They will ask whether an educational institution does not have the power, to protect core values emanating from the Thirteenth and Fourteenth Amendments,[7] to enact reasonable regulations aimed at assuring equal personhood on campus.[8] If one characterizes the issue *this* way, different consequences follow. Now, the defenders of racially scathing speech are required to show that the interest in its protection is compelling enough to overcome the preference for equal personhood;[9] and we will want to be sure that this interest is advanced in the way least damaging to equality. There are again concerns about the decision-maker who will enforce the rules, but from the opposite standpoint: the enforcer of the regulation must be attuned to the nuances of insult and racial supremacy at issue, for example by incorporating multiethnic representation into the hearing process. Finally, a different set of slopes will look slippery. If we do not intervene to protect equality here, what will the next outrage be?

The legal analysis, therefore, leads to opposite conclusions depending on the starting point. But an even deeper indeterminacy looms: both sides invoke different narratives to rally support. Protectors of the First Amendment see campus anti-racism rules as parts of a much longer story: the centuries-old struggle of Western society to free itself from superstition and enforced ignorance. The tellers of this story invoke martyrs like Socrates, Galileo, and Peter Zenger, and heroes like Locke, Hobbes, Voltaire, and Hume who fought for the right of free expression. They conjure up struggles against official censorship, book burning, witch trials, and communist blacklists. Compared to that richly textured, deeply stirring account, the minority protector's interest in freeing a few (supersensitive?) individuals from momentary discomfort looks thin. A textured, historical account is pitted against a particularized, slice-of-life, dignitary one.

Those on the minority-protection side invoke a different, but no less powerful, narrative. They see a nation's centuries-long struggle to free itself from racial and other forms of tyranny, including slavery, lynching, Jim Crow laws, and separate-but-equal schools.[10] They conjure up different milestones—Lincoln's Emancipation Proclamation, *Brown v. Board of Education*; they look to different heroes—Martin Luther King, the early Abolitionists, Rosa Parks, and Cesar Chavez, civil rights protesters who put their lives on the line for racial justice. Arrayed against that richly textured historical account, the racist's interest in insulting a person of color face-to-face looks thin.

One often hears that the problem of campus anti-racism rules is that of balancing free speech and equality. But more is at issue. Each side wants not merely to have the balance struck in its favor; each wants to impose its own understanding of what is at stake. Minority protectors see the injury of one who has been subject to a racial assault as not a mere isolated event, but as part of an interrelated series of acts by which persons of color are subordinated, and which will follow the victim wherever she goes. First Amendment defenders see the wrong of silencing the racist as much more than a momentary inconvenience: protection of his right to speak is part of the never-ending vigilance necessary to preserve freedom of expression in a society that is too prone to balance it away.

Our view is that both stories are equally valid. Judges and university administrators have no easy, a priori way of choosing, of privileging one over the other. They could coin an exception to free speech, thus giving primacy to the equal protection values at stake.[11] Or, they could carve an exception to equality, saying in effect that universities may protect minority populations except where this abridges speech. Nothing in constitutional or moral theory requires one answer rather than the other. Social science, case law, and the experience of other nations provide some illumination. But ultimately, judges and university administrators must choose. And in making this choice, we are in uncharted terrain: we lack a pole star. To gain a sense of the scope of the problem, let us examine recent events at leading universities and reactions to those events.

The Current Controversy

Incidents of racism and other forms of bigotry have been proliferating on the nation's campuses.[12] Some universities have done as little as possible or have focused on specific episodes or perpetrators. Others have instituted broad-based reforms, ranging from curricular changes to adoption of student conduct rules penalizing racist speech and acts.

Major Incidents and Institutional Responses

The Citadel. In October 1986, a black cadet, sleeping in his room, was awakened by five intruders chanting his name. Clad in white sheets and cone-shaped pillowcase masks, the invaders shouted obscenities and fled, leaving behind a charred cross made of newspaper. Five white cadets confessed. The Citadel's president condemned the action but denied it reflected the racial climate on campus. Shortly thereafter, the black cadet resigned from the academy because of harassment for having reported the incident, and filed an $800,000 civil rights action against the school. College officials then issued a report absolving the school of responsibility and recommending only increased ethnic awareness classes for cadets. One year later, a local grand jury indicted the five cadets on charges of illegally wearing masks in violation of a state anti-Klan law. The Citadel promulgated no new rule governing racial insult or hazing.

Dartmouth College. In February 1988, four members of *The Dartmouth Review*, a conservative weekly newspaper, confronted William S. Cole, a black professor, at the conclusion of his music history class. The newspaper had recently published a highly critical review of Cole's course. The confrontation turned into a shouting and pushing match between the professor and *Review* members. Black students charged that the article and classroom incident were racially motivated; the *Review* insisted that they were simply fair criticism of a professor's teaching ability. A university panel found three staff members guilty of disorderly conduct, harassment, and invasion of privacy for initiating and secretly recording the "vexatious exchange" with Cole. The event caused a heated exchange between the *Review* and Dartmouth's president, James O. Freedman, who criticized the newspaper for "poisoning . . . the intellectual environment."[13] For its part, the *Review* charged Freedman with censorship and reverse discrimination.

Racial tensions continued to mount. In two later issues, the *Review* compared President Freedman, a Jew, with Adolf Hitler. The college trustees condemned the newspaper but declared themselves powerless to impose punishment. Shortly thereafter, a superior court judge ordered Dartmouth to reinstate two of the students on the ground that a member of the disciplinary panel had been biased against them. Two months later, a federal district judge dismissed the students' suit against the university. Like The Citadel, Dartmouth took no action to prohibit racial insult and invective.

Columbia University. In March 1987, Michael Jones, a black senior, had an altercation with Matthew Sodl, a white football player and fraternity member, at a campus discotheque.[14] Later, Jones and five black friends brawled with Sodl and a group of his friends outside the discotheque.[15] Each side claimed provocation[16] and charged the other with using racist language.[17] When the university responded slowly, several protests followed, including one in which black demonstrators and their supporters occupied the administration building.[18] The demonstration ended only after New York police arrested fifty demonstrators. Soon after, the university released a report which described the brawl as racial and charged one white male student with "verbal abuse."[19] The report noted that several black students refused to cooperate with the investigation, which prevented the university from proceeding against additional individuals,[20] an assertion many students refused to accept.[21] Their indignation increased when criminal charges were dropped,[22] a university disciplinary panel issued only warnings,[23] and a federal jury found that Columbia discriminated against the only student disciplined for the fight, because he was white.[24] At the time this chapter was written, Columbia had enacted no new student rule forbidding racial behavior or insult.

University of California–Berkeley. An intoxicated fraternity member shouted obscenities and racial slurs at a group of black students as they passed by his fraternity house;[25] later, a campus radio disc jockey told black students to "go back to Oakland" when they asked the station to play rap music. Members of a gay and lesbian group reported that an anonymous caller had left a message on its recorder declaring, "You should be taken out and gassed, like Hitler did with the Jews." Berkeley responded to these and other events by instituting a campuswide Diversity Awareness program, and the statewide system enacted a policy prohibiting "those personally abusive epithets which, when directly addressed to any ordinary person, are likely to provoke a violent reaction whether or not they actually do so."[26] The rule applies to words spoken on university property, at official university functions and events. Penalties range from reprimands to dismissal.

Stanford University. In fall 1988, a group of black and white students debated the racial ancestry of composer Ludwig van Beethoven. The black students correctly maintained that he was a mulatto; some of the white students denied it. Later, two of the whites defaced a poster of Beethoven by scribbling on the face and adding stereotypically black facial features. The incident sparked a sharp confrontation between black and white students. Later, Stanford released a revised student conduct code prohibiting words intended to harm or harass, "directly addressed" to a specific person, and containing "words, pictures or symbols that are commonly understood to convey in a direct and visceral way, hatred or contempt" for a particular race or sex. Nearly ten years later, a local court struck the rule down; Stanford decided not to appeal.

University of Massachusetts. In October 1986, the New York Mets baseball team defeated the Boston Red Sox in the final game of the World Series. At Amherst, over one thousand students who had been watching the game poured out of dormitories onto the campus shortly after midnight. Some were intoxicated. Skirmishes broke out. When a small group of black students arrived, the violence intensified. Ten students were injured, including one black who was left in a neck brace and crutches. A state commission criticized the university, finding the brawl "predictable, preventable and primarily racially motivated." The university punished the instigators and instituted special classes and events on racial tolerance. These measures failed to prevent further racial outbreaks. On March 12, over two hundred minority students occupied the university's African American Studies building. The occupation ended five days later when the university agreed to many of the students' demands, including revision of the student conduct code to punish racially motivated violence.

University of Michigan. In January 1987, a group of black women meeting in a lounge on the Ann Arbor campus found a stack of handbills declaring "open hunting season" on all blacks. A nineteen-year-old white underclassman admitted to distributing them and was disciplined, a result many white students thought too severe. A short time later, a disc jockey for the campus radio station encouraged listeners to call in and tell racist jokes. Other students established a computerized file which contained more such jokes, accessible through a password.

After these and other incidents, the Regents approved a new student conduct code covering several categories of harassment.[27] The policy, which purported to balance free speech with the university's need to deter racist conduct, set varying standards for different locations around the campus. With respect to conduct in classrooms and other academic settings, the policy prohibited any verbal or physical behavior which (1) "stigmatizes or victimizes" any individual on the basis of thirteen different cultural characteristics (including race, sex, ethnicity, and religion), and (2) threatens or interferes with the individual's university activities or "creates an intimidating, hostile or demeaning environment." Sanctions ranged from formal reprimands to expulsion.

A short time later, a graduate student represented by the American

Civil Liberties Union (ACLU) sued Michigan on the ground that its policy violated the First Amendment. A United States District Court struck down the policy in August 1989, finding its provisions unconstitutionally vague.[28] The university replaced the policy with one that bars slurs directed at specific individuals but exempts statements made during classroom discussion.

University of Wisconsin at Madison. In May 1987, members of the Madison chapter of the Phi Gamma Delta (PGD) fraternity sponsored their annual "Fiji Island" party, as part of which they erected a fifteen-foot high plywood caricature of a black man with a bone through his nose and paraded in black face-paint and tropical garb. When black students picketed the house, the caricature was removed only to be erected again the next day. This sparked a further round of protests, which subsided only when the university suspended PGD and ordered its members to undergo sensitivity training. One week later, the predominantly Jewish Zeta Beta Tau (ZBT) fraternity held a closed party. Uninvited PGD members appeared and made racial and ethnic slurs, which provoked a brawl. The university immediately resuspended PGD, but an independent investigator recommended reversal. The acting chancellor lifted the group's suspension and apologized. One month later, the university concluded that, while the racist remarks were "reprehensible," they were not punishable under the existing student conduct code and were protected by the First Amendment. Jewish and black student groups were outraged. In February 1988, Chancellor Donna Shalala unveiled the "Madison Plan," a sweeping program aimed at improving recruitment and retention of minorities of color.

In April 1988, Wisconsin professor Harold Scheub was conducting an exam for his African Storyteller course when six men entered and disrupted the proceedings. Two hours later, Professor Linda Hunter, while teaching an African languages course, was harassed by six men who set off a stink bomb in the classroom before fleeing. University investigators found that the intruders, primarily members of the University of Illinois chapter of the Acacia fraternity, acted with racial motivation and the complicity of the group's Madison chapter. The university suspended the local chapter for one year, and a number of the Illinois members pleaded no contest to criminal charges.

One year after themselves being victimized by ethnic and racial slurs, the Wisconsin chapter of ZBT sponsored a "slave auction" fundraiser at a private home. The auction included several skits, including one in which pledges wore black face paint and Afro wigs, and lip-synched Jackson Five songs; and another in which a male pledge, also in blackface and wig, impersonated Oprah Winfrey while two other males taunted the pledge sexually. When a student committee concluded that the fraternity violated no campus rule and that the skits were protected speech, two hundred demonstrators occupied the administration building in a "day of rage." Chancellor Shalala agreed to some of the group's demands, but refused to expel the ZBT members on the ground that their actions were constitutionally protected. Once again, black students took to the streets. Soon thereafter, the Wisconsin student association stripped the committee of authority over complaints of racism and sexism, and the Interfraternity Council suspended the fraternity for five years. Eventually, Shalala tightened control over campus fraternities and sororities and promulgated a new code of student conduct punishing racial speech and behavior. As happened at Michigan, the Wisconsin ACLU filed suit to declare the university's new policy unconstitutional.

A review of the more celebrated incidents of hate speech and crime indicates that in several cases—Michigan, Wisconsin, Massachusetts, Berkeley, and Stanford—the incidents led to enactment of anti-racism rules. In others—Dartmouth, The Citadel, and Columbia—no rules were enacted, at least immediately. There seems to be little correlation between the seriousness or number of incidents and the enactment of rules. Some universities have responded quickly to a small number of incidents; others have ignored serious unrest or declared themselves unable to act. Whether a campus ultimately adopts an anti-racism rule or not, the mere suggestion of such rules generates controversy.

The Current Debate

In response to the rising number of racial incidents, many colleges and universities have adopted student conduct codes or revised old ones to cope with the new wave of unrest.[29] These rules and policies have drawn fire from commentators ranging from political conservatives to First Amendment absolutists.

The University as "Bastion of Freedom." A frequent argument against campus anti-racism rules is that they run counter to the ideal of the university as a bastion of free thought. Describing the campus as "the locus of the freest expression to be found anywhere," where the unpopular truth may be "pursued—and imparted with impunity," Professor Chester Finn decries any effort to limit that freedom.[30] Many contend that anti-harassment policies, even those aimed only at face-to-face insults, might chill academic exchange or teaching. Further, they argue that "chill" of expression operates only in one direction: Professor Alan Charles Kors charges that at most campuses a white male can be insulted and disparaged with relative impunity.[31] Minority protectors often respond by transferring the debate outside the realm of speech. Martha Minow, for example, focuses on the way racist insults stigmatize the victim and draws a line between speech and harassment.[32] Dartmouth president James O. Freedman responded to criticism of his attack on *The Dartmouth Review* by describing the conflict not as a matter of "expression" but of protecting academic diversity.

In Loco Parentis. Opponents of campus anti-racism rules also charge that the rules represent a throwback to the days when colleges and universities functioned *in loco parentis*. Chester Finn points out that although campuses have refused to regulate student sexuality and alcohol and drug consumption, they are nevertheless anxious to prohibit offensive speech. Martha Minow, on the other hand, points out that "neutrality does not mean no state regulation. The state is not neutral when it permits some private groups to wield power over others."[33]

Protecting the Vulnerable. In his long-running battle with *The Dartmouth Review*, President Freedman emphasized that an academic institution has a responsibility toward the potential victim of racial harassment and insult.[34] Conservatives reject this idea,[35] arguing that speech cannot be bad merely because it permits individuals to say bad things. Contrary views are an inherent part of an intellectual community; persons who are "hurt by strong expressions of disagreement belong not in a university, but in a Trappist monastery."[36] Other writers, however, reply that the injury of a racist insult is not just an individual but a collective one that the community may, and should, address.

The Politics of Tolerance. Many writers who question campus anti-racism rules maintain that the new restrictions are motivated more by politics than the need to protect racial minorities. Robert M. O'Neil views the question as whether "special interests" should override free speech protections.[37] Others see the new policies as thinly veiled efforts to privilege a liberal agenda, pointing out that higher education's tolerance for scathing speech seems to vary with the ideology of the speaker. George Will, for example, questions whether rules banning items offensive to the right—"unpatriotic, irreligious or sexually explicit expressions"—would be graciously accepted by leftist endorsers of anti-racism rules.[38] Thomas Sowell labels anti-racism rules desperate attempts by liberals to cover up the failures of affirmative action.[39] Minority protectors respond that protecting people of color from disparaging treatment is a matter not of politics but human decency, and is deeply rooted in our tradition of constitutional equality.

A Better Way? Some opponents of anti-racism rules urge that "[m]ore speech, not less, is the proper cure for offensive speech." Jon Wiener, for example, calls on universities to speak out forcefully and frequently on why racist speech is objectionable.[40] Others urge that universities focus on underlying racist attitudes, rather than on their outward manifestations, or address racism through teaching and example. The soundness of these and related arguments is addressed later in this chapter.

How Other Societies Have Framed the Issue: International and Foreign Law

A number of international treaties and conventions, many enacted in response to atrocities inflicted upon Jews and other minorities during World War II, condemn racial discrimination and violence.[41] The most important and specific piece of anti-racism legislation, however, is the International Convention on the Elimination of All Forms of Racial Discrimination (CERD).[42] Signed by 104 states,[43] the Convention provides that "[t]he concern of the United Nations with the promotion and protection of human rights and fundamental freedoms is an expression of the ever-increasing interest of the international community in ensuring that these rights and freedoms shall be enjoyed by all human beings everywhere. . . . [R]acial discrimination has been and is considered to be one of the most odious of human rights violations."[44] The convention's central provision is Article 4, which requires member countries to criminalize dissemination of hate propaganda and all organizations that incite racial discrimination.[45] The General Assembly adopted this article only after heated debate,[46] yet most signatory nations have followed its mandate in enacting national legislation.[47] For example, Great Britain's Race Relations Act of 1965[48] was the culmination of several earlier attempts to broaden and conform British law to international trends.[49] The act created a new offense for persons who "with intent to stir up hatred against any section of the public . . . distinguished by colour, race or ethnic or national origins—. . . publish[ ] or distribute[ ] written matter which is threatening, abusive or insulting; or . . . use[ ] in any public place or at any public meeting words which are threatening, abusive or insulting, being matter or words likely to stir up hatred."[50] The act has since been modified a number of times, to reduce the requirement of intent and permit a constable to make an arrest upon reasonable suspicion that an offense is being committed.[51] Although many are still unsatisfied with the law, few advocate doing away with it altogether.[52] In the meantime, British courts interpret the act narrowly to minimize conflict with free speech.[53]

Like Great Britain, Canada has developed a panoply of measures to protect minorities against racism, including the Constitutional Charter of Rights,[54] the Canadian Bill of Rights,[55] certain provisions of the Canadian Criminal Code,[56] and ten provincial human rights codes.[57] Canada's national criminal code prohibited hate speech as early as June 1970. A 1965 Report of the Special Committee on Hate Propaganda provided the impetus for Canada's current legislation. Parliament commissioned the report in an attempt to understand the origin and activity of various hate organizations in the country. Out of the report's recommendations and the desire to harmonize Canada's legislation with international standards, Canada enacted House of Commons Bill C-3, which recognizes four types of hate speech as crimes: advocating genocide, public incitement of hatred, willful promotion of hatred, and spreading false news.[58]

Each of the offenses is subject to a number of defenses, all designed to protect free expression, which together with the requirement of the attorney general's consent to prosecute are aimed at limiting the likelihood of abuse. Although a few civil libertarians continue to express concern, criticism generally has been muted. One commentator has observed that when hate laws were first proposed, the Canadian Civil Liberties Association raised the specter of the slippery slope; yet, the evils they warned about have not come to pass, even in the wake of recent Canadian

Supreme Court decisions upholding laws against pornography and hate speech. As in Great Britain, the current debate concerns how broad or narrow the rules should be and details of their effectuation.

The German penal code, like that of the Netherlands, France, and Austria, outlaws the spreading of hatred, promotion of genocide, and inciting of hatred against minority groups in a manner tending to breach the peace.[59] It also outlaws the organization of unconstitutional political parties (neo-Nazi) and dissemination of propaganda and use of the emblems of these parties, and prohibits writings that "incite to racial hatred or which depict cruel and otherwise inhumane acts of violence against persons in such a manner as to glorify or deny the wrongfulness of such acts of violence."[60] Further, it is a punishable offense to deny the Holocaust's existence.

Italy, which at the time of Article 4's enactment expressed concern that the article might jeopardize the right of free expression, nevertheless enacted one of the strongest laws implementing it. The first sentence under the law was imposed on October 28, 1980, after eleven Italian youths carried wooden crosses and shouted "Jews to the ovens" and "Hitler taught us it's no crime to kill Jews" during a basketball game between Israel and Italy. The judge imposed a sentence of three years and four months.[61]

The Scandinavian countries have long protected individual liberty. Yet, Sweden's constitution[62] permits punishment of hate speech and acts of persecution against national or ethnic-origin groups, while Norway recently amended its penal code in the wake of anti-semitic violence to provide "Anyone who threatens, insults, or exposes any person or groups of persons to hatred, persecution or contempt on account of their religion, race, colour, or national or ethnic origin by means of a public utterance or by other means of communication brought before, or in any other way disseminated among the general public, shall be punished by fines or imprisonment up to two years."[63]

Australia has adopted the Racial Discrimination Act of 1975,[64] which makes it "unlawful for a person to publish or display . . . an advertisement or notice that indicates . . . an intention to do an act that is unlawful by reason of a provision of this Part."[65] New Zealand's Race Relations Act of 1971, amended in 1977,[66] makes incitement to racial disharmony a criminal offense.

Naturally one must extrapolate cautiously from the experiences of other societies. And what holds true of a nation may not hold true for a university. Still, it would be a mistake to ignore the experience of Canada, whose constitutional approach to regulation of speech resembles our own; or of Great Britain, with whom we share a common-law tradition. With these provisos, some cautious generalizations seem possible. In some countries, for example Britain and Canada, anti-racism laws met with initial resistance, which has largely subsided. In others, for example Scandinavia, the laws have been accepted and have remained largely unchallenged. In no country's experience does there seem to have been a snowball effect toward censorship. We discuss various countries' attitudes toward, and recent experiences with, anti-hate legislation in greater detail in chapter 8.

Social Science and Racism

The debate surrounding campus anti-racism rules has not only proceeded in an empirical vacuum, ignoring the experience of other societies; it has also proceeded in a theoretical one, blind to the insights of social scientists who have studied race and racism. Critics of anti-racism rules, for example, often assert that (1) rules forbidding racist remarks will simply cause racism to go underground or surface in a more virulent form; (2) racist speech serves as a form of release, allowing prejudiced individuals to blow off steam harmlessly; (3) punishing racist speech is ineffective because it does not deal with the "root" causes of racism; and (4) the harm of a racial insult is *de minimis*. For their part, defenders of anti-hate rules maintain that racial speech causes serious harm to the psyche and educational prospects of its victims, with little if any documentation of these effects. Social science research sheds light on these and other assertions central to the debate about anti-racism rules.

Nature and Origin of Prejudice

Social scientists have put forward a number of overlapping theories—psychodynamic, socioeconomic, and social-psychological—that explain how persons come to harbor prejudiced attitudes toward members of outgroups. No theory dominates; indeed, more than one approach may be essential to understand the complex phenomenon of racism.

Psychodynamic theories find the source of racism in personality traits of particular individuals.[67] For example, Adorno and his co-authors write that the most severe forms of racism are associated with a group of traits labeled the "authoritarian personality."[68] Authoritarian personalities are rigid, conventional, and have difficulty accepting impulses they consider deviant—fear, weakness, sex, and aggression. Because they reject these impulses in themselves, they are prone to displace them onto others, particularly members of disfavored groups.

Other social scientists believe that understanding racism requires going beyond personal pathology to broader currents in society.[69] Many hold that two principal sources of racism and prejudice toward out-groups are economic dislocation and competition.[70] The anxiety produced by rapid social change requires a scapegoat—but that group must then be assigned traits of inferiority, in order to preserve the myth that America is fair and just.[71] Scapegoating also channels aggression and strengthens group loyalty against outsiders who are perceived as at fault for societal ills.[72]

Finally, the social-psychological approach[73] holds that racial antipathies are not innate but learned, often as an aspect of group membership. Humans have a natural propensity to generalize. Ethnic categories serve this purpose, as well as satisfy the basic human need for group identity. Loyalties to the in-group are accompanied by dislike of out-groups. The dislike increases the distance between the individual and the out-group, so that the attitude becomes self-reinforcing.

The combined effect of all these forces—personal dynamics, scapegoating, economic dislocations, and in-group-out-group categories—is powerful: studies indicate that a majority of Americans harbor some degree of prejudice toward groups other than their own. Yet, not all act on these attitudes; at times, we hold our prejudices in check. Under what conditions is the racial impulse restrained and what may society do to promote that restraint?

Controlling Racism

Unlike with racism's etiology, there is relative agreement on the part of social scientists on how to control its expression. Much prejudice is situational—individuals express it because the environment encourages or tolerates it.[74] The attitude may be relatively constant, but most of us express it selectively—at times we hold it in check, at other times we feel freer to express it in action. The main inhibiter of prejudice is the certainty that it will be remarked and punished. This "confrontation theory"[75] for controlling racism holds that most individuals are ambivalent in matters of race. We realize that the national values—those enshrined in the "American Creed"—call for fair and respectful treatment of all. But the fair-mindedness of our public norms is not always matched by our private behavior. During moments of intimacy we feel much freer to tell or laugh at an ethnic joke, to make a racist or sexist remark. (See chapter 1.)

Rules, formalities, and other environmental reminders put us on notice that the occasion requires the higher formal values of our culture. The very existence of rules forbidding certain types of racist acts causes us not to be inclined to carry them out. Moreover, threat of public notice and disapproval operates as a reinforcer—the potential racist refrains from acting out of fear of notice and sanction. The confrontation theory is probably today the majority view among social scientists on how to control racism. Most who subscribe to this approach hold that laws and rules play a vital role in controlling racism. According to Allport, they "create a public conscience and a standard for expected behavior that check overt signs of prejudice."[76] Nor is the change merely cosmetic. In time, rules are internalized, and the impulse to engage in racist behavior weakens.

The current understanding of racial prejudice thus lends some support to campus anti-racism rules. The mere existence of such rules will often cause members of the campus community to behave in a less racist way, particularly when others may be watching. Even in private settings, some people will refrain from acting because the law has set an example. Those whose prejudice is associated with authoritarianism will do so because the rules represent society's legitimate voice. Further, social science casts doubt on both the "hydraulic" theory of racism, according to which controlling racism in one arena will simply cause it to crop up somewhere else, as well as the theory that racist remarks are relatively harmless. A large body of literature shows that incessant racial categorization and treatment seriously impair the prospects and development of persons of minority race, deepen rigidity, and set the stage for even more serious transgressions on the part of persons so disposed.

Legal Paradigms: The Emerging Stand-Off

As mentioned earlier, campus anti-racism rules can be analyzed from two directions. One perspective puts speech at the center and demands that proponents of anti-racism rules justify the abridgment of that liberty. Another puts equal dignity at the center and regards the speech-act as a violation. Proponents of the latter view argue that the university has the power (perhaps the duty) to protect vulnerable populations from racial abuse, and demand that advocates of free speech show why the interest in hurling invective should nevertheless prevail. Typically, they cite some of the harms associated with racist speech detailed in the preceding section and in chapter 1.

A First Amendment View

The First Amendment appears to stand as a formidable barrier to campus rules prohibiting group-disparaging speech. Designed to assure that debate on public issues is "uninhibited, robust, and wide open,"[77] the First Amendment protects speech that we hate as much as that which we hold dear.[78] Yet racial insults implicate powerful social interests in equality and equal personhood. When uttered on university campuses, racial insults bring into play additional concerns. Few would question that the university has strong, legitimate interests in teaching students and teachers to treat each other respectfully; protecting minority-group students from harassment; and protecting diversity, which could be impaired if students of color become demoralized and leave the university, or if parents of minority race decide to send their children elsewhere.

Only on one occasion has the United States Supreme Court weighed free speech against the equal-protection values endangered by race-hate speech. In *Beauharnais v. Illinois,*[79] the defendant was convicted under a statute prohibiting dissemination of materials promoting racial or religious hatred. Citing the "fighting words" doctrine of *Chaplinsky v. New Hampshire,* Justice Frankfurter ruled that libelous statements aimed at groups, like those aimed at individuals, fall outside First Amendment protection.[80] Later decisions, notably *New York Times v. Sullivan,*[81] and *R.A.V. v. St. Paul,*[82] have increased protection for libelous speech, with the result that some commentators and courts question whether *Beauhar-*

nais today would be decided differently.[83] Yet, *Beauharnais* has never been overruled, and in the meantime many courts have afforded redress in tort for racially or sexually insulting language, with few finding any constitutional problem with doing so.[84] (See chapter 1).

Moreover, over the past century the courts have carved out or tolerated dozens of "exceptions" to free speech. These exceptions include speech used to form a criminal conspiracy or an ordinary contract; speech that disseminates an official secret; speech that defames or libels someone; speech that is obscene; speech that creates a hostile workplace; speech that violates a trademark or plagiarizes another's words; speech that creates an immediately harmful impact or is tantamount to shouting fire in a crowded theater; "patently offensive" speech directed at captive audiences or broadcast on the airwaves; speech that constitutes "fighting words"; speech that disrespects a judge, teacher, military officer, or other authority figure; speech used to defraud a consumer; words used to fix prices; words ("stick 'em up—hand over the money") used to communicate a criminal threat; and untruthful or irrelevant speech given under oath or during a trial.

Much speech, then, is unprotected. The issues are whether the social interest in reining in racially offensive speech is as great as that which gives rise to these "exceptional" categories, and whether the use of racially offensive language has speech value. Because little recent Supreme Court law directly addresses these issues, one might look to the underlying policies of our system of free expression to understand how the Court may rule if an appropriate case comes before it.

As we mentioned earlier, our system of free expression serves a number of societal and individual goals.[85] Included are the personal fulfillment of the speaker; ascertainment of the truth; participation in democratic decision-making; and achieving a balance between social stability and change. Applying these policies to the controversy surrounding campus anti-racism rules yields little support for their detractors. Uttering racial slurs may afford the racially troubled speaker some immediate relief, but hardly seems essential to self-fulfillment in any ideal sense. Indeed, social science writers hold that making racist remarks impairs, rather than promotes, the growth of the person who makes them, by encouraging rigid, dichotomous thinking and impeding moral development.[86] Moreover, such remarks serve little dialogic purpose; they do not seek to connect the speaker and addressee in a community of shared ideals. They divide, rather than unite.

Additionally, slurs contribute little to the discovery of truth. Classroom discussion of racial matters and even the speech of a bigot aimed at proving the superiority of the white race might move us closer to the truth. But one-on-one insults do not. They neither state nor attack a proposition; they are like a slap in the face. By the same token, racial insults do little to help reach broad social consensuses. Indeed, by demoralizing their victim they may actually reduce speech, dialogue, and participation in political life. "More speech" is rarely a solution. Epithets often strike suddenly, immobilizing their victim and rendering her speechless. Often they are delivered in cowardly, anonymous fashion—in the form of a defaced poster or leaflet slipped under a student's door, or hurled by a group against a single victim, rendering response foolhardy. Nor do they help strike a healthy balance between stability and social change. Racial epithets could be argued to relieve racial tension harmlessly and thus contribute to racial stability, but this strained argument has been called into question by social science. (See chapter 6.)

Yet racial epithets are speech, and as such we ought to protect them unless there is a very good reason for not doing so. A recent book by Kent Greenawalt suggests a framework for assessing laws against insults.[87] Drawing on First Amendment principles and case law, Greenawalt writes that the setting, the speaker's intention, the forum's interest, and the relationship between the speaker and the victim must be considered. Moreover, abusive words (like kike, nigger, wop, and faggot) are punishable if spoken with intent, cause a harm capable of formulation in clear legal language, and form a message essentially devoid of ideas. Greenawalt offers as an example of words that could be criminally punishable, "You Spic whore," uttered by four men to a woman of color at a bus stop, intended to humiliate her. He notes that such words can have long-term damaging effects on the victim and have little if any cognitive content; that meaning which the words convey may be expressed in other ways.

Under Greenawalt's test, narrowly drawn university guidelines penalizing racial slurs might well withstand scrutiny. The university forum has a strong interest in establishing a nonracist atmosphere. Moreover, most university rules are aimed at face-to-face remarks that are intentionally abusive. Most exclude classroom speech, speeches to a crowd, and satire published in a campus newspaper. Under Greenawalt's nonabsolutist approach, such rules might well be held constitutional.[88]

An Equal Protection View

The First Amendment perspective thus yields no clear-cut result. Society has a strong interest in seeing that expression is as unfettered as possible, yet racial slurs have no great social worth and can cause serious harm. Unfortunately, looking at the problem of racist speech from the perspective of the equality-protecting amendments yields no clearer result.

Equality and equal respect are highly valued principles in our system of jurisprudence. Three constitutional provisions and a myriad of federal and state statutes are aimed at protecting the rights of racial, religious, and sexual minorities to be free from discrimination in housing, education, jobs, and many other areas of life. Moreover, universities have considerable power to enact regulations protecting minority interests. Yet the equality principle is not without limits. State agencies may not redress breaches by means that too broadly encroach on the rights of whites, or on other constitutional principles. Rigorous rules of intent, causation, standing, and limiting relief circumscribe what may be done.[89] New causes of action are not lightly recognized; for example, the legal system has resisted efforts by feminists to have pornography deemed a civil rights offense against women.[90] And, as we have seen, even tort law has been slow to recognize a civil cause of action for racist speech (see chapter 1).

Moreover, courts have held or implied that a university's power to effectuate campus policies, presumably including equality, is also limited. Cases stemming from efforts to regulate the wearing of armbands, what students may publish in the school newspaper, or their freedom to gather in open areas for worship or speech have shown that individual liberty will sometimes limit an institution's interest in achieving its educational objectives—students do not abandon all their constitutional rights at the schoolhouse door. According to the author of a leading treatise on higher-education law, rules bridling racist speech will be found constitutional if there is a local history of racial disruption; if the rules are narrowly tailored to punish only face-to-face insults and avoid encroaching on classroom and other protected speech; if they are consistently and even-handedly applied; and if due process protections such as the right to representation and a fair hearing are present.[91] The author's guidelines seem plausible, but have yet to be tested. One set of rules was promulgated, then withdrawn; others were declared overly broad and subsequently redrafted. In several jurisdictions, the ACLU has announced that it is monitoring developments and may file suit.

In the meantime, analogous authority continues to develop. In *Bob Jones University v. United States,*[92] the Supreme Court held that universities may not discriminate in the name of religion. In *University of Pennsylvania v. EEOC,*[93] the Supreme Court held that a university's desire to protect confidential tenure files did not insulate the university from review in connection with discrimination investigations. Both cases imply that the anti-discrimination imperative will at times prevail over other strong interests, such as freedom of religion or academic freedom—and possibly speech. In the recent Minnesota "cross-burning" case (discussed later), however, the Court held that criminal laws regulating hate messages must be broadly and neutrally drawn.

Reconciling the First and Fourteenth Amendments: Stigma-Pictures and the Social Construction of Reality

Class Subordination and the Problem of Concerted Speech

As we have seen, neither the constitutional narrative of the First, nor of the Thirteenth and Fourteenth, Amendments clearly prevails in connection with campus anti-racism rules. Judges must choose. The dilemma is embedded in the nature of our system of law and politics: we want and fear both equality and liberty. We think the problem of campus anti-racism rules can yield to a postmodern insight: that speech by which society constructs a stigma picture of minorities may be regulated consistently with the First Amendment. Indeed, regulation may be necessary for full effectuation of the values of equal personhood we hold equally dear.

The first step is recognizing that racism is, in almost all its aspects, a class harm—the essence of which is subordination of one people by another. The mechanism of this subordination is a complex, interlocking series of acts, some physical, some symbolic. Although the physical acts (like lynchings and cross burnings) are often the most striking, the symbolic acts are the most insidious. By communicating and constructing a shared cultural image of the victim group as inferior, we enable ourselves to feel comfortable about the disparity in power and resources between ourselves and the stigmatized group. Even civil rights law may contribute to this stigmatization: the group is so vulnerable that it requires help. The shared picture also demobilizes the victims of discrimination, particularly the young. Indeed, social scientists have seen evidence of self-hatred and rejection of their own identity in children of color as early as age three.

The ubiquity and incessancy of harmful racial depiction are thus the source of its virulence. Like water dripping on sandstone, it is a pervasive harm which only the most hardy can resist. Yet the prevailing First Amendment paradigm predisposes us to treat racist speech as an individual harm, as though we had only to evaluate the effect of a single drop of water. This approach—corresponding to liberal, individualistic theories of self and society—systematically misperceives the experience of racism for both victim and perpetrator. This mistake is natural, and corresponds to one aspect of our natures—our individualistic selves. In this capacity, we want and need liberty. But we also exist in a social capacity; we need others to fulfill ourselves as beings. In this group aspect, we require inclusion, equality, and equal respect. Constitutional narratives of equal protection and prohibition of slavery—narratives that encourage us to form and embrace collectivity and equal citizenship for all—reflect this second aspect of our existence.

When the tacit consent of a group begins to coordinate the exercise of individual rights so as seriously to jeopardize participation by a smaller group, the "rights" nature of the first group's actions acquires a different character and dimension.[94] The exercise of an individual right now poses a group harm and must be weighed against this qualitatively different type of threat.

Greenawalt's book[95] has made a cautious move in this direction. Although generally a defense of free speech in its individual aspect, his book also notes that speech is a primary means by which we construct reality. Thus, a wealthy and well-regarded citizen who is victimized by a vicious defamation is able to recover in tort. His social "picture," in which he has a property interest, has been damaged, and will require laborious reconstruction. It would require only a slight extension of Greenawalt's observation to provide protection from racial slurs and hate speech. Indeed, the rich man has the dominant "story" on his side; repairing the defamation's damage will be relatively easy.

Racist speech, by contrast, is not so readily repaired—it separates the victim from the storytellers who alone have credibility. Not only does racist speech, by placing all the credibility with the dominant group, strengthen the dominant story, it also works to disempower minority groups by crippling the effectiveness of their speech in rebuttal. This situation makes free speech a powerful asset to the dominant group, but a much less helpful one to subordinate groups—a result at odds, certainly, with marketplace theories of the First Amendment. Unless society is able to deal with this incongruity, the Thirteenth and Fourteenth Amendments and our complex system of civil rights statutes will be of little avail. At best, they will be able to obtain redress for episodic, blatant acts of individual prejudice and bigotry. This redress will do little to alleviate the source of the problem: the speech that creates the stigma-picture that makes the acts hurtful in the first place, and that renders almost any other form of aid—social or legal—useless.

Operationalizing the Insight

Could judges and legislators effectuate our suggestion that speech which constructs a stigma-picture of a subordinate group stands on a different footing from sporadic speech aimed at persons who are not disempowered? It might be argued that all speech constructs the world to some extent, and that every speech act could prove offensive to someone. Traditionalists find modern art troublesome, Republicans detest left-wing speech, and some men hate speech that constructs a sex-neutral world. Yet race—like gender and a few other characteristics—is different; our entire history and culture bespeak this difference. Thus, judges easily could differentiate speech which subordinates blacks, for example, from that which disparages factory owners. Will they choose to do so? There is cause for doubt: low-grade racism benefits the status quo. Moreover, our system's winners have a stake in liberal, marketplace interpretations of law and politics—their seeming neutrality and meritocratic nature reassure the decision-makers that their social position is deserved.

Still, resurgent racism on our nation's campuses is rapidly becoming a national embarrassment. Almost daily, we are faced with headlines featuring some of the ugliest forms of ethnic conflict and the specter of virtually all-white universities. The need to avoid these consequences may have the beneficial effect of causing courts to reflect on, and tailor, constitutional doctrine. As Harry Kalven pointed out twenty-five years ago, it would not be the first time that insights born of the cauldron of racial justice yielded reforms that ultimately redounded to the benefit of all society.[96]

We began by pointing out a little-noticed indeterminacy in the way campus anti-racism rules are analyzed. Such rules may be seen either as posing a First Amendment problem or falling within the ambit of the equality-protecting amendments. The survey of the experience of other nations in regulating hate speech and the writings of social scientists on race and racism do not dispel this indeterminacy. Each view is plausible; each corresponds to a deeply held narrative; each proceeds from one's life experiences; each is backed by constitutional case law and principle. Each lays claim to the higher education imperative that our campuses reflect a marketplace of ideas.

The gap between the two approaches can be addressed by means of a postmodern insight: racist speech is different because it is the means by which society constructs a stigma-picture of disfavored groups. It is tacitly coordinated by its speakers in a broad design, each act of which seems harmless but which, in combination with others, crushes the spirits of its victims while creating culture at odds with our national values. Only by taking account of this group dimension can we capture the full power of racially scathing speech—and make good on our promises of equal citizenship to those who have so long been denied its reality.

5

Images of the Outsider

Why the First Amendment Marketplace Cannot Remedy Systemic Social Ills. Social Science and Narrative Theory Are Questioning Faith in the Freemarket of Ideas

Conventional First Amendment doctrine is beginning to show signs of strain. Outsider groups and women charge that free-speech law protects them inadequately against certain types of harm. On a more theoretical level, some scholars are questioning whether free expression can perform the lofty functions of community building and consensus formation that society assigns to it.[1]

We believe that in both situations the source of the difficulty is the same: failure to take account of the ways language and expression work. The results of this failure are more glaring in some areas than others. Much as Newtonian physics enabled us to explain phenomena of daily life but required modification to address ones lying on a larger scale, First Amendment theory will need revision to deal with issues lying at its farthest reaches. Just as the new physics ushered in considerations of perspective and positionality,[2] First Amendment thinking will need to incorporate these notions as well.

Conventional First Amendment doctrine is most helpful in connection with small, clearly bounded disputes. Free speech and debate can help resolve controversies over whether a school disciplinary or local zoning policy is adequate, whether a new sales tax is likely to increase or decrease net revenues, or whether one candidate for political office is a better choice than another. Speech is less able, however, to deal with systemic social ills, such as racism or sexism, that are widespread and deeply woven into the fabric of society. Free speech, in short, is least helpful where we need it most.

Consider racial depiction, for example. Several museums have featured displays of racial memorabilia from the past.[3] One exhibit recently toured the United States;[4] another opened a few years ago.[5] Filmmaker Marlon Riggs produced an award-winning one-hour documentary, *Ethnic Notions*, with a similar focus.[6] Each of these collections depicts a shocking parade of Sambos, mammies, coons, uncles, bestial or happy-go-lucky, watermelon-eating African Americans. They show advertising logos and household commodities in the shape of blacks with grotesquely exaggerated facial features. They include minstrel shows and film clips depicting blacks as so incompetent, shuffling, and dim-witted that it is hard to see how they survived to adulthood. Other images depict primitive, terrifying, larger-than-life black men in threatening garb and postures, often with apparent designs on white women.

Seeing these haunting images today, one is tempted to ask: "How could their authors—cartoonists, writers, film-makers, and graphic designers—individuals, certainly, of higher than average education, create such appalling images?[7] And why did no one protest?" The collections mentioned focus on African Americans, but the two of us, motivated by curiosity, examined the history of ethnic depiction for each of the four main minority subgroups of color—Mexicans, African Americans, Asians, and Native Americans—in the United States. In each case we found the same story: each group is depicted, in virtually every epoch, in terms that can only be described as demeaning or worse. In addition, we found striking parallels among the stigma-pictures that society disseminated of the four groups. The stock characters may have different names and appear at different times, but they bear remarkable likenesses and seem to serve similar purposes for the majority culture.

To answer the "How could they" question, we hold that those who composed and disseminated these images simply did not see them as grotesque. Their consciences were clear—their blithe creations did not trouble them. It is only today, decades later, that these images strike us as indefensible and shocking. Our much-vaunted system of free expression, with its marketplace of ideas, cannot correct serious systemic ills such as racism or sexism simply because we do not see them as such at the time. No one can formulate an effective contemporaneous message to challenge the vicious depiction; this happens only much later, after consciousness shifts and society adopts a different narrative.[8] Our own era is no different. This is the dominant, overpowering lesson we draw from reviewing two centuries of ethnic depiction.

We call the belief that we can somehow control our consciousness despite limitations of time and positionality the *empathic* fallacy.[9] In literature, the *pathetic* fallacy holds that nature is like us, that it is endowed with feelings, moods, and goals we can understand.[10] The poet, feeling sad, implores the world to weep with him or her.[11] Its correlate, which we term the *empathic* fallacy, consists of believing that we can enlarge our sympathies through linguistic means alone. By exposing ourselves to ennobling narratives, we broaden our experience, deepen our empathy, and achieve new levels of sensitivity and fellow-feeling. We can, in short, think, talk, read, and write our way out of bigotry and narrow-mindedness, out of our limitations of experience and perspective. As we illustrate, however, we can do this only to a very limited extent.

Not only does our system of free speech fail to correct the repression and abuse subjugated groups must face, it often deepens their dilemma. If not remonstrance, then what? We suggest a program of social reform that includes speech as only one element, and limn a new, variable theory of the First Amendment that incorporates the insights articulated in this chapter.

Images of the Outsider

A small but excellent literature chronicles the depiction in popular culture of each of the major minority subgroups of color—African Americans, Native Americans, Asians, and Mexicans.[12] Let us examine this history and see what parallels we find among the ways that society has traditionally depicted the four groups.

African Americans

Early in our history, as everyone knows, slave traders rounded up African villagers and transported them to the New World in chains. En route, many died; those who survived were sold and forced to work in the fields and houses of a colonial nation bent on economic development and expansion. By the eve of the Civil War, over four million African Americans were condemned to exist in some form of this American Nightmare.

Slave codes regulated behavior, deterring rebellion and forbidding intermarriage. They also prohibited Southern blacks from learning to read and write, thereby denying them access to the world of print then replete with arguments about "the rights of man." The dominant image of blacks in the popular theater and literature of the late eighteenth century was that of the docile and contented slave[13]—childlike, lazy, illiterate, and dependent on the protection and care of a white master. The first appearance of Sambo, a "comic Negro" stereotype, occurred in 1781 in a play called *The Divorce.*[14] This black male character, portrayed by a white in blackface, danced, sang, spoke nonsense, and acted the buffoon. The black man's potential as a sexual and economic competitor was minimized by portraying him as an object of laughter.

Blackface minstrelsy found a new popularity in the 1830s when Thomas D. Rice created Jim Crow, modeled on an elderly, crippled black slave who shuffle-danced and sang.[15] It is thought that Rice even borrowed the old man's shabby clothes for a more authentic stage performance. Rice's performance of Jump Jim Crow won him immediate success in the United States and England. By the 1840s minstrel shows were standard fare in American music halls. There, whites in blackface created and disseminated stereotypes of African Americans as inept urban dandies or happy childlike slaves.[16] Probably more whites—at least in the North—received their understanding of African American culture from minstrel shows than from first hand acquaintance with blacks or their ideas.

Because laws forbade slaves to learn to read or write, slave culture was primarily oral. Thus, it is highly significant that former slaves such as Frederick Douglass and William Wells Brown published accounts of captivity, life on plantations, and escapes to freedom.[17] These early slave narratives, published in the North and circulated among abolitionist societies, presented counterimages to the prevailing myths of the day. The abolitionist movement reached its apogee with the publication of Harriet Beecher Stowe's *Uncle Tom's Cabin.* Though Stowe was successful in presenting the slave master as villain, her portrayal of Uncle Tom changed the stereotype of the black slave only a little: previously he had been docile, content, or comic, while in her depiction he became gentle, long-suffering, and imbued with Christian piety.[18]

After the Civil War, the black image bifurcated. The "good slave" image continued, but was soon joined by an ominous "shadow" figure. The Uncle Tom character became romanticized, a black mouthpiece espousing an apologia for the beliefs of the old genteel white Confederacy. Though never overtly sexual, his masculine form reemerged as the avuncular storyteller Uncle Remus, as well as various other "uncles." His feminine form evolved into a "mammy" figure—cook, washerwoman, nanny, and all-round domestic servant—responsible for the comfort of the Southern white household.[19] With no life of her own, but a fount of practical wisdom, she took an intense interest in the welfare and well-being of the white family she cared for.

During the tumultuous Reconstruction period, the sexuality denied to uncles and mammies found a crude outlet in a new stereotype of the recently freed male Negro as brutish and bestial.[20] The Ku Klux Klan and other illegal raiding parties justified their reign of terror as necessary to control newly freed blacks, whom they believed ready to force sex on any white woman they might encounter. This stereotype, appearing in novels with titles like *The Negro as Beast*, was offered to justify the widespread lynching that took 2,500 black lives between 1885 and 1900.

The myth of the out-of-control ambitious black was fueled by currents prevalent in the marketplace of Western thought during the late nineteenth century: (1) the growth of American imperialism; (2) the absorption of "inferior races"; (3) the white man's burden mentality—the white South bearing the burden in the U.S.; (4) the manifest destiny belief of the Anglo-Saxons; and (5) the new social science theory concerning genetic inferiority.[21]

Many of these ideas found expression in the powerful, crass, and influential writings of Thomas Dixon, whose work represented an effort to satisfy his two goals in life: making money and converting people to racism. He believed that whites, both Northern and Southern, were dutybound to protect the Anglo-Saxon heritage, particularly white women, who were destined to produce a superior race.[22] In 1905, Dixon wrote *The Clansman*, a tale of two families, one Northern, one Southern, united through marriage. It proved a sensation, particularly in the South. Ten years later, filmmaker D. W. Griffith used the plots of this and another of Dixon's novels[23] for his epic three-hour film, *The Birth of a Nation*.

The film transformed Dixon's novels into vivid visual images, featuring uncles, mammies, buffoons, an interfering mulatto mistress, and a chase scene in which a black man with animal-like traits pursues a young white woman until she leaps to her death from a pedestal-like perch at the edge of a cliff. The film played to audiences throughout the country. Recent white immigrants from eastern and southern Europe saw the film in movie houses in poor neighborhoods, where it played for almost a year. In the South it played for fifteen years. A special screening was held at the White House for Dixon's former classmate, President Woodrow Wilson, his guests, and the entire Supreme Court. Wilson later described the film as "like writing history with lightning."[24]

Blacks could do little to confront the overwhelming popularity of *The Birth of a Nation*. The NAACP, by then established with its own newspaper, mobilized opposition. But the film's momentum was unstoppable. Film critics, many of them liberal, though decrying its racism, praised the film for its undeniable technical and artistic merits.

In contrast, efforts to present the story of Reconstruction from a black point of view were less successful. Novelist Albion Tourgee, a white superior court judge and activist, used black characters who spoke in their own voices to show the freed man as a person who worked hard and attempted to succeed, but was victimized by the Ku Klux Klan.[25] Tourgee believed the answer to racism lay in portraying blacks as normal—like everyone else. His novel, *Bricks without Straw*, attracted a devoted but small audience; the South's treatment of blacks no longer interested many Northerners, and few Southerners were willing to listen. Black writers suffered a similar fate. While Charles Chesnutt, author of *The Conjure Woman*, was included in a list of the foremost storytellers of the time, his publisher refused to release his next novel because the previous two about racial themes had been commercially unsuccessful.[26] As two authorities point out, "[M]essages only reach those people who are willing to listen. Only when a later audience became receptive . . . could [their] tales be . . . appreciated."[27]

Although blacks had gained formal legal equality, the Supreme Court in 1896 upheld segregation in *Plessy v. Ferguson*.[28] Lynchings continued; racist stereotypes prevailed. Blacks had little access to the press or the film industry and could do little to change the racism that both industries promulgated. Nevertheless, blacks joined the army in droves during World War I. They found that segregation in the ranks was rigidly enforced, however, and many returned angry and disheartened. After the war, unrest in the country led to at least twenty-five urban race riots, many in the previously peaceful North. Repressive images immediately increased and prevailed for a little over a decade. Then, as the disruption abated, a few writers, such as Eugene O'Neill and Sinclair Lewis, portrayed blacks and their plight sympathetically. Black writers and artists in New York created the Harlem Renaissance.[29] Blacks' image metamorphosed yet again. Excited and enthusiastic over this new artistic rapprochement with blacks, whites quickly praised them and their work for elements of the exoticism and primitivism popularized by Gauguin. Echoing early images of good-natured, happy-go-lucky blacks, white society began to regard African Americans as musically talented, rhythmical, passionate, and entertaining. Although these developments heralded a somewhat more positive image, nevertheless the new ones retained elements of condescension and previous stereotypes. The majority-race critics, intellectuals, and artists who were entranced by the Renaissance may have intended no harm, yet they perpetuated views of African Americans as the exotic other.[30]

With World War II, black soldiers and workers again were needed for the war effort; the more virulent forms of racism were held in abeyance. However, when the war ended and the soldiers returned, racial hostilities again sharpened. Having experienced a relatively racism-free environment during the war, black workers and soldiers were not prepared to return to lives of menial work and subservience to whites. For many, expectations of improvement were fed by war propaganda depicting the U.S. as fighting for freedom.[31] Activism sprang up; the civil rights movement began, and once again the dominant image of blacks took on new forms: the cocky, street-smart black who knows his rights; the unreasonable, opportunistic community leader and militant; the safe, comforting, cardigan-wearing ("nice") black of TV sitcoms; and the Black Bomber of superstud films, all mutations of, and permutations of, old familiar forms.[32]

Native Americans

The experience of other groups parallels that of blacks. For example, when the colonists arrived in Virginia and Massachusetts in the seventeenth century, they brought with them images of the Indian created in England and Europe. Early explorers described native peoples of the new world as innocent, ingenuous, friendly, and naked.[33] At first, relations between the two groups were cordial. Later, however, more settlers arrived, bringing with them English concepts of property—land transfer, titles, deeds—that were foreign to Indian thought. Indians who did not cooperate with the settlers' plans were forced off their lands; eventually hostilities broke out,[34] resulting in a conflict that lasted over two centuries.

Early writings about Native Americans reflected two romanticized images—"the Indian princess," incarnated most notably in Pocahantas, and "the man Friday," found in *Robinson Crusoe*,[35] earlier as the troublesome servant Caliban,[36] later as the faithful loyal Chingachgook,[37] and in the twentieth century the buffoon and sidekick Tonto.[38] The first instance of the "captivity narrative" appeared in Massachusetts in 1682 with Mary Rowlandson's "Captivity and Restoration."[39] Early fiction portrayed Indians as looters, burners, and killers—but not rapists,[40] because New Englanders knew that Indians rarely committed rape.[41] But the erotic elements of Rowlandson's story, although mild and subordinated to her religious message, made it the prototype for later such tales that emphasized sexual aggression directed toward Simon-pure captives.

Other writers followed suit without Rowlandson's delicacy, portraying Indians as animal-like and subhuman, a characterization whose roots go back to Paracelsus (1493–1541), who proposed that Indians were not among "the sons of Adam."[42] Shakespeare explored this theme when he wrote *The Tempest* and created a servant for Prospero—Caliban—whose name was an anagram of the newly coined word "cannibal."[43] Cotton Mather and other Puritan writers called Indians wolves, lions, sorcerers, and demons possessed by Satan.[44] By the nineteenth century, the image of the Indian had been rendered savage, barbarous, and half-civilized. In early movies restless natives and jungle beasts were practically interchangeable elements.[45] No wonder, then, that Native Americans were removed, with little protest from the dominant society, to reservations, just as wild and rare beasts were confined to animal reserves.

Later movies of the "cowboys and Indians" genre built on these images when they featured war dances, exotic dress, drunkenness, surprise attacks, scalping, raiding, raping, tomahawks, tomtoms, and torture.[46] D. W. Griffith, creator of *The Birth of a Nation*, incorporated these elements and more in *The Battle at Elderbush Gulch* (1913). In that movie, a white woman, trapped in a cabin surrounded by Indians, awaits her fate, not knowing whether the Indian attackers will kill her or whether one of her white defenders will shoot her before letting the Indians take her alive. By 1911, portrayal of Native Americans in film had become so demeaning that representatives of four Western tribes protested to President William Howard Taft and to Congress. But little change occurred until World War II, when Hollywood transferred the enemy role to the Japanese and Germans. Many of these early Indian movies are still shown on television, feeding the psyches of new generations of Americans with the familiar stereotypes.[47]

Shortly after the end of the war, Hollywood released *Broken Arrow* (1950), the first movie ever to feature an Indian as hero—Cochise of the Apaches. Though artistically and historically flawed, it was widely praised.[48] Other "noble savage" films reversed the stereotype in the opposite direction, portraying Native Americans with exaggerated nobleness—a striking parallel to the treatment adulating whites gave black writers during the Harlem Renaissance.

In 1969, N. Scott Momaday, a Kiowa-Cherokee writer, won the Pulitzer Prize for his novel *House Made of Dawn*. In 1972, PBS ran a BBC production of *The Last of the Mohicans*. In each of these cases, much of the audience was struck by the intelligence of the Native American voice—a far cry from the earlier steady diet (still heard today) of chiefs saying "ugh," braves shrieking war whoops, and Tonto saying "me gettum." It was not always so. Thomas Jefferson wished Congress could speak half as well as orators of Indian nations.[49] William Penn praised the Lenni Lanape language of the Delaware for its subtlety.[50] Yet, the speech of Native Americans—as well as that of African Americans, Mexicans, and Asians—has been mangled, blunted, and rendered inarticulate by whites who then became entitled to speak for them. Like the other groups of color, Native Americans have been disempowered by the very element which, they are told, will save them.

Asian Americans

With Asian Americans, we find much the same pattern we found elsewhere: the dominant depiction in popular culture is negative—although rarely seen as such at the time—and the stereotype shifts to accommodate society's changing needs.

In the middle years of the nineteenth century, Chinese were welcomed into the land for their labor. Needed to operate mines, build railroads, and carry out other physical tasks necessary to the country's develop-ment,[51] the industrious immigrants soon, however, began to surpass white American workers. They opened small businesses, succeeded in making profitable mines that others had abandoned. Not surprisingly, Chinese became the scapegoats for the 1870s depression. Unionists and others exaggerated negative traits thought to be associated with them—opium smoking, gambling—and succeeded in having anti-Chinese legislation enacted.[52] By 1882 public sentiment had mobilized sufficiently so that Congress was able to pass an Exclusion Act, which reduced the number of Chinese in the U.S. from 105,000 in 1880 to 65,000 in 1908.[53] During this period, Japan's international position was on the rise, yet U.S. writers and politicians depicted all Asians as inferior, unassimilable, willing to work unhuman hours at low wages, and loyal to foreign despots.[54] When Japan defeated first China and then Russia, it began to replace China as the "yellow peril." By 1924, all Asians were barred, an exclusion the Supreme Court had upheld for the Chinese in 1889.[55] During a period of increasing tension between the two countries, the film industry portrayed Japanese and other Asians—during this period few distinctions were made—in unremittingly negative terms. As with African Americans and Native Americans, Asian men were depicted as cunning, savage, and as potential rapists interested in defiling white women. (In sharp contrast, white male actors were seen as having legitimate access to Asian women.)

As U.S. militancy grew, films began to devalue Asian—principally Japanese—life. Not even *they* valued life, the narratives of the day said. Why should we value theirs? During earlier periods, when racism against Asians was relatively quiescent, writers and filmmakers employed the stock character of Charlie Chan[56]— the hapless, pidgin-talking Asian, in many respects the functional equivalent of the Sambo or uncle. But as anti-Japanese sentiment increased, we began depicting even domestic Asians as foul and tricky.[57] Anti-Asian films were easy to produce and profitable; Hollywood would often assign a Japanese actor to play a Chinese villain and vice versa.[58]

W. R. Hearst sponsored *Patria*, an anti-Asian film serial that began in 1919 and continued for several years, depicting Asians as a Yellow Men-ace.[59] At one point, Woodrow Wilson became so disturbed by the viru-lence of Hearst's production that he wrote to him, asking him to soften it.[60] Hearst responded by changing the series so that it became domi-nantly anti-Mexican. In the period immediately preceding and following

World War II, anti-Japanese images continued to proliferate. A stock character was the master Oriental criminal, often played by Anglo actors in makeup.[61] By this time, films and novels were distinguishing between Chinese (who were good), and Japanese (who were bad). After Pearl Harbor, intense anti-Japanese propaganda resulted in federal action to intern 110,000 Japanese Americans, many of whom had lived in the United States all their lives.[62] Many lost farms, houses, and other property.[63] It later came to light that most of the evidence of sabotage and fifth-column activities had been fabricated.[64]

Following World War II, depictions of blacks and Indians were upgraded to some extent, but those of Asians only a little. Many of James Bond's villains, for example, have been Asian. In recent days, Japan has once again become a serious economic rival of the United States, producing automobiles, computers, and other products at a price and quality American industry has proven unable to match. Predictably, a further wave of anti-Asian sentiment and stereotyping is reemerging.

Mexican Americans

Images of Mexican Americans (Chicanos) fall into three or four well-delineated stereotypes—the greaser; the conniving, treacherous bandido; the happy-go-lucky shiftless lover of song, food, and dance; and the tragic, silent, "Spanish," tall, dark, and handsome type of romantic fiction—which change according to society's needs.[65] As with blacks, Asians, and Indians, most Americans have relatively few interpersonal contacts with Mexican Americans; therefore, these images become the individual's only reality. When such a person meets an actual Mexican American, he or she tends to place the other in one of the ready-made categories.[66] Stereotyping thus denies members of both groups the opportunity to interact with each other on anything like a complex, nuanced human level.

During and just after the conquest, when the U.S. was seizing and then settling large tracts of Mexican territory in the Southwest, "Western" or "conquest" fiction depicted Anglos bravely displacing shifty, brutal, and treacherous Mexicans.[67] After the war ended and control of the Southwest passed to American hands, a subtle shift occurred. Anglos living and settling in the new regions were portrayed as Protestant, independent, thrifty, industrious, mechanically resourceful, and interested in progress; Mexicans, as traditional, sedate, lacking in mechanical resourcefulness and ambition.[68] Writers both on and off the scene created the same images of indolent, pious Mexicans—ignoring the two centuries of enterprising farmers and ranchers who withstood or negotiated with Apaches and Comanches and built a sturdy society with irrigation, land tenure, and mining codes.

In the late conquest period, depiction of this group bifurcated. As happened at a different period with African Americans, majority-race writers created two images of the Mexican: the "good" (loyal) Mexican peon or sidekick, and the "bad" fighter/greaser Mexican who did not know his place. The first was faithful and domestic; the second, treacherous and evil. As with other groups, the second ("bad") image had sexual overtones: the greaser coveted Anglo women and would seduce or rape them if given the opportunity.[69] Children's books of this time, like the best-selling Buffalo Bill series, were full of Mexican stereotypes used to reinforce moral messages to the young: *they* are like this, *we* like that. The series ended in 1912.

The first thirty years of this century saw heavy Mexican immigration of mainly poor workers. The first Bracero programs—official, temporary importation of field hands—appeared. With increasing numbers, white-only signs and segregated housing and schools appeared, aimed now at Mexicans in addition to blacks.[70] Since there was now an increased risk of interaction and intermarriage, novels and newspaper writing reinforced the notion of these immigrants' baseness, simplicity, and inability to assimilate.[71]

The movies of this period depicted Latins as buffoons, sluts, or connivers; even some of the titles were disparaging: for example, *The Greaser's Gauntlet*.[72] Films featured brown-skinned desperados stealing horses or gold, lusting after pure Anglo women, shooting noble Saxon heroes in the back, or acting the part of hapless buffoons. Animated cartoons and short subjects, still shown on television, featured tequila-drinking Mexicans, bullfighters, Speedy Gonzalez and Slowpoke Rodriguez, and clowns—as well as Castilian caballeras, light-skinned, upper class, and prone to wearing elaborate dresses and carrying castanets.

World War II brought the need for factory and agricultural workers and a new flood of immigrants. Images softened to include "normal" or even noble Mexicans, like the general of Marlon Brando's *Viva Zapata*. Perhaps realizing it had overstepped, America diminished the virulence of its anti-Mexican imagery. Yet the Western genre, with Mexican villains and bandits, continues; and the immigrant speaking gibberish still makes an appearance. Even the most favorable novel and film of the postwar period, *The Milagro Beanfield War,* dissolves in stereotypes.[73]

A few writers found their own culture alienating or sick and sought relief in a more serene Southwest culture. As with the Harlem Renaissance, these creative artists tended to be more generous to Mexicans, but nevertheless retained the Anglo hero as the central figure or Samaritan who uplifts the Mexican from his or her traditional ignorance.

How Could They? Lessons from the History of Racial Depiction

As we have seen, the depiction of ethnic groups of color is littered with negative images, although the content of those images changes over time. In some periods, society needed to suppress a group, as with blacks during Reconstruction. Society then coined an image to suit that purpose—that of primitive, powerful, larger-than-life blacks, terrifying and barely under control. At other times, for example during slavery, society needed reassurance that blacks were docile, cheerful, content with their lot. Images of sullen, rebellious blacks dissatisfied with their condition would have made white society uneasy. Accordingly, images of simple, happy blacks, content to do the master's work, were disseminated.

In every era, then, ethnic imagery comes bearing an enormous amount of social weight. Nevertheless, we sense that we are in control, that things need not be that way. We believe we can use speech, jiujitsu fashion, on behalf of oppressed peoples. We believe that speech can serve as a tool of destabilization. It is virtually a prime tenet of liberal jurisprudence that by talk, dialogue, exhortation, and so on, we present each other with passionate, appealing messages that will counter the evil ones of racism and sexism and thereby advance society to greater levels of fairness and humanity.

Recall the debate about campus speech codes. In response to a rising tide of racist incidents, many campuses have enacted student conduct codes that forbid certain types of face-to-face insult. As we have seen, these codes invariably draw fire from free-speech absolutists and others on the ground that they would interfere with free speech. Campuses, they argue, ought to be "bastions of free speech." Racism and prejudice are matters of "ignorance and fear," for which the appropriate remedy is more speech. Suppression, it is said, merely drives racism underground, where it will fester and emerge in even more hateful forms. Speech is the best corrective for error; regulation risks the specter of censorship and state control. Efforts to regulate pornography, Klan marches, and other types of race baiting often meet similar responses.

But modernist and postmodern insights about language and the social construction of reality show that reliance on countervailing speech that will, in theory, wrestle with bad or vicious speech is often misplaced. This is so for two interrelated reasons: first, the account rests on simplistic and erroneous notions of narrativity and change; and second, it rests on a misunderstanding of the relation between the subject, or self, and new narratives.

The First Reason—Time Warp: Why We (Can) Only Condemn the Old Narrative

Our review shows that we simply do not see many forms of discrimination, bias, and prejudice as wrong at the time. The racism of other times and places does stand out, does strike us as glaringly and appallingly wrong. But this happens only decades or centuries later; we acquiesce in today's version with little realization that it is wrong, that a later generation will ask "How could they?" about *us*. We only condemn the racism of another place (South Africa) or time. But that of our own place and time strikes us, if at all, as unexceptional, trivial, or well within literary license. Every form of creative work (we tell ourselves) relies on stock characters. What's so wrong with a novel that employs a black who . . . , or a Mexican who . . . ? Besides, the argument goes, those groups are disproportionately employed as domestics, are responsible for a high proportion of our crime, are they not? And some actually talk this way; why, just last week, I overheard. . . .

This time-warp aspect of racism makes speech an ineffective tool to counter it. Racism is woven into the warp and woof of the way we see and organize the world—it is one of the many preconceptions we bring to experience and use to construct and make sense of our social world. Racism forms part of the dominant narrative, the group of received understandings and basic principles that form the baseline from which we reason. How could these be in question? Recent scholarship shows that the dominant narrative changes very slowly, resisting alteration. We interpret new stories in light of the old. Ones that deviate too markedly from our preexisting stock are dismissed as extreme, coercive, political, and wrong. The only stories about race we are prepared to condemn, then, are the old ones giving voice to the racism of an earlier age, ones that society has already begun to reject. We can condemn Justice Brown for writing as he did in *Plessy v. Ferguson,* but not university administrators who refuse remedies for campus racism, failing to notice the remarkable parallels between the two.[74]

The Second Reason: Our Narratives, Our Selves

Racial change is slow, then, because the story of race is part of the dominant narrative we use to interpret experience. The narrative teaches that race matters, that people are different, with the differences lying always in a predictable direction. It holds that certain cultures, unfortunately, have less ambition than others, that the majority group is largely innocent of racial wrongdoing, that the current distribution of comfort and well-being is roughly what merit and fairness dictate. Within that general framework, only certain matters are open for discussion: How different? In what ways? (Are some of them, perhaps, good at sports?) With how many exceptions? And what measures are called for to deal with this unfortunate situation and at what cost to whites?[75] This is so because the narrative leaves only certain things intelligible; other arguments and texts would seem alien.

A second and related insight from modern scholarship focuses not on the role of narratives in confining change to manageable proportions, but on the relationship between our selves and those narratives. The reigning First Amendment metaphor—the marketplace of ideas—implies a separation between subjects who do the choosing and the ideas or messages that vie for their attention.[76] Subjects are "in here," the messages "out there." The preexisting subjects choose the idea that seems most valid and true— somewhat in the manner of a diner deciding what to eat at a buffet.

But scholars are beginning to realize that this mechanistic view of an autonomous subject choosing among separate, external ideas is simplistic. In an important sense, we *are* our current stock of narratives, and they us. We subscribe to a stock of explanatory scripts, plots, narratives, and understandings that enable us to make sense of—to construct—our social world. Because we then live in that world, it begins to shape and determine *us*, who we are, what we see, how we select, reject, interpret, and order subsequent reality.[77]

These observations imply that our ability to escape the confines of our own preconceptions is quite limited. The contrary belief—that through speech and remonstrance alone we can endlessly reform ourselves and each other—we call the *empathic fallacy*. It and its companion, the pathetic fallacy, are both based on *hubris*, the belief that we can be more than we are. The empathic fallacy holds that through speech and remonstrance we can surmount our limitations of time, place, and culture, can transcend our own situatedness. But our examination of the cultural record, as well as postmodern understandings of language and personhood, both point to the same conclusion: the notion of ideas competing with each other, with truth and goodness emerging victorious from the competition, has proven seriously deficient when applied to evils, like racism, that are deeply inscribed in the culture.[78] We have constructed the social world so that racism seems normal, part of the status quo, in need of little correction. It is not until much later that what we believed begins to seem incredibly, monstrously wrong. How could we have believed *that?*

True, every few decades an occasional genius will rise up and offer a work that recognizes and denounces the racism of the day.[79] Unfortunately, they are ignored—they have no audience. Witness, for example, the recent "discovery" of long-forgotten black writers such as Charles Chesnutt, Zora Neale Hurston, or the slave narratives.[80] Consider that Nadine Gordimer won the Nobel Prize after nearly forty years of writing about the evils of apartheid;[81] Harriet Beecher Stowe's book sold well only after years of abolitionist sentiment and agitation had sensitized her public to the possibility that slavery was wrong. One should, of course, speak out against social evils. But we should not accord speech greater efficacy than it has.

The Nature of the Evil

Another way of approaching speech's role in correcting racism is by examining not language but the referent, race. This examination discloses that racism contains features that render it relatively unamenable to redress through words. Racism, even when blatant, resists efforts to rally others against it. Indeed, talking often makes matters worse.

How Much Racism Exists? The Difference Perspective Makes

As we have shown, much racism is not seen as such at the time of its commission. But the extent of even the blatant variety is often underappreciated by whites. The reason is simple: few acts of clear-cut racism take place within their view.[82] Racism is often covert; the vignettes tend to be played out behind the scenes when no one else is watching. A merchant who harasses well-behaved black teenage shoppers will probably not do so if other whites are watching. A white apartment owner or employer will probably not deny a superbly qualified black applicant an apartment or job if a friend or observer is present.

As a result of its often covert nature, many persons of the majority race, even those of good will, consistently underestimate the extent of racism in society. Persons of color, on the receiving end of racism, generally report much more of it than do whites and naturally place greater priority on its remedying. This puzzles some whites, who wonder whether blacks are exaggerating or trying to guilt-trip them to gain an unfair advantage. The problem is perspective: imagine that one's body were somehow magnetically charged. One would go through life astonished at how many metal filings there are in the world and how much we need a clean-up operation. Those not caught in this Kafkaesque dilemma would naturally fail to appreciate the situation's urgency.

The Subtle Nuances

Racism's victims become sensitized to its subtle nuances and code words—the body language, averted gazes, exasperated looks, terms such as "you people," "innocent whites," "highly qualified black," "articulate," and so on—that, whether intended or not, convey racially charged meanings. Like an Inuit accustomed to reading the sky for signs of snow or a small household pet skilled at recognizing a clumsy footfall, racism's perpetual victims are alert to the various guises racism and racial signaling take. Sympathizers of majority hue often must labor to acquire the knowledge that for minorities comes all to easily.

On Seeing What One Does Not Want to See

Some refuse to see racism in acts that would trigger suspicion in the mind of any person of color.[83] A well-qualified black applicant fails to get the job. Perhaps it was his tie, his posture, his age, or the way he held himself that caused his rejection. Perhaps he seemed too diffident or too anxious to get the job. Perhaps he had traits, such as voice intonations, that might irritate the firm's customers. Choosing to believe in a race-free world reduces guilt and the need for corrective action. Racism is often a matter of interpretation; when an interpretation renders one uncomfortable and another does not, which will a person often make?[84]

Unlearning the Lessons of the Past

Finally, members of the majority race forget how to see and condemn racism. Society generalizes the wrong lesson from the past, namely that racism has virtually disappeared. We notice, for example, that today there are fewer Sambos than in the past. We thus conclude that those other writers had been acting against conscience, that is, had vicious wills— realized that what they were doing was wrong (as we realize it today), but went ahead and did it anyway. Yet, we think, "*I* do not act against conscience and neither do my friends."

In fact, those earlier writers were acting blithely, not against conscience, any more than we do today in maintaining our own versions of racism and racist imagery. The Willie Horton commercial[85] strikes many as falling within the bounds of fair play, perhaps only slightly exaggerated—at any rate, the sort of thing that one must expect in the rough-and-tumble world of politics. Besides, do not blacks in fact commit a high percentage of violent crime; did I not read that . . . ?

How the System of Free Expression Sometimes Makes Matters Worse

Speech and free expression are not only poorly adapted to remedy racism, they often make matters worse—far from being stalwart friends, they can impede the cause of racial reform. First, they encourage writers, film-makers, and other creative people to feel amoral, nonresponsible in what they do. Because there is a marketplace of ideas, the rationalization goes, another filmmaker is free to make an anti-racist movie that will cancel out any minor stereotyping in the one I am making. My movie may have other redeeming qualities; besides, it is good entertainment and everyone in the industry uses stock characters like the black maid or the bumbling Asian tourist. How can one create film without stock characters?

Second, when insurgent groups attempt to use speech as an instrument of reform, courts almost invariably construe First Amendment doctrine against them. As Charles Lawrence points out, civil rights activists in the sixties made the greatest strides when they acted in defiance of the First Amendment as then understood.[86] They marched, were arrested and convicted; sat in, were arrested and convicted; distributed leaflets, were arrested and convicted. Many years later, after much gallant lawyering and the expenditure of untold hours of effort, the conviction might be reversed on appeal if the original action had been sufficiently prayerful, mannerly, and not too interlaced with an action component. The history of the civil rights movement does not bear out the usual assumption that the First Amendment is of great value for racial reformers.

Current First Amendment law is similarly skewed. Consider the way the many "exceptions" to First Amendment protection favor the interests of the powerful. If one says something disparaging of a wealthy and well-regarded individual, one discovers that one's words were not free after all; that individual has a type of property interest in his or her community image, damage to which is compensable even though words were the sole instrument of the harm. Similarly, if one infringes the copyright or trademark of a well-known writer or industrialist, again it turns out that one's action is punishable. Further, if one disseminates an official secret valuable to a powerful branch of the military or defense contractor, that speech is punishable. If one speaks disrespectfully to a judge, police officer, teacher, military official, or other powerful authority figure, again one discovers that one's words were not free; and so with words used to defraud, form a conspiracy, breach the peace, or untruthful words given under oath during a civil or criminal proceeding. (See chapter 4.)

Yet the suggestion that we create a new exception to protect lowly and vulnerable members of our society, such as isolated, young black undergraduates attending dominantly white campuses, is often met with consternation: minorities (we say), if they knew their own self-interest, should appreciate the need for free speech even more than others. This one-sidedness of free-speech doctrine makes the First Amendment much more valuable to the majority than to the minority.

The system of free expression also has a powerful after-the-fact apologetic function. Elite groups use the supposed existence of a marketplace of ideas to justify their own superior position.[87] Imagine a society in which all A's were rich and happy, all B's were moderately comfortable, and all C's were poor, stigmatized, and reviled. Imagine also that this society scrupulously believes in a free marketplace of ideas. Might not the A's benefit greatly from such a system? On looking about them and observing the inequality in the distribution of wealth, longevity, happiness, and safety between themselves and the others, they might feel guilt. Perhaps their own superior position is undeserved, or at least requires explanation. But the existence of an ostensibly free marketplace of ideas renders that effort unnecessary. Rationalization is easy: our ideas, our culture competed with their more easygoing ones and won. It was a fair fight. Our position must be deserved; the distribution of social goods must be roughly what fairness, merit, and equity call for. It is up to them to change, not us.

A free market of racial depiction resists change for two final reasons. First, the dominant pictures, images, narratives, plots, roles, and stories ascribed to, and constituting the public perception of minorities, are always dominantly negative. Through an unfortunate psychological mechanism, incessant bombardment by images of the sort described above (as well as today's versions) inscribes those negative images on the souls and minds of minority persons. Minorities internalize the stories they read, see, and hear every day. Persons of color can easily become demoralized, blame themselves, not speak up vigorously. The expense of speech also precludes the stigmatized from participating effectively in the marketplace of ideas.[88] They are often poor—indeed, one theory of racism holds that maintenance of economic inequality is its prime function[89]—and hence unlikely to command the means to bring countervailing messages to the eyes and ears of others.

Second, even when minorities do speak they have little credibility. Who would listen to or credit a speaker or writer one associates with watermelon eating, buffoonery, menial work, intellectual inadequacy, laziness, lasciviousness, and demanding resources beyond his or her deserved share?

Our very image of the outsider shows that, contrary to the usual view, society does not really want them to speak out effectively in their own behalf, in fact cannot visualize them doing so. Ask yourself: How do outsiders speak in the dominant narratives? Poorly, inarticulately, with broken syntax, short sentences, grunts, and unsophisticated ideas. Try to recall a single popular narrative of an eloquent, self-assured black (for example) orator or speaker. In the real world, of course, they exist in profusion. But when we stumble upon them, we are surprised: "What a welcome 'exception'!"

Words, then, can wound. But the fine thing about the current situation is that one gets to enjoy a superior position and feel virtuous at the same time. By supporting the system of free expression no matter what the cost, one is upholding principle. One can belong to impeccably liberal organizations and believe one is doing the right thing, even while taking actions that are demonstrably injurious to the least privileged, most defenseless segments of our society.[90] In time, one's actions will seem wrong and will be condemned as such, but paradigms change slowly. The world one helps to create—a world in which denigrating depiction is good or at least acceptable, in which minorities are buffoons, clowns, maids, or Willie Hortons, and only rarely fully individuated human beings with sensitivities, talents, personalities, and frailties—will survive into the future. One gets to create culture at outsiders' expense. And, one gets to sleep well at night, too.

Racism is not a mistake, not a matter of episodic, irrational behavior carried out by vicious-willed individuals, not a throwback to a long-gone era. It is ritual assertion of supremacy, like animals sneering and posturing to maintain their places in the hierarchy of the colony. It is performed largely unconsciously, just as the animals' behavior is. Racism seems right, customary, and inoffensive to those engaged in it, while bringing psychic and pecuniary advantages. The notion that more speech, more talking, more preaching, and more lecturing can counter this system of oppression is appealing, lofty, romantic—and wrong.

What, Then, Should Be Done? If Not Speech, What?

What can be done? One possibility we must take seriously is that *little* can be done—that race, and perhaps sex-based subjugation, is so deeply embedded in our society, so useful for the powerful, that nothing can dislodge it. No less gallant a warrior than Derrick Bell has recently expounded his view of "Racial Realism": things will never get better, powerful forces maintain the current system of white-over-black supremacy.[91] Reformers must labor for what they believe right with no certainty that their programs will ever prove successful. Holding out the hope that reform will one day bear fruit is unnecessary, unwise, and calculated only to induce despair, burnout, and paralysis.

We agree with much of what Bell says. Yet we offer a few suggestions for a program of racial reform growing out of our research and analysis. First, society should act forthrightly in cases of racism that we do see, treating them as stand-ins for the ones we know remain unseen. Second, past mistreatment will generally prove a more reliable basis for remedial action (such as affirmative action or reparations) than future- or present-oriented considerations; the racism of the past is the only kind that we recognize, the only kind we condemn. Third, whenever possible we should encourage and listen to speakers of color, especially on issues of race. As we pointed out in another connection, their reality, while not infallible and certainly not the only one, is what we must heed if we wish to avoid history's judgment. It is likely to be the version society will adopt in thirty years.

Scholars should approach with skepticism the writings of those neo-conservatives, including some of color, who make a practice of telling society that racism is ended.[92] In the sense we have described, there is an "essential" unitary minority viewpoint; the others are wrong. Finally, we should deepen suspicion of remedies for deep-seated social evils that rely on speech and exhortation. The First Amendment is an instrument of variable efficacy, more useful in some settings than others. Overextending it provokes the anger of oppressed groups and casts doubt on speech's value in settings where it is, in fact, useful. With deeply inscribed cultural practices that most can neither see as evil nor mobilize to reform, we should forthrightly institute changes in the structure of society that will enable persons of color—particularly the young—to avoid the worst assaults of racism. As with the controversy over campus racism, we should not let a spurious motto that speech be "everywhere free" stand in the way of outlawing speech that is demonstrably harmful, that is compounding the problem.

Because of the way the dominant narrative works, we should prepare for the near-certainty that these suggestions will be criticized as unprincipled, unfair to "innocent whites," wrong. Understanding how the dialectic works, and how the scripts and counterscripts work their dismal paralysis, may, perhaps, inspire us to continue even though the path is long and the night dark.

Part III

Retreat to Policy Analysis: "Even if What the Crits Say Is So . . ."

In the wake of three recent decisions, one by the United States Supreme Court dealing with punishment for hate crimes, two by the Canadian Supreme Court upholding limitations on pornography and hate speech, interest in campus anti-racism measures has revived. In the late 1980s, a number of U.S. campuses had responded to a wave of racist incidents by enacting student conduct codes forbidding certain types of racist expression. Then, federal courts struck down codes that were in effect at two Midwestern universities. A short time later, the Supreme Court invalidated a St. Paul, Minnesota, hate-speech ordinance under which a white youth had been convicted of burning a cross on the lawn of a black neighbor. Many institutions that had been considering hate-speech rules put them on hold.

But a more recent decision upholding enhanced sentences for defendants convicted of racially motivated crimes, coupled with recent scholarship on the feasibility of tort-based regulation, has spurred renewed interest. Today, many authorities, including university administrators, scholars of color, and even a few detractors of hate-speech rules, believe that properly drafted prohibitions could now be put in place. But will they be?

Not without a fight. No longer certain that wooden, mechanistic First Amendment jurisprudence will hold sway, opponents of hate-speech rules are beginning to argue that even if they could be put in place, they should not be: good policy argues against it. The next chapter addresses one form that resistance takes, namely the deployment of paternalistic objections. In this approach, opponents of hate-speech rules simply announce that there is no dichotomy, no tension at all. Equality and freedom are really not opposed; if minorities truly understood their situation they would not be clamoring for hate-speech rules, but would instead embrace the civil libertarian/free speech position. The following chapter, chapter 7, addresses objections that tend to be associated with neoconservatives— what we call the "toughlove" school. The final chapter, chapter 8, examines the experiences of other Western societies that have enacted hate-speech laws to see what lessons they offer for American institutions.

6

Paternalistic Arguments against Hate-Speech Rules: Pressure Valves and Bloodied Chickens

The Liberals' Response to Crumbling of Certainty

The dominant legal paradigm's resistance to change is not the only obstacle that hate-speech rule advocates confront: what we call *paternalistic* objections are deployed as well.[1] These arguments all urge that hate-speech rules would harm their intended beneficiaries, and thus, if blacks and other minorities knew their own self-interest, they would oppose them. Often the objections take the form of arguing that equality and liberty are not in conflict, since by protecting speech one is also protecting minorities[2] (even though they may not realize it). Our decision to focus on paternalistic objections is sparked by more than mere theoretical interest. Respected writers and commentators, including the national president of the ACLU, make such arguments.[3] Audiences listen and nod agreement. Unless challenged, these arguments may have more effect than they deserve.

In order to understand the interplay of arguments raging in the hate-speech debate, it is necessary briefly to review the development of anti-racism rules. That history has both social and legal aspects. Beginning around fifteen years ago, many campuses began noticing a sharp rise in the number of incidents of hate-ridden speech directed at minorities, gays, lesbians, and others.[4] Experts are divided on the causes of the upsurge. A few argue that the increase is the result of better reporting or heightened sensitivity on the part of the minority community.[5] Most, however, believe that the changes are real, noting that they are consistent with a sharp rise in attacks on foreigners, immigrants, and ethnic minorities occurring in many Western industrialized nations.[6] This general rise, in turn, may be prompted by deteriorating economies and increased competition for jobs. It may reflect an increase in populations of color, due to immigration patterns and high birthrates. It may be related to the ending of the Cold War and competition between the two superpowers.

Whatever its cause, campus racism is of great concern to many educators and university officials. At the University of Wisconsin, for example, the number of black students dropped sharply in the wake of highly publicized incidents of racism. (See chapter 4.) Faced with negative publicity and declining minority enrollments, some campuses established programs aimed at racial awareness. Others broadened their curriculum to include more multicultural offerings, events, and theme houses. Still others enacted hate-speech codes that prohibit slurs and disparaging remarks directed against persons on account of their ethnicity, religion, or sexual orientation. Sometimes these codes are patterned after existing torts or the fighting-words exception to the First Amendment. One at the University of Texas, for example, bars personalized insults that amount to intentional infliction of emotional distress.[7] Another, at the University of California at Berkeley, prohibits "those personally abusive epithets which, when directly addressed to any ordinary person, are . . . likely to provoke a violent reaction whether or not they actually do so."[8]

It was not long before these codes were challenged in court. In *Doe v. University of Michigan*,[9] the university unsuccessfully defended a student conduct code that prohibited verbal or physical behavior that "stigmatizes or victimizes" any individual on the basis of various immutable and cultural characteristics, and that "[c]reates an intimidating, hostile or demeaning environment."[10] Citing Supreme Court precedent that requires speech regulations to be clear and precise,[11] the district court found Michigan's code fatally vague and overbroad. Two years later, in *UWM Post, Inc. v. Board of Regents*,[12] a different federal court considered a University of Wisconsin rule that prohibited disruptive epithets directed against an individual because of his or her race, religion, or sexual orientation. The court invalidated the rule, finding the measure overly broad and ambiguous. The court refused to apply a balancing test that would weigh the social value of the speech with its harmful effect, and found the rule's similarity to Title VII doctrine insufficient to satisfy constitutional requirements.

Finally, the Supreme Court in *R.A.V. v. City of St. Paul*[13] struck down a city ordinance that selectively prohibited certain forms of racist expression. In *R.A.V.*, a white youth had burned a cross on the lawn of a black family. The local prosecutor charged him with disorderly conduct under an ordinance that forbade expression aimed at "arousing anger, alarm or resentment in others on the basis of race, color, creed, religion or gender."[14] Even after adopting the Minnesota Supreme Court's construction of the ordinance to apply only to fighting words, the Supreme Court found it unconstitutional. Fighting words, although regulable in some circumstances, are not entirely devoid of First Amendment protection; in particular, they may not be prohibited based on the content of the message. Not only did the ordinance discriminate based on content, but it further discriminated based on viewpoint by choosing to punish only those fighting words which expressed an opinion with which the city disagreed.

More recent decisions have been more supportive of the efforts of some authorities to take action against racism. In *Wisconsin v. Mitchell*,[15] a black man was convicted of aggravated battery for severely beating a white youth. Because the defendant selected the victim for his race, the defendant's sentence was increased by an additional two years under a Wisconsin penalty-enhancement statute. The United States Supreme Court affirmed the statute's constitutionality, holding that motive, and more specifically racial hatred, can be considered in determining the sentence of a convicted defendant. The Court explained that while "abstract beliefs, however obnoxious" are protected under the First Amendment, they are not protected once those beliefs express themselves in commission of a crime.[16]

In Canada, two recent decisions also upheld the power of the state to prohibit certain types of offensive expression when they cause societal harm. In *Regina v. Keegstra*,[17] a teacher had described Jews in disparaging terms to his pupils and declared that the Holocaust did not take place. The Supreme Court of Canada upheld the national criminal code provision under which the defendant was charged. The court emphasized that this type of hate-speech harms its victims and society as a whole, sufficiently so to justify criminalizing it. In *Regina v. Butler*,[18] the Supreme

Court of Canada reversed a trial court dismissal of criminal pornography charges, based on the social harm caused by the speech and the minimal impairment of legitimate speech that the prohibition presented. Both decisions are notable because Canada's legal and free-speech traditions are similar to those of the United States, and because the Canadian Charter protects speech in terms similar to those of its United States counterpart.

The recent scholarly interest in torts-based approaches provides a final development suggesting the feasibility of regulating hate speech. Several scholars advocate regulating hate speech through the torts of intentional infliction of emotional distress or group defamation.[19] These scholars propose that the law of tort might be tapped to supply models for harm-based codes that would pass constitutional muster. They emphasize that tort law's historic role in redressing personal wrongs, its neutrality, and its relative freedom from constitutional restraints are powerful advantages for rules aimed at curbing hate speech. (See, e.g., chapters 1, 6.)

At present, then, case law and scholarly commentary suggest that hate-speech restrictions may be drafted in compliance with the First Amendment. Given the feasibility of enacting hate-speech codes, coupled with the continued rise of racism on college campuses, the future seems to lie squarely in the hands of policymakers.

Paternalistic Justifications for Opposing Hate-Speech Regulation: Pressure Valves, Bloodied Chickens, and the They-Don't-Know-Their-Own-Self-Interest Argument

Because of the feasibility of drafting constitutional hate-speech regulations, the debate over such rules has shifted to the policy arena. Four arguments made by opponents of anti-racism rules are central to this debate:

- Permitting racists to utter racist remarks and insults allows them to blow off steam harmlessly. As a result, minorities are safer than they would be under a regime of anti-racism rules. We will refer to this as the "pressure valve" argument.
- Anti-racism rules will end up hurting minorities, because authorities will invariably apply the rules against them rather than against

members of the majority group. This we will call the "reverse-enforcement" argument.

- Free speech has been minorities' best friend. Because free speech is a principal instrument of social reform, persons interested in achieving reform, such as minorities, would resist placing any fetters on freedom of expression if they knew their self-interest. This we term the "best friend" objection.

- More speech—talking back to the aggressor—rather than regulation is the solution to racist speech. Because racism is a form of ignorance, dispelling it through reasoned argument is the only way to get at its root. Moreover, talking back to the aggressor is empowering. It strengthens one's own identity, reduces victimization, and instills pride in one's heritage. This we call the "talk back" argument.

Each of these arguments is paternalistic, invoking the interest of the group seeking protection. Each is seriously flawed; indeed, the situation is often the opposite of what its proponents understand it to be. Racist speech, far from serving as a pressure valve, deepens minorities' predicament. Moreover, except in authoritarian countries like South Africa, authorities generally do not apply anti-racism rules against minorities. Free speech has not always proven a trusty friend of racial reformers. Finally, talking back is rarely a realistic possibility for the victim of hate speech.

The Pressure Valve Argument

The pressure valve argument holds that rules prohibiting hate speech are unwise because they increase the danger racism poses to minorities.[20] Forcing racists to bottle up their dislike of minority group members means that they will be more likely to say or do something hurtful later. Free speech thus functions as a pressure valve, allowing tension to dissipate before it reaches a dangerous level. Pressure valve proponents argue that if minorities understood this, they would oppose anti-racism rules.

The argument is paternalistic; it says we are denying you what you say you want, and for your own good. The rules, which you think will help you, will really make matters worse. If you knew this, you would join us in opposing them.

But is this really so? Hate speech may make the speaker feel better, at least temporarily, but it does not make the victim safer. Quite the contrary, the psychological evidence suggests that permitting one person to say or do hateful things to another *increases*, rather than decreases, the chance that he or she will do so again in the future.[21] Moreover, others may believe it is permissible to follow suit.[22] Human beings are not mechanical objects. Our behavior is more complex than the laws of physics that describe pressure valves, tanks, and the behavior of a gas or liquid in a tube. In particular, we use symbols to construct our social world, a world that contains categories and expectations for "black," "woman," "child," "criminal," "wartime enemy," and so on. Once the roles we create for these categories are in place, they govern the way we speak of and act toward members of those categories in the future.

Even simple barnyard animals act on the basis of categories. Poultry farmers know that a chicken with a single speck of blood may be pecked to death by the others.[23] With chickens, of course, the categories are neural and innate, functioning at a level more basic than language. But social science experiments demonstrate that the way we categorize others affects our treatment of them. An Iowa teacher's famous "blue eyes/brown eyes" experiment showed that even a one-day assignment of stigma can change behavior and school performance.[24] At Stanford University, Phillip Zimbardo assigned students to play the roles of prisoner and prison guard, but was forced to discontinue the experiment when some of the participants began taking their roles too seriously.[25] And Diane Sculley's interviews with male sexual offenders showed that many did not see themselves as offenders at all. In fact, research suggests that exposure to sexually violent pornography increases men's antagonism toward women and intensifies rapists' belief that their victims really welcomed their attentions.[26] At Yale University, Stanley Milgram showed that many members of a university community could be made to violate their conscience if an authority figure invited them to do so and assured them this was permissible and safe.[27]

The evidence, then, suggests that allowing persons to stigmatize or revile others makes them more aggressive, not less so. Once the speaker forms the category of deserved-victim, his or her behavior may well continue and escalate to bullying and physical violence. Further, the studies appear to demonstrate that stereotypical treatment tends to generalize—what we do teaches others that they may do likewise. Pressure valves may be safer after letting off steam; human beings are not.

The "Reverse Enforcement" Argument

A second paternalistic argument is that enactment of hate-speech rules is sure to hurt minorities because the new rules will be applied against minorities themselves.[28] A vicious insult hurled by a white person to a black will go unpunished, but even a mild expression of exasperation by a black motorist to a police officer or by a black student to a professor, for example, will bring harsh sanctions. The argument is plausible because certain authorities are racist and dislike blacks who speak out of turn, and because a few incidents of blacks charged with hate speech for innocuous behavior have occurred. Nadine Strossen, for example, asserts that in Canada, shortly after the Supreme Court upheld a federal hate-speech code, prosecutors began charging blacks with hate offenses.[29]

But the empirical evidence does not suggest that this is the pattern, much less the rule. Police and FBI reports show that hate crimes are committed much more frequently by whites against blacks than the reverse.[30] Statistics compiled by the National Institute Against Violence and Prejudice confirm what the police reports show, that a large number of blacks and other minorities are victimized by racist acts on campus each year.[31] Moreover, the distribution of enforcement seems to be consistent with commission of the offense. Although an occasional minority group member may be charged with a hate crime or with violating a campus hate-speech code, these prosecutions seem relatively rare.

Racism, of course, is not a one-way street; some minorities have harassed and badgered whites. Still, the reverse-enforcement objection seems to have little validity in the United States. A recent study of the international aspects of hate-speech regulation showed that in repressive societies, such as South Africa and the former Soviet Union, laws against hate speech have indeed been deployed to stifle dissenters and members of minority groups.[32] Yet this has not happened in more progressive countries. (See chapter 8.) The likelihood that officials in the United States would turn hate-speech laws into weapons against minorities seems remote.

Free Speech as Minorities' Best Friend: The Need to Maintain the First Amendment Inviolate

Many absolutists urge that the First Amendment historically has been a great friend and ally of social reformers. ACLU president Nadine

Strossen, for example, argues that without free speech, Martin Luther King, Jr., could not have moved the American public as he did.[33] Other reform movements also are said to have relied heavily on free speech.[34] This argument, like the two earlier ones, is paternalistic. It is based on the supposed best interest of minorities; if they understood that interest, the argument goes, they would not demand to bridle speech.

The argument ignores the history of the relationship between racial minorities and the First Amendment. In fact, minorities have made the greatest progress when they acted in *defiance* of the First Amendment.[35] The original Constitution protected slavery in several of its provisions, and the First Amendment existed contemporaneously with slavery for nearly one hundred years. Free speech for slaves, women, and the propertyless was simply not a major concern for the drafters, who appear to have conceived the First Amendment mainly as protection for the kind of refined political, scientific, and artistic discourse they and their class enjoyed.

Later, of course, abolitionism and civil rights activism broke out. But an examination of the role of speech in reform movements shows that the relationship of the First Amendment to social advance is not so simple as free-speech absolutists maintain. In the civil rights movement of the 1960s, for example, Martin Luther King, Jr., and others did use speeches and other symbolic acts to kindle America's conscience. But as often as not, they found the First Amendment (as then understood) did not protect them from arrest and conviction. Their speech was seen as too forceful, too disruptive. To be sure, their convictions would sometimes be reversed on appeal, many years later. But the First Amendment, as then understood, served more as an obstacle than a friend.

Why does this happen? Linguistic theory shows that we interpret new stories in terms of the old ones we have internalized and now use to judge reality. When new stories deviate too drastically from those that form our current understanding, we denounce them as false and dangerous. The free market of ideas is useful mainly for solving small, clearly bounded disputes. History shows it has proven much less useful for redressing systemic evils, such as racism. Language requires an interpretive paradigm, a set of shared meanings that a group agrees to attach to words and terms.[36] If racism is deeply inscribed in that paradigm—carved into a thousand scripts, stories, and roles—one cannot speak out against it without appearing incoherent. (See chapter 5.)

An examination of the current landscape of First Amendment exceptions reveals a similar pattern. As we have seen, our system has carved out or tolerated dozens of "exceptions" to the free speech principle: conspiracy; libel; copyright; plagiarism; official secrets; misleading advertising; words of threat; disrespectful words uttered to a judge, teacher, or other authority figure; and many more. These exceptions (each responding to some interest of a powerful group) seem familiar and acceptable, as indeed perhaps they are. But a proposal for a new exception to protect eighteen-year-old black undergraduates immediately produces consternation: the First Amendment must be a seamless web.

It is we, however, who are caught in a web, the web of the familiar. The First Amendment seems to us useful and valuable. It reflects our interests and sense of the world. It allows us to make certain distinctions, tolerates certain exceptions, and functions in a particular way we assume will be equally valuable for others. But the history of the First Amendment, as well as the current landscape of doctrinal exceptions, shows that it is far more valuable to the majority than to the minority, more useful for confining change than for propelling it.

"More Speech"—Talking Back to the Aggressor as a Preferable Solution to the Problem of Hate Speech

Defenders of the First Amendment sometimes argue that minorities should talk back to the aggressor.[37] Nat Hentoff, for example, writes that anti-racism rules teach black people to depend on whites for protection, while talking back clears the air, emphasizes self-reliance, and strengthens one's self-image as an active agent in charge of one's own destiny.[38] The "talking back" solution to campus racism draws force from the First Amendment principle of "more speech," according to which additional dialogue is always a preferred response to speech that some find troubling.[39] Proponents of this approach oppose hate-speech rules not so much because they limit speech, but because they believe that it is good for minorities to learn to speak out. A few go on to offer another reason: that a minority who speaks out will be able to educate the speaker who has uttered a racially hurtful remark.[40] Racism, they hold, is the product of ignorance and fear. If a victim of racist hate speech takes the time to explain matters, he or she may succeed in altering the speaker's perception so that the speaker will no longer utter racist remarks.

How valid is this argument? Like many paternalistic arguments, it is offered blandly, virtually as an article of faith. In the nature of paternalism, those who make the argument are in a position of power, and therefore believe themselves able to make things so merely by asserting them. They rarely offer empirical proof of their claims, because none is needed. The social world is as they say because it is their world: they created it that way.

In reality, those who hurl racial epithets do it because they feel empowered to do so. Indeed, their principal objective is to reassert and reinscribe that power. One who talks back is perceived as issuing a direct challenge to that power. The action is seen as outrageous, calling for a forceful response. Often racist remarks are delivered in several-on-one situations, in which responding in kind is foolhardy.[41] Indeed, many highly publicized cases of racial homicide began in just this fashion. A group began badgering a black person. The person talked back, and paid with his life.[42] Other racist remarks are delivered in a cowardly fashion, by means of graffiti scrawled on a campus wall late at night or on a poster placed outside of a black student's dormitory door. In these situations, more speech, of course, is impossible.

Racist speech is rarely a mistake, rarely something that could be corrected or countered by discussion. What would be the answer to "Nigger, go back to Africa. You don't belong at the University"? "Sir, you misconceive the situation. Prevailing ethics and constitutional interpretation hold that I, an African American, am an individual of equal dignity and entitled to attend this university in the same manner as others. Now that I have informed you of this, I am sure you will modify your remarks in the future"?[43]

The idea that talking back is safe for the victim or potentially educative for the racist simply does not correspond with reality. It ignores the power dimension to racist remarks, forces minorities to run very real risks, and treats a hateful attempt to force the victim outside the human community as an invitation for discussion. Even when successful, talking back is a burden. Why should minority undergraduates, already charged with their own education, be responsible constantly for educating others?

How (and Why) to Draft Campus Anti-Racism Rules—and Why They Are Invariably Resisted

To this point, we have shown that four frequently repeated paternalistic arguments against instituting campus anti-racism rules are flawed. We also believe that, in the wake of recent court decisions, the task of drafting such rules is technically quite feasible. If a few commonsense procedures are followed, such rules should be held constitutional. It now remains for us to sketch a few ways such rules could be written and then to defend them against the claim that they violate the principle and spirit, if not the letter, of First Amendment law.

Two Ways Hate-Speech Rules Could Be Drafted

Campus rules could be drafted either to prohibit expressions of racial hatred and contempt directly through a two-step approach, or to regulate behavior currently actionable in tort. In either case, the rules must be neutral and apply across the board, that is, must not single out particular forms of hateful speech for punishment while leaving others untouched.[44] Moreover, any campus considering enacting such rules should be certain to compile adequate legislative evidence of their necessity.[45]

The direct prohibition approach would couple two provisions. The first would prohibit face-to-face invective calculated seriously to disrupt the victim's ability to function in a campus setting. This provision, which must be race-neutral, could be tailored to capture the content of any recognized First Amendment exception, such as fighting words[46] or workplace harassment.[47] Because of the university's special role and responsibility for the safety and morale of students, even the precaution of working within a recognized exception might not be necessary.[48] A second provision would provide enhanced punishment for any campus offense (including the one just described) which was proven to have been committed with a racial motivation.[49] Such a two-step approach would satisfy all current constitutional requirements. It would promote a compelling and legitimate institutional interest.[50] It would not single out particular types of expression, but rather particular types of motivation at the punishment stage.[51] And it would not abridge rules against content or viewpoint neutrality, since it focuses not on the speaker's message but on its intended effect on the hearer, namely to impair his or her ability to function on campus.

Alternatively, a hate-speech rule could be patterned after an existing tort, such as intentional infliction of emotional distress or group libel, with the race of the victim a "special factor" calling for increased protection, as current rules and the Restatement of Torts already provide.[52] Tort law's neutrality and presumptive constitutionality strongly suggest that such an approach would be valid. This suggestion is strengthened by the two Canadian cases, *Keegstra* and *Butler.* Harm-based rationales for punishing hate speech should be valid if the social injury from the speech outweighs its benefits.

Why Hate-Speech Rules Should Be Valid—Affirmative Considerations

The strongest reason for enacting hate-speech rules on campuses with a history of disruption is that they are necessary to promote equality.[53] But even if one puts aside this consideration and views the controversy purely through the free speech lens, the policy concerns underlying our system of free expression are at best weakly promoted by protecting hate speech. Targeted racist vitriol scarcely advances self-government or the search for consensus. It does not promote the search for truth, nor help the speaker reach self-actualization, at least in any ideal sense. Racist speech thus does little to advance any of the theoretical rationales scholars and judges have advanced as reasons for protecting speech. (See chapters 1 and 4.)

Looking at the hate-speech problem from the perspective of enforcement yields no greater support for the free-speech position. Our system distrusts any form of official speech regulation because we fear that the government will use the power to control the content of speech to insulate itself from criticism.[54] This danger is absent, however, when the government sets out to regulate speech between private speakers, especially about subjects falling outside the realm of politics.[55] When the government intervenes to tell one class of speakers to avoid saying hurtful things to another, governmental aggrandizement is at best a remote concern. This is the reason why regulation of private speech—libel, copyright, plagiarism, deceptive advertising, and so on—rarely presents serious constitutional problems.[56] The same should be true of hate speech.

Another political process concern is also absent. Our legal system resists speech regulation in part because of concern over selective regulation or enforcement.[57] If the state were given the power to declare particular speakers disfavored, it could effectively exclude them from public discourse. We would forfeit the benefit of their ideas, while they would lose access to an important means for advancing their own interest. But none of these dangers is present with hate speech. Allowing the government to create a special offense for a class of persons (even racists) is indeed troublesome, as the Supreme Court recognized in *R.A.V. v. St. Paul.*[58] But the direct prohibition approach we have outlined introduces the racial element only at the sentencing stage, where the dangers and political-process concerns of selective treatment are greatly reduced. The same would be true if the tort approach were adopted. In tort law, it is the intent and injury that matter, not the content of the speech. Enforcement comes from private initiative, not state action. Prevention of harm is the goal, with no speech disfavored as such.

But Will It Happen? Hate Speech and Hubris

In the wake of recent cases, there is little reason today in First Amendment jurisprudence for leaving campus hate speech unregulated. Censorship and governmental nest-feathering are not implicated by rules against private speech. Nor does targeted racial vilification promote any of the theoretical rationales for protecting free speech. Much less does permissiveness toward racist name-calling benefit the victim, as the ACLU and others have argued. Far from acting as a pressure valve which enables rage to dissipate harmlessly, epithets increase their victims' vulnerability. Pernicious images create a world in which some come to see others as proper victims. Like farmyard chickens with a speck of blood, they may be reviled, mistreated, denied jobs, slighted, spoken of derisively, even beaten at will.

The Greeks used the term *hubris* to describe the sin of believing that one may "treat[ ] other people just as one pleases, with the arrogant confidence that one will escape any penalty for violating their rights."[59] Those who tell ethnic jokes and hurl epithets are guilty of this kind of arrogance. But some who defend these practices, including First Amendment purists, are guilty as well: insisting on free speech over all, as though *no* countervailing interests were at stake, and putting forward transparently paternalistic justifications for a regime in which hate speech flows freely is also hubris. Unilateral power can beget arrogance, including the arrogance of insisting that one's worldview, one's interests, and one's way of framing an issue, are the only ones. Unfettered speech, a freemarket in which only some can prevail, is an exercise of power. Some words, we have argued, have no purpose other than to subordinate, injure, and wound.[60] Free speech defenders insist that the current regime is necessary and virtuous, that minorities must acquiesce to this injurious and demeaning definition of virtue, and that their refusal to subordinate their interests to those of the First Amendment is evidence of their childlike simplicity and lack of insight into their own condition. These impositions may well be the greatest hubris of all.[61]

In a hundred years, the hate-speech controversy may well come to be seen as the *Plessy v. Ferguson*[62] of our age. In *Plessy*, the Supreme Court professed to be unable to see a moral difference between two claims—that of blacks to sit in a railroad car with whites, and that of whites to sit in a car without blacks. The hate-speech controversy features the same sort of perverse neutralism. The speaker claims a right to utter face-to-face racial invective. The victim insists he or she has the right not to have it spoken to him or her. A perfect standoff, just like the railroad car case, one right balanced against its perfect reciprocal.

Perhaps because scholars and policymakers realize the hollowness of the neutral principles approach and remember how poorly its predecessor fared in history's judgment, the weight of legal opinion has been slowly swinging in the direction of narrowly drawn hate-speech rules. Free speech traditionalists, focusing solely on one value and ignoring what else is at stake, have been fighting a holding action, using four paternalistic arguments for maintaining the status quo. These arguments each assert that even if hate-speech controls are constitutional, they are unwise because they would injure the very persons sought to be protected. Each of these arguments is invalid, a thin veneer, unsupported by empirical evidence, aimed at rationalizing the current regime.

Tinged with more than a little hubris, the liberals' arguments do not hold. What about those of the conservatives?

7

The Toughlove School: Neoconservative Arguments against Hate-Speech Regulation

("I Just Let It Roll Off My Back")

In *Babette's Feast*,[1] the French housekeeper for two dour Protestant sisters living in a remote Danish village where life is hard decides to mark her fourteenth year of working in this repressed environment by preparing a huge feast. Using money she has just won from the French lottery, she imports turtles, quail, and the finest wines and serves them at a long table to the sisters and their congregation. But she has not counted on the experience's novelty: until now, the God-fearing folks gathered at her table have not touched a drop of liquor or eaten anything other than dried fish and other plain foods in their entire lives. During the dinner, they refuse to acknowledge the delectable dishes they are eating, talking exclusively about the weather, the crops, and God's will.

The response of some neoconservatives[2] to the campus hate-speech controversy reminds us in some ways of Babette's feast. Lacking a ready category for what is taking place under their noses, neoconservatives fail to notice what everyone else sees, or maintain that it is really something else. As with the villagers, ideology plays its part as well. When something happens that conservative thought does not predict, it is forthrightly denied, leading to some strange alliances, as when Babette ends up playing to the returned general, the one diner who allowed himself to appreciate and enjoy the meal.[3]

Here, we examine neoconservatives and the politics of denial. We take a look at mindset and the rhetorical structures and strategies we often unconsciously choose to deal with in an uncomfortable reality and a changing legal environment. As we noted earlier, the rhetorical and logical structure of the hate-speech debate has been undergoing a slow but inexorable shift.[4] As First Amendment formalism, with its various mechanistic doctrines, models, and "tests," has begun giving way to First Amendment legal realism, both the moderate left and the moderate right, who much preferred things the old way, have changed their ground slightly. Realizing, perhaps, that mechanical jurisprudence and case law laid down in an earlier era will not hold the line much longer, they have been urging that even if First Amendment doctrine permits regulating hate speech, wisdom and good policy counsel against it.

Six arguments characterize what we call the "toughlove" or neoconservative position:

- that pressing for hate-speech regulation is a waste of time and resources;
- that white society will never tolerate speech codes, so that the effort to have them enacted is quixotic, symbolic, or disingenuous;
- that racist expression is a useful bellwether that should not be driven underground;
- that encouraging minorities to focus on slights and insults is harmful because it causes them to see themselves as victims;
- that the campaign is classist, since it singles out the transgressions of the blue-collar racist while leaving the more genteel versions of the upper classes untouched; and
- that the cure is worse than the disease, because it institutionalizes censorship, and "two wrongs don't make a right."

What unites these arguments—which we call the "deflection," "quixotic," "bellwether," "victimization," "classist," and "two wrongs" arguments, respectively—are two themes. The first is that struggling against hate speech is a digression ("the real problem is . . ."), and the second is that the effort reinforces the idea of oneself as a victim, rather than an active agent in charge of one's destiny.

We examine the six arguments, then offer an explanation for why neoconservatives take the positions they do on the hate-speech controversy. We believe that the toughlove crowd opposes hate-speech regulations because vituperative speech aimed at minorities forces them to confront the intuition that slurs directed against people of color are simply more serious than ones directed against whites. This intuition, in turn, threatens a prime conservative tenet, the level playing field. We explain why the First Amendment version of that field—namely, the marketplace of ideas—is not level but slanted against people of color, and why talking back to the aggressor is rarely a satisfactory option for hate speech's victims.

The Toughlove Position on Hate Speech: Six Neoconservative Arguments against Regulation

The Deflection (or Waste-of-Time) Argument

Many neoconservative writers who have taken a position against regulation argue that mobilizing against hate speech is a waste of precious time and resources. Donald Lively, for example, writes that civil rights activists ought to have better things to do, and that concentrating on hate-speech reform is myopic and calculated to benefit only a small number of blacks and other minority persons.[5] Instead of "picking relatively small fights of their own convenience,"[6] racial reformers should be examining "the obstacles that truly impede" racial progress, namely bad laws and too little money.[7]

Other toughlove writers echo Lively's conclusions. Dinesh D'Souza writes that campus radicals espouse hate-speech regulation because it is easier than studying hard and getting a first-rate education.[8] Stephen Carter also has little good to say about the hate-speech crusade, describing it as a digression and a distraction.[9] Henry Louis Gates expresses perhaps the sharpest disdain for anti-hate-speech activism, wondering why this ephemeral subject attracts the attention of so many academics and thinkers when so much more serious work remains to be done.[10] In a cover story in *The New Republic* reviewing *Words That Wound*, Gates, chair of the department of African American studies at Harvard, writes that addressing racist speech does lip service to civil rights without dealing with the material reality of economic subordination.[11]

But is it so clear that efforts to control hate speech are a waste of time and resources, at least compared to other problems that the campaigners could be addressing? What neoconservative writers ignore is that eliminating hate speech goes hand in hand with reducing what they consider "real racism." Certainly, being the victim of hate speech is a less serious affront than being denied a job, a house, or an education. It is, however, equally true that a society that speaks and thinks of minorities derisively is fostering an environment in which such discrimination will occur frequently. This is so for two reasons. First, hate speech, in combination with an entire panoply of media imagery, constructs and reinforces a picture of minorities in the public mind. This picture or stereotype varies from era to era, but is rarely positive: persons of color are happy and carefree, lascivious, criminal, devious, treacherous, untrustworthy, immoral, of lower intelligence than whites, and so on. (See chapter 5.)

This stereotype guides action, accounting for much misery in the lives of persons of color. Examples include motorists who fail to stop to aid a stranded black driver, police officers who hassle African American youths innocently walking or speaking to each other on the streets, or landlords who act on hunches or unarticulated feelings in renting an apartment to a white over an equally or more qualified black or Mexican. Once the stage is set—once persons of color are rendered one-down in the minds of hundreds of actors—the selection of minorities as victims of what even the toughlove crowd would recognize as real discrimination increases in frequency and severity. It also acquires its capacity to sting. A white motorist who suffers an epithet ("goddam college kid!") may be momentarily stunned. But the epithet does not call upon an entire cultural legacy the way a racial epithet does, nor deny the victim her status and personhood.

A second reason why even neoconservatives ought to pause before throwing their weight against hate-speech regulation has to do with the nature of latter-day racism. Most neoconservatives, like many white people, think that acts of out-and-out discrimination are rare today. The racism that remains is subtle, "institutional," or "latter-day."[12] It lies in the arena of unarticulated feelings, practices, and patterns of behavior (like promotions policy) on the part of institutions as well as individuals. A forthright focus on speech and language may be one of the few means of addressing and curing this kind of racism. Thought and language are inextricably connected. A speaker asked to reconsider his or her use of language may begin to reflect on the way he or she thinks about a subject.

Words, external manifestations of thought, supply a window into the unconscious. Our choice of word, metaphor, or image gives signs of the attitudes we have about a person or subject. No readier or more effective tool than a focus on language exists to deal with subtle or latter-day racism. Since neoconservatives are among the prime proponents of the notion that this form of racism is the only (or the main) one that remains, they should think carefully before taking a stand in opposition to measures that might make inroads into it. Of course, speech codes would not reach every form of demeaning speech or depiction. But a tool's unsuitability to redress every aspect of a problem is surely no reason for refusing to employ it where it is effective.

The Quixotic Argument

Neoconservatives also argue against hate-speech regulation on the ground that the effort is doomed or quixotic. White people will never accede to such rules. Proponents of hate-speech regulation surely must know this, they reason, hence their objectives are probably symbolic, tactical, or at any rate something other than what they say. Lively, for example, writes that the U.S. Supreme Court has consistently rejected laws regulating speech, finding them vague and overbroad.[13] He also writes that the anti-hate speech campaign lacks vision and a sense of "marketability"—it simply cannot be sold to the American people.[14] Gates asks how hate-speech activists can possibly believe that campus regulations will prove effective even if enacted. If campuses are the seething arenas of racism that activists believe, how will campus administrators and hearing officials provide nondiscriminatory hearings on charges brought under the codes?[15] Elsewhere he accuses hate-speech activists of pressing their claims for merely "symbolic" reasons,[16] while ignoring that the free-speech side has a legitimate concern over symbolism, too. Carter is less negative about the motivations of hate-speech reformers, but does question whether their campaign is not "unwinnable."[17]

But is the effort to curb hate speech doomed or misguided? It might be seen this way if indeed the gains to be reaped were potentially only slight. But, as we argued earlier, they are not: the stakes are large, indeed our entire panoply of civil rights laws and rules depends for its efficacy on controlling the background of harmful depiction against which the rules and practices operate. In a society where minorities are thought and spoken of respectfully, few acts of out-and-out discrimination would take place. In one that harries and demeans them at every turn, even a determined judiciary will not be able to enforce equality and racial justice.

Moreover, success is more possible than the toughlove crowd would like to acknowledge. A host of Western industrialized democracies have instituted laws against hate speech and hate crime, often in the face of initial resistance. Some, like Canada, Great Britain, and Sweden, have traditions of respect for free speech and inquiry rivaling ours. (See chapter 8.) Determined advocacy might well accomplish the same here. In recent years, many—perhaps several hundred—college campuses have seen fit to institute student conduct codes penalizing face-to-face insults of an ethnic or similar nature, many in order to advance interests that the campus straightforwardly identified as necessary to its function, such as protecting diversity or providing an environment conducive to education.[18] Moreover, powerful actors like government agencies, the writers' lobby, industries, and so on have generally been quite successful at coining free speech "exceptions" to suit their interest—libel, defamation, false advertising, copyright, plagiarism, words of threat, and words of monopoly, just to name a few. (See chapter 4.) Each of these seems natural and justified—because time-honored—and perhaps each is. But the magnitude of the interest underlying these exceptions seems no less than that of a young black undergraduate subject to hateful abuse while walking late at night on campus. New regulation is of course subject to searching scrutiny in our laissez-faire age. But the history of free speech doctrine, especially the landscape of exceptions, shows that need and policy have a way of being translated into law. The same may happen with hate speech.

The Bellwether Argument

A further argument one hears from the anti-rule camp is that hate speech should not be driven underground, but rather allowed to remain out in the open. The racist whom one does not know is far more dangerous than the one whom one does. Moreover, on a college campus, incidents of overt racism or sexism can serve as useful spurs for discussion and institutional self-examination. Carter, for example, writes that regulating racist speech will leave minorities no better off than they are now, while screening out "hard truths about the way many white people look at . . . us."[19] D'Souza echoes this argument, but with a reverse twist, when he points out that hate-speech crusaders are missing a valuable opportunity. When racist graffiti or hateful fraternity parties proliferate, minorities should reflect on the possibility that this may signal something basically wrong with affirmative action.[20] Instead of tinkering futilely with the outward signs of malaise, we ought to deal directly with the problem itself. An editor of *Southern California Law Review* argues that anti-racism rules are tantamount to "[s]weeping the problem under the rug," whereas "[k]eeping the problem in the public spotlight . . . enables members [of the university community] to attack it when it surfaces."[21]

How should we see the bellwether argument? In one respect, the argument does make a valid point. All other things being equal, the racist who is known is less dangerous than the one who is not.[22] What the argument ignores is that there is a third alternative, namely the racist who is cured, or at least deterred by rules, policies, and official statements so as no longer to exhibit the behavior he or she once did. Since most conservatives believe that rules and penalties change conduct (indeed are among the strongest proponents of heavy penalties for crime), the possibility that campus guidelines against hate speech and assault would decrease those behaviors ought to be taken seriously.[23] Of course, the conservative may argue that regulation has costs of its own—something even we would concede—but this is a different argument from the bellwether one.[24]

What of the notion that silencing the racist through legislation might deprive the campus community of the "town hall" opportunity to discuss and analyze issues of race when incidents of racism occur?[25] But campuses could hold those meetings and discussions anyway. The rules are not likely to suppress hate speech entirely; even with them in force, there will continue to be some number of incidents of racist speech and behavior. The difference is that now there will be the possibility of campus disciplinary hearings, which are even more likely to spark the "town hall" discussions the argument assumes are desirable. The bellwether argument ignores that rules will have at least some edifying effect and that there are other ways of having campuswide discussions short of allowing racial confrontation to flourish uncontrolled.

The Victimization Argument: Do Hate-Speech Rules Encourage Passive, Dependent Behavior?

A fourth argument many neoconservative critics of hate-speech regulations make is that prohibitions against verbal abuse are unwise because they encourage minorities to see themselves as victims. Instead of rushing to the authorities every time they hear something that wounds their feelings, persons from minority groups ought to learn to speak back or ignore the offending behavior. A system of rules and complaints reinforces in their minds that they are weak and in need of protection, that their lot in life is to be victimized rather than to make use of those opportunities that are available to them. Carter, for example, writes that anti-hate-speech rules cater to "those whose backgrounds of oppression make them especially sensitive to the threatening nuances that lurk behind racist sentiment."[26] Lively warns that the rules reinforce a system of "supplication and self-abasement,"[27] D'Souza that they distort and prevent interracial friendships and encourage a "crybaby" attitude;[28] Gates that they reinforce a "therapeutic" mentality and an unhealthy preoccupation with feelings.[29]

Would putting into place hate-speech rules induce passivity and a victim mentality among minority populations? Certainly not, for other alternatives will remain available as before. No African American or lesbian student is required to make a complaint when targeted by vicious verbal abuse. He or she can talk back or ignore it if he or she sees fit. Hate-speech rules simply provide an additional avenue of recourse to those who wish to take advantage of them. Indeed, one could argue that filing a complaint constitutes one way of taking charge of one's destiny: one is active, instead of passively "lumping it" when verbal abuse strikes. It is worth noting that we do not make the "victimization" charge in connection with other offenses that we suffer, such as having a car stolen or a house burglarized, nor do we encourage those victimized in this fashion to "rise above it" or talk back to their victimizers. If we see recourse differently in the two sets of situations it may be because we secretly believe that a black who is called "nigger" by a group of whites is in reality not a victim. If so, it would make sense to encourage him not to dwell on or sulk over the event. But this is different from saying that filing a complaint deepens victimization; moreover, many studies have shown it simply is untrue.[30] Racist speech is the harm. Filing a complaint is not. No empirical evidence suggests that filing a civil rights complaint causes otherwise innocuous behavior to acquire the capacity to harm the complainant.

The "Classist" Argument

A further argument some neoconservatives make is that the effort to limit hate speech through enactment of campus rules is classist. The rules will end up punishing only what naive or blue-collar students do and say. The more refined, indirect, but more devastating expressions of contempt of the more highly educated classes will pass unpunished. Henry Louis Gates offers the following comparison:

(A) LeVon, if you find yourself struggling in your classes here, you should realize it isn't your fault. It's simply that you're the beneficiary of a disruptive policy of affirmative action that places underqualified, underprepared and often undertalented black students in demanding educational environments like this one. The policy's egalitarian aims may be well-intentioned, but given the fact that aptitude tests place African Americans almost a full standard deviation below the mean, even controlling for socioeconomic disparities, they are also profoundly misguided. The truth is, you probably don't belong here, and your college experience will be a long downhill slide.

(B) Out of my face, jungle bunny.[31]

Lively and D'Souza make versions of the same argument, Lively urging that the codes reach only blue-collar racism and are backed only by academic elites;[32] D'Souza that the rules aim to enforce a "social etiquette among students, while ignoring the higher-echelon racism of meaningful glances and rolling of eyes of university higherups."[33]

In one respect, the classist argument is plainly off target. Both blue-collar and upper-class people will be prohibited from uttering certain types of slurs and epithets. Many hate-speech codes penalize serious face-to-face insults based on race, ethnicity, and a few other factors. Such rules would penalize the same harmful speech—for example, "Nigger, go back to Africa; you don't belong at this university"—whether spoken by the millionaire's son or the coal miner's daughter. If, in fact, the prep school product is less likely to utter words of this kind, or to utter only intellectualized versions like the one in Gates's example, this may be because he is less racist in a raw sense. If, as many social scientists believe, prejudice tends to be inversely correlated with educational level and social position, the wealthy and well educated may well violate hate-speech rules less often than others. And, to return to Gates' example, there is a difference between his two illustrations, although not in the direction he seems to suggest. "Out of my face, jungle bunny" is a more serious example of hate speech because it is not open to argument or a more-speech response, and has overtones of a direct physical threat. The other version, while deplorable, is unlikely to be coupled with a physical threat, and is answerable by more speech.

The "Two Wrongs" Argument

The "two wrongs" argument, which holds that hate speech may be wrong but prohibition is not the way to deal with it, is one of the relatively few arguments that both the moderate right and the moderate left put forward, although they do so in slightly different forms and for different reasons. The moderate left opposes hate-speech restrictions in part because although it detests racism it loves free speech even more. (See chapter 6.) Neoconservatives oppose regulation because it is government (in most cases) that would be doing the regulating, and especially because in the area of speech, governing to them is synonymous with censorship. Gates, for example, writes that "there is also a practical reason to worry about the impoverishment of the national discourse on free speech. If we keep losing the arguments, then we may slowly lose the liberties that they were meant to defend."[34] He also warns that two wrongs don't make a right and laments that our society and legal system have fallen away from Harry Kalven's ideal of civil rights and civil liberties as perfectly compatible goods for all.[35] Lively writes that history teaches that campaigns to limit speech always end up backfiring against minorities because free speech is a vital civic good and even more essential for them than others.[36] Virtually all the authors of the moderate right persuasion (and some of the moderate left as well) cite the fear of censorship or governmental aggrandizement. If we allow an arm of the state to decide what is harmful speech, soon little of it will survive.[37]

Our response to the two wrongs argument is elaborated in greater detail later, but one aspect of it is worth mentioning now. The term "censorship" is appropriately attached to regulation by which the heavy hand of government falls on weaker, unpopular private speakers, or else on political dissidents who are attempting to criticize or change government itself.[38] But with hate-speech regulation, few of the concerns that underlie our aversion to censorship are present. Hate-speakers are not criticizing government, but someone weaker than themselves. In prohibiting it, universities are not attempting to insulate themselves from criticism; the political-process concerns over governmental self-perpetuation are not present. The speech being punished is far from the core of political expression—it carries few ideas at all except "I hate and reject your personhood."[39] Indeed, hate speech silences the victim and drives him away.[40] Thus, when the government regulates hate speech, it enhances and adds to the potential social dialogue, rather than subtracts from it.

What Underlies the Neoconservative Position on Hate Speech: Anathema, or the Fear That the First Amendment Playing Field Will Turn Out Not to Be Level

Why does the toughlove crowd embrace the six arguments that we examined in the last section and found wanting? We believe the reason has to do with the way hate speech casts doubt on a principal tenet of the conservative faith: the level playing field. In First Amendment theory, the name of that playing field is the marketplace of ideas, in which messages and communications of all sorts supposedly vie on equal terms to establish themselves, and out of which, in theory, truth—the best idea of all—will emerge.[41]

The core difficulty that hate speech poses for the conservative mind is, simply, that there is no correlate—no analog—for hate speech directed toward whites, no countering message which cancels out the harm of "Nigger, you don't belong on this campus—go back to Africa." Vituperation aimed at blacks wounds;[42] there is nothing comparably damaging that whites have to undergo. The word "honky" is more a badge of respect than a put-down. "Cracker," although disrespectful, still implies power, as does "redneck." The fact is that terms like "nigger," "spic," "faggot," and "kike" evoke and reinforce entire cultural histories of oppression and subordination. They remind the target that his or her group has always been and remains unequal in status to the majority group. Even the most highly educated, professional-class African American or Latino knows that he or she is vulnerable to the slur, the muttered expression, the fishy glance on boarding the bus, knows that his degree, his accomplishments, his well-tailored suit are no armor against mistreatment at the hands of the least-educated white.[43]

But not only is there no correlate, no hate speech aimed at whites, there is no means by which persons of color and others can respond effectively to this form of speech within the current system. Our culture has developed a host of narratives, mottoes, and presuppositions that render it difficult for the minority victim to talk back in individual cases, and to mobilize effectively against hate speech in general. These include: feelings are relatively unimportant, words hurt only if you let them; rise above it; don't be so sensitive; don't be so humorless; talk back—show some backbone. Stated or unstated narratives like these form part of the linguistic and narrative field on which minority victims must play in responding to taunts and epithets, and of course limit the efficacy of any such response.

And when campus minorities do mobilize for measures that would curb hate speech in general, they encounter additional obstacles. Although our system of free speech has carved out or tolerated dozens of "exceptions" and special doctrines, opponents conveniently forget this, treating the demand for even narrowly tailored anti-hate-speech rules as a shocking request calculated to endanger the entire edifice of First Amendment protection.

Hate speech, then, is individually wounding in a way that finds no analog with respect to whites; there is no effective way for a victim to speak back or counter it, even when it is physically safe to do so;[44] and the most frequently targeted groups evoke little sympathy from society or the legal system when they ask for protection. In other settings, the combination of the three features just enumerated would cause us to conclude that the playing field is not level, but sharply slanted. Imagine, for example, an athletic competition in which one side is denied a powerful weapon (say, the forward pass); in which the other side is permitted to deploy this weapon freely, because the rules prevent the first from doing anything to counter it when it is used (such as knocking down the ball); and changes in the rules are not permitted because this is said to violate the charter that established the game in the first place.

Surely, we would say that such a competition is unfair. Yet, something like that characterizes the predicament of minority victims of hate speech. Conservatives cannot allow themselves to see this, however, since it goes against some of their most basic assumptions, including free competition and merit. We believe this accounts for the contortions and maneuverings among neoconservatives, including some of color who ought to know better. But the problem of hate speech will not go away by merely insisting on ideologically based truths that "must be so," nor by responses that ought to work, much less by blaming the victim or telling him that the problem is all in his head. Hate speech renders campuses uncomfortable and threatening to substantial numbers of students at vulnerable points in their lives. It helps construct and maintain a social reality in which some are constantly one-down in encounters that everyone agrees matter. And it tolerates and creates culture at odds with our deepest national values and commitments.

Coming to grips with hate speech does pose serious problems for a society committed both to equality and to individual freedom and autonomy. But resorting to facile arguments like those discussed in this chapter does little to advance the discussion. Neoconservatives should allow themselves to see what everyone else sees—that hateful slurs and invectives are a virulent form of inequality reinforcement—and join the serious search now beginning for cures to this national disease.

8

"But America Wouldn't Be America Anymore"

The Experience of Other Countries Shows That Adopting Hate-Speech Rules Would Not Cause the Sky to Fall; America Would Be Even More American

To this point, we have argued that hate speech of all kinds (including hard core pornography) is socially pernicious, with few redeeming qualities. We have also shown that the emerging conception of the First Amendment allows regulation, and that no policy argument stands in the way of it. Sometimes, however, one hears vague references to other societies that have prohibited racist or sexist hate speech, with ill effects.

Now, at last, it is possible to examine these claims. In April 1991, ARTICLE 19, a London-based international organization devoted to freedom of expression and the press, held a three-day conference at Essex University. Distinguished lawyers, activists, and diplomats from several dozen countries discussed the question of hate speech under domestic and international law. The conference papers were published a year later under the title, *Striking a Balance*.[1] Edited by American attorney Sandra Coliver and published in London by ARTICLE 19, International Centre Against Censorship, the book features an impressive list of contributors, including major figures in the international human rights community, delegates from European and Third World nations, and legal scholars from the United States and other countries. *Striking a Balance* is worth describing in some detail.

Two overviews of the international situation, one by Kevin Boyle, professor of law and director of the Human Rights Centre, University of Essex,[2] the other by Paul Gordon, senior research officer, Runnymede Trust, introduce the volume.[3] Boyle's essay succinctly poses the issue with which the book is concerned: namely, how recent outbreaks of racial, ethnic, and religious hostilities require society to reconsider the relationship between freedom of expression and freedom from verbal harassment for minority groups. He notes that the United States stands virtually alone in extending freedom of expression to what has come to be called hate speech. Most countries tolerate some degree of regulation. But First Amendment jurisprudence and our unique "history as a society born in rebellion against . . . censorship" militate against regulation of any but the most pernicious forms of speech in the United States.[4] Boyle reminds us that "[t]here is a communal as well as an individual dimension to human rights and freedoms," and that "the individual's right to promote racist views must . . . be defended [not only] in terms of individual rights, but in terms of the communal interests in equality."[5] He implies that a sensible society would limit speech when it begins to endanger these interests.

A second essay, by Paul Gordon, focuses on European racism and xenophobia.[6] Gordon describes the nature and extent of racist violence, identifies the affected parties, and relates these conflicts to the larger political context of emerging nationalism and the end of the Soviet empire. A following group of essays discusses international treaties and declarations concerning freedom from discrimination and freedom of expression, such as the Convention on the Elimination of all Forms of Racial Discrimination (CERD) and the International Covenant on Civil and Political Rights (ICCPR). Commentaries by noted human rights advocates, including Karl Josef Partsch, Danilo Turk, and Louis Joinet, examine the history of these documents and their current interpretations.

Although this part of the book will undoubtedly prove of great use to scholars wishing to acquaint themselves with the international dimension of hate-speech law, the next part, an imposing 240-page compilation of Country Experiences, is likely to prove of greater benefit to scholars in the United States.[7] In this section, twenty-five legal thinkers and human rights activists present the experiences of fifteen countries in coping with racial, ethnic, and religious violence, and the legal framework each has put into place to deal with the problem. The countries include Argentina, Australia, Canada, the Commonwealth of Independent States (formerly the Soviet Union), Denmark, France, Germany, India, Israel, the Netherlands, South Africa, Sri Lanka, the United Kingdom, the United States, and Uruguay.

Following the country reports, policy statements appear from eleven national human rights organizations, such as the ACLU (U.S.) and ARTICLE 19 (UK), and from ethnic and religious defense organizations, such as the American-Arab Relations Committee and the Anti-Defamation League of B'nai B'rith.[8] A short concluding part contains essays evaluating laws against insult and incitement, including a summary by the book's editor, Sandra Coliver.

Lessons from the International Arena: What Light Do Experiences of Other Countries Shed on the U. S. Debate?

Will Suppressing Racist Speech Cause It to Go Underground Only to Surface in More Virulent Forms Later?

The experiences detailed do not sustain this "hydraulic" view of racism frequently put forward by opponents of regulation in the United States. (See also chapter 6.) Most countries find that all but a small group of extremists accept some regulation, agreeing that such regulation is a step toward restoring and maintaining racial harmony. The sole exceptions are two countries with long histories of racial or ethnic oppression, South Africa[9] and Sri Lanka,[10] where censoring hate speech does seem to increase the incidence of ethnic hatred.

"Hate Speech Is Not the Root of the Problem; Regulating It Is a Diversion"

Some opponents of United States regulation of hate speech urge that laws against racial insults divert attention from what should be the main goal—getting at the core of discrimination itself. (See also chapter 7.) They maintain that better means, such as education, counseling, teaching, voluntary restraint, and civil rights litigation, are available. Focusing on hate-speech regulation can deflect us from other more important tasks. Though most countries appear to agree that these other measures are necessary and useful, only two (Israel and South Africa) argue that "efforts to fight racism should be concentrated on racist and discriminatory actions"[11] and not on hate speech itself. Most nations appear to find that regulating hate speech is a useful adjunct to other measures for maintaining intergroup harmony. The experiences of most of the nations covered in the book appear not to support a "diversion" charge.

Will Societies Inevitably Turn Race-Hatred Rules against Minorities or Political Dissidents?

The experience of more progressive countries like Canada does not bear out the charge that regulation backfires, harming those it is designed to protect. In more repressive societies, however, such as South Africa and the former Soviet Union, ruling majorities have deployed laws against hate speech to stifle minority-group members and blacks who spoke out against oppression.[12] Under apartheid, virtually all reported prosecutions were of those on the left wing of the political spectrum; black victims of racial abuse by whites rarely found protection in these laws.[13] Israel[14] and Sri Lanka[15] report similar experiences.

Will Hate-Speech Regulation Lead to Further Erosion of Freedom of Speech?

Many in the United States who take the position that hate-speech laws are unwise argue that such measures inevitably lead down the "slippery slope" to greater regulation of speech. Although some of the essayists mentioned this concern, no country report did. Indeed, the experiences of Canada, Denmark, France, Germany, and the Netherlands—countries whose commitment to freedom of inquiry arguably is comparable to that of the United States—imply that limited regulation of hate speech does not invariably, or even frequently, weaken the respect accorded free speech.[16] Citizens seem to regard anti-hate-speech laws as limited exceptions comparable to libel or official-secret rules necessary to preserve a decent society.

"Talking Back Is Better"

Some opponents of hate-speech regulation argue that laws are substitutes for a much preferable response to hate speech, namely, encouraging victims to speak out and denounce the practice. (See chapter 7.) This argument appears not to be in broad currency as no country report addressed this assertion. In the meantime, recent reports of minority-group members who were attacked and seriously injured as a result of talking back to their harassers cast doubt on the wisdom of this counsel.

Will Laws against Hate Speech Chill Discussion, Especially in Sensitive Settings Like University Campuses?

This argument, analogous in structure to the "slippery slope" argument discussed earlier, receives similar treatment in the country reports. France[17] and Germany[18] argue that academic freedom is not absolute and therefore must be weighed against such countervailing values as the human dignity of students. In the new South Africa, however, "race issues and politics substantially overlap. . . . Regulation of . . . speech and publications would, therefore, [unacceptably] chill political debate within that country."[19] Like other slippery-slope concerns, the likelihood that these laws will chill vital expression depends on how societies view hate speech. If it is perceived as abhorrent and far removed from speech's core functions, most will consider they may regulate it without chilling other speech.

Prosecution Makes Hate Mongers into Martyrs

Some opponents of hate-speech regulation argue that punishing utterers of racial insult and invective simply focuses attention on hate mongers and enables them to paint themselves as martyrs. If acquitted, they claim vindication; if convicted, they portray themselves as hounded and harassed victims of intolerance. The reports provide some support for this assertion. In two countries, Canada[20] and the United Kingdom,[21] prosecution of hate groups produced this effect. Yet other countries did not report such experiences. Moreover, Great Britain and Canada did not see fit to discontinue their approach to regulation because of the occasional racist martyr it produced.

In addition to casting doubt on these common arguments against hate-speech regulation, *Striking a Balance* offers support for a number of assertions associated with the pro-regulation position.

Racism Is Increasing throughout the World and Needs to Be Addressed through Law

Most United States proponents of regulation, and even some detractors, believe that hate speech and hate crimes are increasing. In particular, many believe that the last few years have witnessed a strong upsurge. Reports from nine other countries verify that this is so. Indeed, since 1990, racial and religious incitement appears to have increased around the world, most markedly in democratic societies.

In Canada, a recent unprecedented rise of anti-Semitism, Holocaust denial, and revisionism resulted in the historic litigation of a trilogy of cases.[22] An escalation of interethnic conflict has emerged in the former Soviet Union,[23] while a wave of xenophobia and violence against immigrants and refugees has swept over Denmark.[24] In France, Africans and Jews are targets for group libel and incitement.[25] Publications advocating Holocaust revisionism and outbreaks of violence against aliens, asylum seekers, Jews, and Gypsies are occurring more frequently in Germany[26] and throughout Europe.[27] India, though remarkably successful in creating a diverse democratic society, nonetheless has suffered considerable incitement to religious and communal hatred in recent years.[28] Jewish-Arab hostilities in Israel also increased over the past several years.[29] Sri Lankans—Buddhists, Tamils, and Muslims—have struggled through an ethnic and religious civil war during the past seven years.[30] In the United Kingdom, an estimated 70,000 racist attacks occur per year and hate propaganda is increasing.[31] In Europe, one in three citizens believes that there are too many persons of other races or nationalities living in that citizen's country; only 19% disapprove completely of racist movements.[32] In Austria, nearly one-half believe the Jews were partly to blame for their own persecution. The German reporter described the situation in his country as a "frightening revival."[33]

Hate Speech Harms Its Victims

Though some delegates disagreed on the extent of the harm, few disagreed that hate speech injures its victims. The Supreme Court of Canada acknowledged this by using a harm-based rationale to justify criminalizing hate speech in the *Keegstra* decision.[34] The French country report recognized that, in addition to psychological and moral harm, hate speech damages the individual and collective reputations of its victims.[35] Germans view a racial or ethnic attack as an affront to a person's core identity.[36] Uruguay professes to have one of the few laws that expressly acknowledges the pain caused by racist words or acts.[37] The Netherlands recognizes racist statements as insulting and distressing;[38] South Africa, that the racial insult "harms souls."[39] In the United Kingdom, racial vilification is a form of defamation.[40]

Hate Speech Harms Society

Canadian, French, and German statutory documents, reprinted as excerpts in this volume, affirm a corollary proposition about the broader effect of hateful speech on the community. The *Keegstra* decision notes that hate propaganda can harm society as a whole.[41] In France, the preamble to a longstanding statute on group libel declares that such "aggression is directed against the whole body politic and its social and moral fabric."[42] Article 131 of the German Criminal Code seeks to protect the "social harmony" endangered by incitement to racial hatred. Common law in the United Kingdom restricts racist speech in part to avoid harm to the public order.[43]

Regulating Hate Speech Sends an Important Message to Potential Offenders

Although it is difficult to show any immediately discernible deterrent effects of anti-hate-speech laws, many societies remain convinced that they serve an important symbolic function. Hate speech laws place offenders on notice that racial vilification will earn official disapproval. Hate-speech regulation also strengthens those in the society who promote racial harmony. The reporter for the former Soviet Union writes that laws against hate speech are an essential tool for curbing ethnic hostilities.[44] Reporters for Israel declare that its new law "has reinforced anti-racist ideology and influenced modes of behavior through its normative proscription against racism."[45] A government report from the Netherlands states that the purpose of its hate-speech regulation is to bring about a change in social attitudes.[46] British[47] and Australian[48] officials justify outlawing hate speech by emphasizing that doing so expresses official condemnation of bigotry and ethnic hatred.

Implications for Finding the Right Balance

As is discussed elsewhere in this book, recent scholarship sheds light on how expression and interpretation are interwoven with the idea of community—"a social formation that inculcates norms into the very identities of its members."[49] Frank Michelman echoes these words when he states:

This view [civic republicanism] of the human condition implies that self-cognition and . . . self-legislation must, to a like extent, be socially situated; norms must be formed through public dialogue and expressed as public law. Normative reason . . . cannot be a solitary activity. Its exercise requires knowledge, including self-knowledge, obtainable only by encounter with different outlooks in public argument. Thus its requisite forum is "a political community of equals."[50]

If this is so, it seems to follow that a culture that has achieved what it sees as a desirable measure of community would resist perceived threats to that community, including ones from hate speech. Hate speech, of course, vilifies and excludes its victims. When class-based, as it generally is, it threatens to fracture community by whipping up resentment and hostility. When concerted and extended over time, it may create enduring castes that will prove highly resistant to change. (See chapters 1 and 9.)

A reasonable hypothesis, then, is that a nation which values preexisting harmony and fears an upsurge in racism or other types of group hatred will act reflexively to curb hateful utterances that endanger its own interpretive community. Certainly, these restorative measures could take many forms, only one of which is legal regulation. Yet societies with a history of respect for legality are likely to turn to solutions of this sort if the threat to the community is serious or persistent.

The case for this proposition is not so much empirical as interpretive. Yet, viewing the responses of societies to ethnic and religious unrest as communities striving for self-preservation does seem to shed light on the complex web of arguments, counterarguments, and resistance laid out in the United States's controversy and on the pages of the country reports in *Striking a Balance*. India, for example, has both a strong commitment to democracy and a recent history of bitter ethnic and religious conflict. Our interpretive community hypothesis predicts that such a society would take strong action to curb violence, discourage racist speech, and restore the fragile interpretive community that is part of its democratic heritage and ideals; indeed, this is what it has done.[51]

A country like the former Soviet Union, by contrast, is marked by balkanization and a tradition of centralized repressive government. Such a society would not likely rely on shared expression, dialogue, and other forms of communication to bind itself together. Rather, centralized authority serves that purpose. When intergroup conflict breaks out, the impulse to restore a communicative paradigm will be weak. Consequently, laws against hate speech will not be in force. If they are, they are apt to be used eccentrically, as in the case of dissidents.[52]

Finally, the United States has a history of severe and prolonged friction embracing at least four racial minority groups and exceeding that found in most other developed nations. At the same time, the United States has a strong commitment to the use of a common language, common traditions, and common ideals and symbols as means of maintaining national identity. The commitment to free expression is strong. Moreover, the United States was founded, in part, as a reaction to the oppression of crown and church. Freedom of expression was a core Enlightenment value shared by many of the nation's framers. In this respect, the United States resembles nations such as Australia and South Africa, which either do not enforce anti-hate laws or do so grudgingly. In the United States, demographic changes and the increasing political force of minorities, combined with diversity and multicultural movements on campuses, indicate that this unsettled situation will likely continue into the future until a new interpretive community and First Amendment paradigm are finally agreed upon.

This insight leads to a conclusion that the editors and authors of *Striking a Balance* may have overlooked. There may be no single balance that will work for all cultures, or even for the same culture at different times. The appropriate balance between equality and freedom of expression may be a complex, shifting matrix that includes several different forces: the value placed on community historically and aspirationally; the value placed on equality among the various national groups; the perception that minority populations are unfairly excluded or stigmatized; the degree to which speech is considered an important individual prerogative rather than a means of achieving community; and finally, the perception that minority groups lack the means to assert and defend themselves against vilification.

A slight change in the strength of any of these components in a given setting may cause the balance and attitudes toward hate-speech regulation to shift. For example, many university campuses have witnessed an increase in the number of students of color and women seeking and gaining admission coupled with increased competition for slots and scholarships. All the while, a sharp debate rages about the role of multiculturalism in admission, curriculum, and faculty employment. Racist speech and insults occur frequently. Institutions where these divisive events occur are likely to turn to speech regulation to preserve or restore peace and community. Yet these same measures will draw fire from proponents of radical individualism[53] and those who benefit from the current regime. The balance, then, is inherently unstable and likely to provoke repeated challenges.

Liberty, including free speech, and community exist in a reciprocally dependent tension. Each presupposes the other. As defenders of hate-speech regulation argue, dialogue is fruitless without something approaching equality among the speakers. Defenders of protected speech point out, with equal justification, that free speech is an important instrument for achieving social justice—equality presupposes liberty. Either value may be used rhetorically, or in the real world, to suppress the other. The demand for community may lead to conformity, censorship, and group-think. Speech, if misused, can be used concertedly to oppress minority groups.

Thus, neither value seems logically prior; each is necessary for the full expression of the other. Interpretive communities are necessary for speech; speech is a necessary tool to restore, adjust, and refine community. Societies struggle to reach that balance in light of their own needs, histories, and ethnic compositions. Perhaps the most valuable lesson to be gleaned from *Striking a Balance* is that there are no simple answers.

Part IV

"From Where I Sit"—The Special Problems of Judges and Progressive Lawyers

Up to this point, we have argued that hate speech harms its victims; that nothing in the emerging realist view of the First Amendment prevents society from taking steps to control that harm; and that good social policy does not stand in the way, either. Yet some judges and many progressive lawyers have been slower than others—particularly legal scholars and civil rights activists—in accepting the need for reform. In this part we offer a sympathetic treatment of the judges' dilemma. We also show how a kind of romantic totalism afflicts some lawyers, journalists, and other First Amendment absolutists, causing them to prefer defending Nazis and pornographers to defending their victims—the minorities and women who suffer as a result of racist and misogynist speech and invective.

9

Hateful Speech,
Loving Communities

*Why Judges Are Sometimes Slower than Others
at Seeing the Need for Reform*

As we mentioned earlier, the debate about hate speech features two camps, each of which views the controversy in quite different terms.[1] One group, on learning about a proposed hate-speech code, immediately declares the proposal a free speech question. If one places speech at the center in this fashion, a number of things immediately follow. The civil rights advocates are immediately placed on the offensive, seen as aggressors attempting to curtail a precious liberty. The burden shifts to them to show that the speech restriction is not content-based, is supported by a compelling interest, is the least restrictive means of promoting that interest, and so on.[2] (See chapter 4).

Concerns about slippery slopes and dangerous administrators also arise: if we allow racial invective to be bridled, will we not soon find ourselves tolerating restrictions on classroom speech or political satire in the school newspaper?[3] If we permit our fragile web of speech protection to suffer one rent, might not others soon follow? Moreover, someone will have to adjudicate complaints brought under the new rules. Is there not a danger that the judge or administrator will turn into a narrow-minded censor, imposing his or her notion of political orthodoxy on a campus climate that ought to be as free as possible?[4]

Hate-speech rule advocates will see the controversy in quite different terms, however. For them, the central issue is whether campuses are free to impose reasonable rules to protect the dignity and self-regard of vulnerable young minority undergraduates and other targets of hate speech.[5] Placing equality at the center of the controversy, they will see defense of racist invective as endangering values emanating from the equality-protecting Constitutional amendments.[6] Since these values are vital to our system of justice, they will insist that the free speech advocate show that the hate-speaker's interest in hurling racial invective rises to the requisite level of constitutional urgency. They will insist this interest be advanced in the way least onerous to equality. They, too, will raise line-drawing and slippery slope concerns: If society does *not* intervene to protect equality from this intrusion, where will it all stop? They will raise concerns about the administrator who will make decisions under the code, but from the opposite direction: they will want to make sure that the hearing officer is sensitive to the delicate nuances of racial supremacy in the incidents likely to come before him or her.[7]

Differences between the two camps run deeper than matters of doctrine and enforcement ability, however. The two sides invoke different narratives to make their view of the matter seem the only one. The free-speech defenders depict the current struggle as just the latest in a centuries-long succession of battles to keep speech free. They evoke a deeply stirring account, including early struggles against censorship by king and church.[8] They see a history of book burning, inquisitions, official blacklists, and imposed orthodoxy.[9] They cite heroes—Galileo, Voltaire, Locke—who in word or deed resisted imposed orthodoxy or ignorance.[10] The story the speech defenders tell is deeply rooted in the myths, history, and traditions of our people.

The minority defenders have their own narrative, however, one which taps cultural myths no less rooted, no less stirring than those invoked by the free speech defenders. For them, the struggle over hate speech is a continuation of our nation's centuries-long battle over equality and brotherhood,[11] one that includes early abolitionists who worked to subvert an evil institution—Quakers and others who operated the underground railroad—and 1960s-era civil rights protesters who marched for racial justice. They, too, have their heroes: Frederick Douglass, Rosa Parks, Martin Luther King, Jr., Cesar Chavez, and Justice Harlan, author of the dissent in *Plessy v. Ferguson*.[12]

Each side of the controversy thus wants not merely to have the balance struck in its favor, but also to place its interpretation of what is at stake at the center of the characterization. Yet on closer inspection it turns out that the two stories are closely connected. Although on the surface they are contradictory and in tension, the paradigms stand in an intricate relation. Like lovers locked in a death embrace, each depends on, yet threatens, the other. This chapter describes this interconnection and shows what it means for our system of law and politics. When confronted with competing values, a common response is to entrust the decision to a wise judge who will balance the concerns at stake.[13] The peculiar relation of speech and equality, however, shows how difficult this balancing can be.

How Speech and Equality Both Presuppose and Threaten Each Other

Free speech and equality presuppose and threaten each other. Insult and invective, brought to bear by a powerful majority on a helpless minority, can oppress. It can harm directly, either through injury to the psyches of its victims or by encouraging others to take immediate hostile action. It can also harm indirectly, constructing an image or stigma-picture according to which the victim is less than human. (See chapters 1, 4.) But the call for respectful treatment itself can stifle and oppress.[14] Imagine, for example, a community that enacted a rule prohibiting all expression that any individual in the group might find unsettling. This call for civility could easily lead to a bland form of group-think in which little change could occur. Speech and equality are thus in tension.

Yet speech and communitarian values also depend on each other. As civil libertarians like the ACLU's Nadine Strossen point out, speech has served as a powerful instrument for social reform,[15] something minorities (if they knew their own history) ought to know as well as anyone. But her counterparts point out with equal logic that speech, at least in the grand dialogic sense, presupposes rough equality among the speakers.[16] Speech among persons who are markedly unequal in power and standing is not democratic dialogue at all, but something else—a sermon, a rant, an order, a summons—like speech to a child.[17]

Speech and community are thus both interdependent and in tension;

yet practical challenges force us to act. Minorities clamor for greater protection from campus insults, hate crimes, and symbolic acts such as cross burning. The ACLU and other liberal organizations demand that campuses refrain from enacting hate-speech regulations, and threaten suit if they do. The situation is often binary. If minorities demand a speech code, we can either oblige them or not. If the ACLU challenges a speech code, we can strike it down or not.

The usual approach in our system of politics whenever principles clash is to try to balance the competing values in some fashion.[18] We hope that an ingenious decision-maker can find a way to protect minorities from invective and insult while allowing speakers some liberty to say what is on their minds.

But the difficulty is not just the practical one of finding the right compromise. Speech and equality are not separate values, but rather opposite sides of the same coin. Their interdependence arises because they are integral aspects of a more basic phenomenon, namely the interpretive community.[19] Recent scholarship points out that communication requires a group of persons who agree to see the world roughly in the same way. It presupposes a community of speakers and listeners who abide by certain conventions, who assign particular meanings and interpretations to words and messages. Without such an interpretive community, communication is impossible.

The notion of an interpretive community explains the precarious interdependence of speech and equal-protection values. Speech requires community—without it communication is virtually impossible. At the same time, community requires speech because it is our only way of doing what communities must do. Yet, concerted speech can isolate or exclude a weak minority, just as majoritarian limitations on what is said can freeze social change.[20] It is this precarious interdependence that makes the hope of balancing the interests of the two sides in the hate-speech controversy problematic. In effect, a judge weighing any nontrivial proposal for regulating hate speech is deciding whether to throw the state's weight behind a new interpretive community.[21] That new speech community will have different bounds from the old. In it, minorities, gays, or women will be treated with greater respect, or less. Their image, their self-regard, will be treated with greater solicitude, or less. Their speech will be given greater credibility, or less. Terms and customs dear to them will be included in the lexicon, or not.

When judges make decisions with respect to speech codes, then, they are not simply balancing two discrete things, like Smith's desire to have a twelve-foot fence against Jones's desire to have more sunlight in his living room. They are deciding between competing conceptions of speech equality, between different worlds we might live in. This is at once a more portentous and difficult task than deciding whether the interest of a young black undergraduate in not being called a "N . . ." late at night on his or her way home from the library "outweighs" the interest of the would-be speaker in shouting it.

How might judges approach this task? It is not the run-of-the-mill judicial assignment, like the backyard fence case. As we explain later in this chapter, deciding between one speech community and another requires a dialogue.[22] Judges will have discussions with other judges or carry on internal monologues with themselves, all conducted through a set of conventions using words with established meanings.[23] These dialogues-about-dialogue will be heavily weighted in favor of the current regime.[24] Thus, most radical reformers and members of movements which aim to transform the speech-community should be under no illusion that judges can readily and fairly balance the two competing values—one established and entrenched, the other foreign and "new." For judges to weigh proposed speech regulations fairly and dispassionately requires them, in effect, to stand outside their own interpretive community. They must be unsituated, have no experience, attach no particular meanings to words and arguments. This is no easy task.[25] History shows that when reformers have asked the dominant society to restructure itself radically, the response has often been incomprehension, if not ridicule. The would-be reformer is heard as urging that black be redefined as white, night as day, a thing as its opposite. After a brief review of such responses, we return to the question of why this happens.

What Happens When Reformers Ask Us to Change the Existing Speech Paradigm

At many points in human history, activists and innovators have asked society to transform radically the way it thought and spoke about a subject or group. Often the request was tantamount to a change in consciousness, requiring adoption of a new definition of the human community or community of concern, of the "we" in the "we are this." In most cases, this request was greeted initially with skepticism and disbelief. This was so in large part, we believe, because reformers were heard as asking for something that could not be said, or heard, within the current speech paradigm and was therefore unthinkable.

Consider, for example, society's responses to the early abolitionist movement. For decades, the principal response was ridicule and disbelief. Many whites, including some mainline church leaders, believed blacks were inferior to whites, childlike, and ill-prepared to assume the responsibilities of citizenship. Even President Pierce reacted to the prospect of abolition with shock and dismay. In a message to Congress, he charged that granting blacks full rights was beyond lawful authority and could only be accomplished by the "forcible disruption of a country" he considered the best and most free in human history.[26] He charged the abolitionists with appealing to passion, prejudice, and hatred. To be sure, part of the resistance to abolition was economic, especially in the South. But at least as much was conceptual, stemming from a failure of imagination or empathy.

Many citizens reacted to the abolitionist message with surprise or scorn: What, free *them?* Early feminists and children's rights advocates met similar resistance. More recently, environmentalists, gay and lesbian activists, and animal rights advocates have encountered the same opposition. In response to the early movements, society eventually changed its paradigm or way of thinking about the group in the direction of greater inclusion. In the cases of animal rights and of gay and lesbian rights, we will probably do so in the future. We think this contrast is general: proposals that entail a reconstitution of the human community or community of concern always spark much greater resistance than ones that do not, such as a change in the way we finance schools. The request that we change our speech and our thoughts with respect to minorities and women taps much of the same resistance that accompanied previous broad social reforms.

The Mechanisms of Cultural Resistance, and How to Double-Cross Them

We construct the social world, in large part, through speech. How we speak to and of others determines whether and on what terms we accept them into our world as groups and as individuals.[27] The leaders of the reform movements just mentioned were asking for more than better treatment in material respects for certain people or things. They were also asking that these people or things be thought of, spoken of, constructed, differently. They were asking that terms like human, creature, decent, good, nice, precious, and worthy of respect apply to them. In short, they were asking for membership in the human community. Respectful speech, even more than willingness to rent a house or offer a job to someone, indicates the degree to which we accept that person's humanity.

Yet speech, including the reformer's, is paradigm-dependent;[28] unfortunately, both exclusion and inclusion are built into the very narratives and thought structures by which we communicate. Recent focus on our common language reveals that the "image of the outsider" in American law and culture has always included a host of stories, pictures, and stock characters that are demeaning yet seldom seen as such at the time. During each era, a few reformers complained of the unfairness of a Sambo, a Charlie Chan, or a Tom image, but the usual response was incomprehension: isn't that the way they actually are? Our system of ethnic depiction constructs reality so that the images seem true, or at most, are perceived as humorous exaggerations well within the bounds of artistic license. (See chapter 5.)

We coined the term "empathic fallacy" to describe the belief that we may somehow escape the confines of our own internalized narratives, that we may easily and endlessly reform ourselves and each other through argument, exhortation, exposure to great literature, and other verbal means. If even modest alterations in our system of imagery, such as abandoning a stereotype that a group finds demeaning, provoke strong resistance, how much more will we resist requests that appear to require radical restructuring of our self-concept as a people? In proposing rules that change the way we speak about women or persons of color, the reformer is heard as saying something verging on incoherent. The reformer, we learn, is asking that "us" be defined to include them, that justice means consideration of those others, that "nice" refers to those we have learned are "not nice," those who were excluded from the paradigm by which we first learned how to use that term.

Judges are no quicker than others to surmount their own limitations of culture and experience.[29] In cases containing a radical reform component, even eminent justices often fail to appreciate the moral force of the new vision being urged on them. Years later, such cases are labeled "anomalies," failures that mar the reputation of an otherwise great jurist.[30]

A judge is always free, within the limits of precedent, to modify the current understanding of terms like justice, fairness, discrimination, and equal protection. But given the limitations of the courtroom situation, that modification could occur only through a process of dialogue among the judge, the lawyers, and the relevant community. Such a dialogue is necessarily heavily weighted in favor of the status quo. Long ago, empowered actors and speakers enshrined their meanings, preferences, and views of the world into the common culture and language.[31] Now, deliberation within that language, purporting always to be neutral and fair, inexorably produces results that reflect their interests.[32]

Only a judge with no experience, history, or community—virtually with no language—could render an unbiased decision in a case calling for reformulation of the terms by which we define that community, change our history, alter our language. There is no such judge. Tools of thought primarily facilitate "normal science"—minor, incremental refinements in the current structures by which we see and rule ourselves. Law is no exception. After its passage, even the Fourteenth Amendment was primarily used to protect corporations and then later to rationalize a regime of segregation in which blacks were "separate but equal."[33] The result of free speech, including the courtroom variety, is most often to ensure stasis, not to facilitate change.

Blacks, women, gays and lesbians, and others were not part of the speech community that framed the Constitution and Bill of Rights.[34] They fell outside the original definition of "we the people"—they were not allowed to speak. Later, when they did, their speech was deemed incoherent, self-interested, worthy of scorn. Who would credit a member of a group whose members—according to thousands of images, plots, narratives, stories, and songs—are stupid, bestial, happy-go-lucky, and sexually licentious? Words apportion credibility and define the community.[35] Because those assigned a stigma are by virtue of that separated from mainstream society, few judges will know them. How many judges are good friends with an African American, send their children to schools with more than a token black presence, attend social clubs where blacks or Mexicans appear in roles other than gardener or waiter? Excluded groups fall outside most judges' experience.[36] What can they fall back on other than what they hear and read?

Much of what they hear and read comes, of course, from the law, an interpretive community of its own. At a recent annual meeting of the

Association of American Law Schools, participants explored the question, "Does the law have a canon?"[37] Some answered no, the law has only cases, statutes, administrative regulations, and the like, all of which are the same for everyone, black or white, conservative or liberal.

But the law does have a canon. It consists of terms like "just," "fair," "equal," "equal opportunity," "unfair to innocent whites," "nice," "deserving," and "meritorious," all with canonical meanings that reflect our sense of how things ought to be, namely, much as they are.[38] The terms reassure us that all is well, that our own situations in life are deserved (because fairly won), and that change generally ought to be resisted because the demand for it is incoherent or unprincipled.[39] Many years ago, the majority of us learned what "principled" means, and it certainly doesn't mean the strange thing that reformer is saying! Words, once they enter the canon, freeze community, enabling us to resist transformation without even noticing how we do so. The suggestion that they are like us is heard as an impossibility.

When a reformer demands that we look at things in a different way, our first response is outrage or incredulity: what they are asking for simply does not fit our paradigm. What happens if the reformer persists?

Resistance

Any serious proposal to transform society radically is apt to provoke a number of predictable responses.[40] We can fail to hear what the reformer is saying, or translate the message into something else. We can declare that the reformer is obviously aiming to avert a particular evil, and then pretend not to find any evidence that the evil is in fact occurring. We can deprecate the reformer as extreme, politically motivated, self-interested, or bizarre. (See chapter 2.)

Running through most of these forms of resistance is the idea that the reformer is imposing on the status quo. Civil rights are fine, up to a point. But with each successive demand, the reformers are decried as having exceeded all reasonable bounds. "We have already admitted some of them into the workplace, made places for them at our schools. Now they want to control how we speak, how we think. They are going too far." No longer victims, minorities become the aggressors and the majority the innocent victim. Resistance is now not only morally permissible, it is in order.

The point of canonical ideas is to resist attack.[41] If one places at the center of one's belief system the notion that all speech should be free and that equality must accommodate itself to that regime, then all equality arguments but the most moderate will appear extreme and unjust. The canon defines the starting point, the baseline from which we decide what other messages, ideas, concepts, and proposals are acceptable. Only moderate ones that effect minor incremental refinements within the current regime pass the test. All preconceptions—that women's place is with home and children, that minorities are here at our sufferance, that we have given blacks too much already, that speech ought to be free regardless of its cost—resist change. Reason and argument prove unavailing; the point of the canon is to define what *is* a reasoned, just, principled demand. Because hate-speech rules fall outside this boundary, if one begins (as most of us do) with a free-speech paradigm, reason fails and the status quo prevails.

Strategies

Even though reform proposals predictably evoke stubborn resistance, history shows that there are a number of means by which reformers can nevertheless bring about a degree of change. These include rearranging interest convergence, tricking the trope, and the narrative strategy of the double cross. Each of these tools is potentially available to reformers who wish to institute hate-speech rules.

Rearranging Interest Convergence

Societies rarely restructure themselves in response to a reasoned plea, but they do readily transform themselves in response to changes in material conditions.[42] For example, the American workplace quickly accepted women once the slipping economic position of the United States plus the advent of information technology made women's entry both necessary and feasible. Reformers on behalf of women's rights had been advocating the virtues of equality in the workplace for centuries, while making little headway. Once the nation became persuaded that its economic well-being required women workers, change quickly followed. Derrick Bell interprets the tortuous course of civil rights progress in similar fashion:

black people have made progress only when that progress also benefited members of the majority group.[43] The same is probably true for other disadvantaged groups, such as inmates of mental facilities, children, and the aged.[44]

How will interest convergence bear on the fortunes of hate-speech reformers? Municipal and collegiate hate-speech regulations do little to advance the tangible self-interest of powerful whites. At one time, the United States was engaged in competition with the Soviet Union for the loyalties of the uncommitted Third World, most of which is black, Asian, or brown. During this period, it behooved us to be on our best behavior toward our own minority populations. We could scarcely portray ourselves as superior to godless communism, all the while visibly mistreating our own populations of color.[45] Moderate reforms were enacted; the Supreme Court even upheld a group libel law in a single case.[46] With the collapse of the Soviet Union, the need for such exemplary behavior today largely has disappeared. Blacks are a relatively weak group, while the forces arrayed against them in the hate-speech controversy are well financed, certain they are right, and able to command the legal expertise to bring and win test suits.[47] Interest convergence is not a particularly promising avenue for blacks and others interested in promoting the cause of hate-speech regulation. Indeed, a certain amount of unanswered, low-grade racism and hassling on the nation's campuses may even confer a benefit on the *status quo*. [48]

"Tricking the Trope": Verbal Jujitsu

In the absence of interest convergence, reformers may employ other avenues for achieving redress. The first we call "tricking the trope." One can identify and enumerate the rhetorical strategies the dominant culture deploys to deny one moral legitimacy and to portray one as extreme, as an aggressor, as interested in trammeling others' rights, and so on. Then one can proceed to turn these rhetorical strategies against the dominators.

Martin Luther King, Jr., was an expert at this strategy. Innumerable times he brought the lofty language of the Declaration of Independence, the Bible, and other basic cultural documents to bear in the cause of racial justice for blacks.[49] This sometimes stopped Southern racists in their tracks—their own rhetoric and beliefs were being used against them. King's most effective speeches and letters thus were replete with references to Moses leading the people out of bondage and to the political rights of all men, and reminding us of this nation's commitment to brotherhood and equality for all.[50]

In the hate-speech controversy, reformers might remind their opponents that our founding as a nation grew out of complaints over disrespectful treatment and petty annoyances at the hands of the British aristocracy, that the Pledge of Allegiance ends with the words, "With liberty and justice for all," and that, more recently, the Third Reich prepared the way for atrocities visited on Jews, Gypsies, and homosexuals by first stigmatizing them and portraying them as less than human.[51] The powerful rhetoric of the ACLU and other organizations committed to expanding free speech can be turned around. Why do black undergraduates not have an equal right to go where they please without harassment and personal assault?

Double-Crossing the Narrative: The Counterstory

A third strategy that can be deployed is the double-cross or "trickster" tale. In black history, oral storytellers and later black novelists and poets have used the double-cross to register their disagreement with a regime that oppressed and demeaned them at every turn.[52] The Spanish *picaro* was a similar figure. The trickster was one who employed slyness and clever strategy to win justice from a more powerful master; the double-cross was, similarly, a means to avenge unfair treatment.[53]

Currently, a new generation of civil rights scholars, known as critical race theorists, is developing a form of legal scholarship that uses narratives or storytelling. Writers who adopt this approach employ anecdotes, chronicles, dialogues, and similar tales to analyze, criticize, and expose mindset. Some such accounts take the form of stories from personal experience, illustrating a point about racial justice. Others take a different approach. Instead of aiming at bringing to life the minority perspective or experience, these accounts focus on some majoritarian narrative, for example the notion of the innocent white male, or that racial discrimination does not exist unless it is intentional, or that role modeling is a good idea. These "counterstories" are aimed at displacing one or more of these comforting majoritarian myths and tales in order to call into question the accuracy, impartiality, and correctness of the current story or account of progress toward racial equality. Derrick Bell's "Geneva Chronicles" are prime examples, but there are many more.

Could storytellers of color or their sympathizers employ these tools to shake the complacency of the forces resisting hate-speech rules? Perhaps so. Irony, the demonstration of how self-interest operates in the current regime, and the "flip," the change of frame or perspective, are powerful means of introducing doubt or "suspicion" where they did not exist before. Minority storytellers have already begun the task of deploying such tools.

Cultural Nationalism

Each of the preceding approaches—interest convergence and the two narrative strategies—presupposes that the insurrectionist group wishes to merge with the dominant society, but merely on more favorable terms. A fourth strategy consists of withdrawal, either permanent or strategic. The trend toward cultural nationalism among Chicano and African American groups is a recent example.[54]

In the controversy about hate speech, we see the beginnings of such an approach. Parents of minority children, concerned about their well-being and safety at white-dominated institutions, are beginning to send their college-age offspring to predominantly black schools where the atmosphere will be more supportive. This strategy has the advantages of avoiding the need for hate-speech rules altogether, building black institutions and culture, and allowing the next generation of African American leaders to develop in relative safety.

It is ironic that the threat of black flight may prove the spur that college and university administrators need to begin the serious process of assessing their own institutional cultures and environments. The University of Wisconsin, for example, enacted a speech code precisely at a point when concern over dwindling black numbers on the state's campuses had reached real alarm. The very onset of defensive nationalism may supply a vital (because self-interest based) argument for reform.

We have argued that speech and equality, freedom of expression and the call for community, both presuppose and threaten each other. Speech, at least in the grand dialogic sense, presupposes rough equality among the speakers, while equality depends on activism and mass action, both of which are unthinkable without speech. Insult and invective by a powerful majority can oppress a minority. Likewise, imposition of a dominant community's values and beliefs can stifle speech and thought.

Efforts to balance these competing values are rendered difficult because the values are inextricably interdependent aspects of a more basic structure, the interpretive community. Judges asked to strike a balance between free speech and minority protection are in effect deciding the contours of a new interpretive community. They must decide whose views count, whose speech is to be taken seriously, whose humanity afforded full respect. Can they do so fairly and open-mindedly given that most of them come from the dominant speech community? This is a formidable task.

We called attention to reform movements whose members asked society to transform radically the way it thought or spoke about a subject or group. Their proposals were greeted initially with skepticism and disbelief because the messages were heard as asking the unthinkable according to the communicative paradigm of the time. Social decision-makers asked to decide in favor of one interpretive community over another are situated in a speech paradigm. Their deliberations are carried out through words already carrying established meanings, almost always heavily weighted in favor of the status quo. Thus, reformers provoke predictable responses. We either fail to hear their message, or mistranslate it when we do. We misdirect the point of their critique, then fail to find evidence of social ill. We deprecate their intent or declare that we are the ones suffering imposition.

Hate-speech reform invokes a plausible constitutional paradigm, with its own history, case law, and genuine heroes. Yet prospects for change, through the courts at any rate, are not particularly good. Because of the way we are situated and because there is little in the self-interest of elite groups to cause them to want change, reform of laws against hate speech is certain to continue to evoke sharp resistance. At some future time, the United States will probably join the majority of Western nations that impose limitations on racial incitement and invective. We will then look back on our current stance and wonder how we could have thought it "principled."

10

"The Speech We Hate"

The Romantic Appeal of First Amendment Absolutism. Does Defending Nazis Really Strengthen the System of Free Speech?

In *The Brothers Karamazov*, Alyosha, an impressionable young man, visits his mother's grave, where he has an intense religious experience.[1] Transformed, he declares "I want to live for immortality, and I will accept no compromise."[2] Having discovered God—the most important thing in life—nothing else matters to Alyosha. He enters a monastery, devotes himself single-mindedly to his spiritual mentor Father Zossima, prays fervently, counsels the young, rescues animals, and effects a reconciliation between feuding schoolboys before the death of one of them.

In many respects, certain free speech absolutists (such as the ACLU) remind us of Alyosha. Until recently, they have held the line in every case of a proposed free speech exception, invoking such doctrines and shibboleths as: no content regulation; no viewpoint regulation; speech is different from action; more speech is the cure for bad speech; and governmental censorship and self-aggrandizement are evils always to be feared and avoided.[3]

But as legal realism[4] has finally arrived in First Amendment jurisprudence, more than fifty years after its appearance in other areas of law, sweeping aside the various mechanical doctrines and "tests" that prevailed until recently, the old-timers, who much preferred things the way they were, have been shifting their ground slightly. Nowhere is this shift more evident than with regulation of hate speech and pornography. With publication of a number of influential law review articles and books, and the handing down of a trio of decisions by the U.S. and Canadian supreme courts,[5] it now seems likely that cautiously drafted hate-speech codes will be found constitutional. But are they wise? Formerly assured that formalistic categories and doctrines such as the prohibition against content or viewpoint discrimination would hold, the ACLU and others who oppose hate-speech rules have until recently ignored these questions. Now, like an Alyosha beginning to doubt his faith, they are starting to hedge their bets and argue that even if hate-speech rules are constitutional, they are a bad idea and that colleges, universities, and other institutions should not adopt them, even if they could.

In previous chapters, we examined two sets of policy arguments that opponents of such rules have advanced.[6] On the left, the ACLU and others have put forward policy arguments based on paternalism. These include what we call the "pressure valve," "reverse enforcement," "best friend," and "talk back" arguments, all of which have in common the insistence that hate-speech rules would injure minorities, whether they know it or not, and should be avoided for that reason. A second set of arguments characterizes the moderate right. These include that mobilizing against hate speech is a waste of time—minorities ought to have better things to do; that hate speech is a useful bellwether that ought not be driven underground; that running to the authorities every time one suffers a minor indignity merely deepens victimization; and that minorities ought to toughen up or learn to talk back. Each of these arguments, which make up what we call the "toughlove" position, just like the ones the liberals offer, has answers. Some are empirically groundless, others assume a social world unlike the one we live in, others are inconsistent with other values that we hold.

Here we examine one argument that is neither paternalistic nor of the toughlove variety, but structural. Associated with the ACLU and others who take a relatively purist position with respect to the First Amendment, the argument holds that hate speech, pornography, and similar forms of expression ought to be protected precisely because they are unpopular. The speech we hate, it is said, must be protected in order to safeguard that which we hold dear. The only way to assure protection of values that lie at the core of the First Amendment is to protect speech lying at its periphery.[7] And this inevitably means protecting unpopular speakers: Nazis, anti-Semites, the Ku Klux Klan, utterers of campus hate speech, and promulgators of hard-core pornography.[8]

What can be said about this argument? As we will show, it is fairly often put forward by lawyers, legal commentators, special interest groups, and even an occasional judge as a reason for protecting odious speech. The argument takes two or three forms, each of which boils down to the insistence that to protect speech of one sort it is necessary to protect another. The argument in all its guises, however, is paradoxical and groundless. We address how an argument with so little foundation can be put forward with seeming sincerity by otherwise intelligent people. We show that the argument's contradictions disappear once one understands that hate speech today lies not at the periphery, but at the center, and political speech at the periphery of First Amendment ideology. The center and the periphery have traded places in a second sense, as well: in a striking reversal of Harry Kalven's thesis, injuries to whites are now placed at the fore of constitutional jurisprudence, with redress to blacks' historical injustices allowed only when it coincides with benefits to whites.

Single-Valued Jurisprudence: Examples in Commentary and Judicial Opinions

As we indicated, the "speech we hate" (core/periphery) argument has been put forward by commentators, including ones associated with special interest groups like the ACLU, as well as by a few courts. In no case that we have found has anyone attempted to argue for its truth or validity; instead, it has been repeated as though a kind of mantra: we must protect X in order to protect Y.[9]

The Commentators' and Special Interest Groups' Argument

The argument that we must protect the speech we hate in order to protect that which we hold dear is a special favorite of certain commentators who advocate an unfettered First Amendment. For example, Samuel Walker, the author of a recent history of the ACLU[10] and another of the hate-speech controversy, writes that the ACLU believes that "every view, no matter how ignorant or harmful we may regard it, has a legal and moral right to be heard."[11] He explains that banning ignorant and hateful propaganda against Jews, for instance, "could easily lead to the suppression of other ideas now regarded as moderate and legitimate."[12] The free speech victories that have been won in defending Nazi and other unpopular speech, Walker points out, have also been used to protect pro-civil rights messages.[13] In two recent books and a series of law review articles, Nadine Strossen, the president of the ACLU, echoes Walker's views. "If the freedom of speech is weakened for one person, group, or message," according to Strossen, we will soon have no free speech right left at all.[14] Thus, for example, "the effort to defend freedom for those who choose to create, pose for, or view pornography is not only freedom for this particular type of expression but also freedom of expression in general."[15] In *Speaking of Race, Speaking of Sex: Hate Speech, Civil Rights, and Civil Liberties*, Anthony Griffin and Henry Louis Gates advance positions similar to Strossen's. Gates writes that when the ACLU defended the right of neo-Nazis to march in Skokie, a predominantly Jewish suburb of Chicago where a number of Holocaust survivors lived, it did so to protect and fortify the constitutional right of free speech.[16] If free speech can be tested and upheld to protect even Nazi speech, "then the precedent will make it that much stronger in all the less obnoxious cases."[17] Griffin, who forfeited his position with the Texas NAACP in order to defend a Klan organization, reiterates the ACLU position through a series of three fables, all of which reinforce the notion that the only way to have a strong, vibrant First Amendment is to protect Nazi speech, racist speech, and so on.[18] Otherwise, the periphery will collapse and the government will increasingly regulate speech we regard as central to our system of politics and government.[19]

This type of argument is not just the favorite of the ACLU and its friends. Respected constitutional commentators have employed similar reasoning. Lee Bollinger, for instance, posits that Nazi speech should be protected not because people should value their message in the slightest or believe it should be seriously entertained, but because protection of such speech reinforces our society's commitment to tolerance.[20] Laurence Tribe advances a variant of the same theme. In explaining that there is no principled basis for regulating speech based on content or viewpoint, Tribe states, "If the Constitution forces government to allow people to march, speak, and write in favor or preach brotherhood, and justice, then it must also require government to allow them to advocate hatred, racism, and even genocide."[21] As put forward by these and other commentators, then, the "speech we hate" argument takes on a small number of variants. Some argue that there must be a wall around the periphery to protect speech that we hold dear. Others reason that speech that lies at the periphery must be protected if we are to strengthen impulses or principles, such as toleration, that are important to society.

The Courts' Version

Many years ago, Justice Oliver Wendell Holmes laid the groundwork for the periphery-to-center reasoning by declaring that, "[I]f there is any principle of the Constitution that more imperatively calls for attachment than any other it is the principle of free thought—not the free thought for those who agree with us but freedom for the thought that we hate."[22] He urged that "we should be eternally vigilant against attempts to check even the expression of opinions that we loathe and believe to be fraught with death."[23] Later, in *Brandenburg v. Ohio*, the Supreme Court issued a ringing defense of an unfettered right of free speech. In vindicating the Ku Klux Klan's right to express hatred and violence toward Jews and blacks, the Court held that unless the Klan's speech is likely to incite imminent lawless action, our Constitution has made such speech immune from governmental control.[24] And in the "Nazis in Skokie" case, the Seventh Circuit's opinion reverberated with Justice Holmes's reasoning.[25] In upholding the neo-Nazi's right to march in that city, the court wrote that its result was dictated by the fundamental proposition that if free speech is to remain vital for all, courts must protect not only speech our society deems acceptable, but also that which it justifiably rejects and despises.

Courts, then, make many of the same versions of the core/periphery argument that commentators do: without protection for speech we hate, the free marketplace of ideas will collapse; in order to protect speech that our society finds acceptable we must also protect speech we find repugnant. The argument in each of its guises is essentially the same: to protect the most central, important forms of speech—political and artistic speech, and so on—we must protect the most repugnant, valueless forms including hate speech directed against minorities and degrading pornographic stereotypes of woman.

Difficulties with the Extreme-Case, or "Speech We Hate," Argument

As we mentioned, the extreme-case argument is rarely if ever defended or justified. Rather, its supporters put it forward as an article of faith, without reason or support, as though it were self-evidently true. But is it?

Lack of Empirical Support

If protecting hate speech and pornography were essential to safeguarding freedom of inquiry and a flourishing democratic politics, we would expect to find that nations that have adopted hate-speech rules and curbs against pornography would suffer a sharp erosion of the spirit of free inquiry. But this has not happened. A host of Western industrialized nations, including Sweden, Italy, Canada, and Great Britain, have instituted laws against hate speech and hate propaganda, many in order to comply with international treaties and conventions requiring such action. Many of these countries have traditions of respect for free speech at least the equal of ours. No such nation has reported any erosion of the atmosphere of free speech or debate. (See chapter 8.) At the same time, the United States, which until recently has refused to put such rules into effect, has a less than perfect record of protecting even political speech. We persecuted communists,[26] hounded Hollywood writers out of the country,[27] and harassed and badgered such civil rights leaders as Josephine Baker,[28] Paul Robeson,[29] and W. E. B. DuBois[30] in a campaign of personal and professional smears that ruined their reputations and denied them the ability to make a living. In recent times, conservatives inside and outside the Administration have disparaged progressives to the point where many are now afraid to use the "liberal" word to describe themselves.[31] Controversial artists are denied federal funding.[32] Museum exhibits that depict the A-bombing of Hiroshima have been ordered modified.[33] If political speech lies at the center of the First Amendment, its protection seems to be largely independent of what is taking place at the periphery. There may, indeed, be an inverse correlation. Those institutions most concerned with social fairness have proved to be the ones most likely to promulgate anti-hate-speech rules. Part of the reason seems to be recognition that hate speech can easily silence and demoralize its victims, discouraging them from participating in the life of the institution.[34] If so, enacting hate-speech rules may be evidence of a commitment to democratic dialogue, rather than the opposite, as some of their opponents maintain.

A Paradoxical Metaphor

A second reason why we ought to distrust the core-periphery argument is that it rests on a paradoxical metaphor that its proponents rarely if ever explain or justify. Suppose, for example, that one were in the business of supplying electricity to a region. One has competitors—private utility companies, suppliers of gas heaters, and so on. Ninety-nine percent of one's business consists of supplying electricity to homes and businesses, but one also supplies a small amount of electricity to teenagers to recharge the batteries of their Walkmans. It would surely be a strange business decision to focus all or much of one's advertising campaign on the much smaller account. Or take a more legal example. Protecting human security is surely a core value for the police. Yet, it would be a peculiar distribution of police services if a police chief were to reason: human life is the core value which we aim to protect; therefore, we will devote the largest proportion of our resources toward apprehending shoplifters and loiterers.

There are situations in which the core-periphery argument does make sense. Providing military defense of a territory may be one; ecology, where protecting lizards may be necessary in order to protect hawks, may be another. But ordinarily the suggestion that to protect a value or thing at its most extreme reaches is necessary in order to protect it at its core requires, at the very least, an explanation. Defenders of hate speech who deploy this argument have not provided one.[35] And, in the meantime, a specious argument does great harm. It treats in grand, exalted terms the harm of suppressing racist speech, drawing illegitimate support from the broad social justification—social dialogue among citizens.[36] The harm to hate speech's victims, out on the periphery, by contrast is treated atomistically, as though it were an isolated event, a mere one-time-only affront to feelings.[37] An injury characterized in act-utilitarian terms obviously cannot trump one couched in broad rule-utilitarian terms.[38] The Nazi derives a halo effect from other, quite legitimate and valuable cases of speech, while the black is seen as a lone, quirky grievant with hypersensitive feelings. But, in reality, hate speech is part of a concerted set of head-winds, including many other cases of such speech, that this particular African American victim will experience over the course of his or her life. (See, e.g., chapter 4.) If we are willing to defend speech in broad social terms, we should be able to consider systemic, concerted harms as well.

The speech-we-hate argument draws plausibility only by ignoring this symmetry. It draws on a social good to justify an evil deemed only individual, but which in fact is concerted and societywide. The unfairness of collapsing the periphery and the center as absolutists do would be made clear if we rendered the argument: "We protect the speech *they* hate in order to protect that which we love." But not only is the argument unfair in this sense, it ignores what makes hate speech peripheral *as speech* in the first place. Face to face hate speech—slurs, insults, put-downs, and epithets—are not referential. The recipient learns nothing new about himself or herself.[39] Rather, they are more like performatives, relocating the speaker and victim in social reality. Hate speech is not about the real, but the hyperreal; a Willie Horton ad is like an ad about jeans that makes no factual claim but merely shows a woman and a car.[40]

Mistaking Principles for People

There is one setting in which it does make good sense to argue from the extreme or peripheral case, namely where human beings, as opposed to abstract principles, are concerned. For example, one sometimes hears it said that the test of a civilized society is the degree of protection it affords its least privileged, most despised members. Thus prison reformers argue that a society that locks up and warehouses prisoners under crowded and inhumane conditions with little opportunity for recreation, acquisition of jobs skills, or rehabilitation is not deserving of the term "civilized." And so with treatment of the mentally ill, juvenile offenders, the mentally retarded, and the desperately poor. Here, what we do at the periphery does say something about the way society values things like compassion, forgiveness, and the fair distribution of resources. But people, unlike abstract principles, retain their value and distinctive nature even at the furthest reaches. Human beings are always ends in themselves—there is no continuum of humanness.[41] But our constitutional system recognizes not one, but many values.[42] As we shall show, we cannot treat principles, not even the First Amendment, in that fashion.

The Nature of Constitutional Continuums

Every periphery is another principle's core; that is the nature of a multivalent constitutional system like ours. Principles limit other ones: X's right to privacy limits Y's right to freedom of action, and so on. Indeed, the idea of a constitutional principle, like free speech, that has a core and a periphery would be incoherent without the existence of other values (such as privacy or reputation) to generate the limit that accounts for the periphery. Thus commercial and defamatory speech, which have a lesser degree of constitutional protection than political speech, are subject to limits not because they are not speech at all but because they implicate other values that we hold.[43] And the same is true of speech that constitutes a threat, provokes a fight, defrauds customers, or divulges an official secret. All these and dozens of other "exceptions" to the First Amendment are peripheral, and subject to limits, precisely because they reflect other principles, such as security, reputation, peace, and privacy.[44] To argue, then, that speech must be protected at the extremest case even more assiduously than when its central values are at stake is either to misunderstand the nature of a constitutional continuum, or to argue that the Constitution in effect has only one value.

Violation of the Principle of Dialogic Politics

Moreover, to argue in such fashion is to violate a principle that is inherent in our constitutional structure and jurisprudence: the principle of dialogic politics.[45] Law has not one value, but many. The district attorney wants the ability to protect the community from offenders; all citizens have an interest in not being randomly seized, frisked, and searched. A wants to speak. B does not wish to be defamed. In situations of competing values, judges attempt to "balance" the principles, trying to fashion a solution that gives the appropriate weight to each.[46](Not an easy task. See chapter 9.) They are guided by lawyers and briefs arguing both sides of the case, as well as case law showing how rights have been balanced in previous decisions. Inherent in this process is what we call dialogic politics, the notion that in cases where interests and values conflict, people and principles (through their defenders, to be sure) ought to be made to talk to each other. In close cases, judges ought to heed both sides; lawyers representing polar views ought to be made to respond to each other's arguments.

But the totalist view admits of no compromise: one's favorite principle remains supreme everywhere it has a bearing, no matter how slight. This means that one is not obliged to talk to those other persons, not obliged to address those other values. If the whole purpose of the First Amendment is to facilitate a system of dialogue and compromise, this is surely a paradoxical view for a defender of that amendment to be taking.

Totalism versus Totalism: When Extremism Cancels Itself Out

Every totalist argument is indeterminate because it can easily be countered by an opposite and equally powerful countervailing totalism. To continue with the hate-speech example, imagine that someone (say, the NAACP Legal Defense Fund) argued in the following fashion: (1) equality is a constitutional value; (2) the only way effectively to promote equality is to assure that it is protected everywhere; (3) therefore, whenever equality collides with another value, such as free speech, equality must prevail. "We must protect the equality we hate, as much as that which we hold dear." Now we would have two values, the defenders of which are equally convinced should reign supreme. Each regards the other's periphery as unworthy of protection. To be sure, balancing may be troublesome because it can disguise the political value judgments a judge makes on his or her way to a decision. But totalism is worse—it gives the possessor permission not even to enter the realm of politics at all. At least, balancing encourages the decision-maker to be aware and take account of the various values and interests at stake in a controversy. With totalism, one has no need to compromise or consider the other side. One finds oneself outside the realm of politics, and instead inside that of sheer power.

First Amendment Romanticism versus the Social Construction of Racial Reality

With hate speech and pornography, heeding the ACLU's totalist argument introduces special dangers of its own. Hate speech lies at the periphery of the First Amendment, as the proponents of the argument quickly concede. Yet the reason why hate speech does so is that it implicates the interest of another group, minorities, in not being defamed, reviled, stereotyped, insulted, badgered, and harassed. Permitting a society to portray a relatively powerless group in this fashion helps construct a stigma-picture or stereotype according to which its members are lascivious, lazy, carefree, immoral, stupid, and so on. (See chapter 5.) This stereotype guides action, making life much more difficult for minorities in transactions that clearly matter: getting a job, renting an apartment, hailing a cab. But it also diminishes the credibility of minority speakers, inhibiting their ability to have their points of view taken seriously, in politics or anywhere else—surely a result that is at odds with the First Amendment and the marketplace of ideas. This is an inevitable result of treating peripheral regions of a value as entitled to the same weight we afford that value when it is centrally implicated: we convey the impression that those other values—the ones responsible for the continuum in the first place—are of little worth. And when those other values are central to the social construction of a human being or social group, the dangers of undervaluing their interests rise sharply. Their interests are submerged today—in the valuing a court or decision-maker is asked to perform. And they are submerged in the future, because their owners are thereafter the bearers of a stigma, one which means they need not be taken fully into account in future deliberations. Permitting one social group to speak disrespectfully of another habituates and encourages speakers to continue speaking that way in the future. This way of speaking becomes normalized, inscribed in hundreds of plots, narratives, and scripts; it becomes part of culture, what everyone knows. The reader may wish to reflect on changes he or she has surely observed over the last fifteen years or so. During the civil rights era of the sixties and early seventies, African Americans and other minorities were spoken of respectfully. Then, beginning in the late seventies and eighties, racism was spoken in code. Today, however, op-ed columns, letters to the editor, and political speeches deride and blame them outspokenly. Anti-minority sentiment need no longer be spoken in code but is right out in the open. We have changed our social construct of the black from unfortunate victim and brave warrior to welfare leeches, unwed mothers, criminals, and untalented low-IQ affirmative action beneficiaries who take away jobs from more talented and deserving whites. The slur, sneer, ethnic joke, and most especially face-to-face hate speech are the main vehicles that have made this change possible.

The Core-Periphery Argument: Why It Persists

As we have seen, the extreme case (or core-periphery) argument rests on an unexamined, paradoxical metaphor. It adopts a view of the Constitution and of dialogue that is at odds with the one we hold, and it makes the mistake of treating subordinate principles as though they were people and ends in themselves. It treats the interests of minorities as though they were of little weight, or as fully protected by merely protecting speech, including slurs. It ignores the experience of other Western nations that have instituted hate-speech reforms without untoward consequences. What accounts for this argument's rhetorical attraction and staying power? We believe the principal reason is that hate speech and pornography today do not lie at the periphery of the First Amendment, as the ACLU and other advocates urge, but at its center. In former times, society was much more structured than it is now. Citizens knew their places. Women and blacks understood they were not the equals of white men—the Constitution formally excluded them,[47] and coercive social and legal power reminded them of that if they were ever tempted to step out of line.[48] It was not necessary constantly to reinforce this—an occasional reminder would do.[49] Today, however, the formal mechanisms that maintained status and caste are gone or repealed. All that is left is speech and the social construction of reality. Hate speech has replaced formal slavery, Jim Crow laws, female subjugation, and Japanese internment as means to keep subordinate groups in line. In former times, political speech was indeed the center of the First Amendment. Citizens (white, property-owning males, at any rate) did take a lively interest in politics. They spoke, debated, wrote tracts, corresponded with each other about how the Republic ought to be governed. They did not much speak about whether women were men's equals, should be allowed to hold jobs or vote, whether blacks were the equals of whites, because this was not necessary—the very ideas were practically unthinkable.

Today, the situation is reversed. Few Americans vote, or can even name their representative in Washington.[50] Politics has deteriorated to a once-every-four-years ritual of attack ads, catch phrases, sound bites, and image manicuring.[51] At the same time, however, politics in the sense of jockeying for social position has greatly increased in intensity and virulence. Males are anxious and fearful of advances by women;[52] whites fear crime and vengeful behavior from blacks; and so on.[53] Hate speech today is a central weapon in the struggle by the empowered to maintain their position in the face of formerly subjugated groups clamoring for change. It is a means of disparaging the opposition while depicting one's own resistance to sharing opportunities as principled and just. Formerly, the First Amendment and free speech were used to make small adjustments within a relatively peaceful political order consisting of propertied white males. Now it is used to postpone macroadjustments and power-sharing between that group and others: it is, in short, an instrument of majoritarian identity politics. Nothing in the Constitution (at least in the emerging realist view) requires that hate speech receive protection. But ruling elites are unlikely to relinquish it easily, since it is an effective means of postponing social change.

In the sixties, it was possible to believe Harry Kalven's optimistic hypothesis that gains for blacks stemming from the gallant struggle for civil rights would end up benefiting all of society.[54] It was true for a time, at least, that the hard-won gains by a decade of civil rights struggle did broaden speech, due process, and assembly rights for whites as well as blacks.[55] Today, however, there has been a stunning reversal. Now, the reciprocal injury—inhibition of the right to injure others—has been elevated to a central place in First Amendment jurisprudence. The injury—of being muffled when one would otherwise wish to disparage, terrorize, or burn a cross on a black family's lawn—is now depicted as a prime constitutional value.[56] The interest convergence between black interests and broadened rights for whites lasted but a short time. Now, the ACLU defends Aryan supremacists, while maintaining that this is best for minorities, too. Blanket resistance to hate-speech regulations, which many college and university administrators are trying to put into place in order to advance straightforward institutional interests of their own—preserving diversity, teaching civility, preventing the loss of black undergraduates to other schools—generates a great deal of business for the ACLU and similar absolutist organizations. In a sense, the ACLU and conservative bigots are hand-in-glove. Like criminals and police, they understand each other's method of operation, mentality, and objectives. There is a tacit understanding of how each shall behave, how each shall gain from the other. Indeed, primarily because the Ku Klux Klan and similar clients are so *bad*, the ACLU gets to feel romantic and virtuous[57]—and the rest of us, who despise racism and bigotry, are seen as benighted fools because we do not understand how the First Amendment really works.

But we do. The bigot is not a stand-in for Tom Paine. The best way to preserve lizards is not to preserve hawks. Reality is not paradoxical. Sometimes, defending Nazis is simply defending Nazis.

Notes

Notes to Chapter 1

1. 88 Wash. 2d 735, 565 P.2d 1173 (1977) (en banc).
2. 88 Wash. 2d at 736, 565 P.2d at 1174.
3. *Id.* at 741, 565 P.2d at 1177.
4. 578 F.2d 1197 (7th Cir.), *cert. denied*, 439 U.S. 916 (1978).
5. *Id.* at 1200.
6. *See generally* A. HIGGINBOTHAM, IN THE MATTER OF COLOR (1978).
7. *See* G. ALLPORT, THE NATURE OF PREJUDICE 77–78 (1954) (studies led researchers to estimate that four-fifths of American population harbored enough antagonism toward minority groups to influence their daily conduct); *id.* at 197–98 (84% agreement among college students for stereotype of blacks as superstitious). *See generally* REPORT OF THE NATIONAL ADVISORY COMMISSION ON CIVIL DISORDERS (KERNER COMMISSION) 203–82 (N.Y. TIMES ed., 1968).
8. Despite recent civil rights activism, verbal racism has not disappeared. *See, e.g., Racism Flares on Campus,* TIME, Dec. 8, 1980, at 28 ("stinking black monkeys" and other messages sent to black students at Williams College; black student leader at Harvard University found her office calendar defaced with racist slogans; crosses burned at Purdue University; letter addressed to black student dormitory at Wesleyan University spoke of "wip[ing] all g.d. niggers off the face of the earth"). A black dean at Harvard University attributed the recent upsurge in racist slurs and acts to a change in national mood, which has made such acts "once again . . . respectable." *Id. See also* McQueen, *The Anguish and Humiliation of Interracial Couples,* SACRAMENTO BEE, Feb. 5, 1981, at C4, col. 1; Trescott, *Is Social Racism Now Becoming "Acceptable?"* L.A. TIMES, June 12, 1981, at V2, col. 1 ("the veiled insult, contempt masquerading as a joke, [and] the direct slur," underground in 1960s and early 1970s, now being "recycled . . . as a protest against minority gains"). *See also* chapter 4, on campus racism in the present era.
9. P. MASON, RACE RELATIONS 2 (1970).
10. O. COX, CASTE, CLASS AND RACE 383 (1948).
11. K. CLARK, DARK GHETTO 63–64 (1965).
12. *See* G. ALLPORT, *supra* at 152.
13. J. KOVEL, WHITE RACISM: A PSYCHOHISTORY 195 (1970).

14. *See* E. GOFFMAN, STIGMA 7 (1963). *See also* J. GRIFFIN, BLACK LIKE ME (1960) (white journalist dyed skin, assumed black identity, traveled through South, was treated as a black; began to assume physical demeanor and psychological set of black itinerant).

15. *See, e.g.*, G. ALLPORT, *supra* at 9, 148–49; M. GOODMAN, RACE AWARENESS IN YOUNG CHILDREN 46–47, 55–58, 60 (rev. ed. 1964). *See also* Cota Robles de Suarez, *Skin Color as a Factor of Racial Identification and Preference of Young Chicano Children*, CHI. J. SOC. SCI. & ARTS, Spring 1971, at 107; Stevenson & Stewart, *A Developmental Study of Racial Awareness in Young Children*, 29 CHILD DEV. 399 (1958).

16. J. MARTIN & C. FRANKLIN, MINORITY GROUP RELATIONS 3 (1979).

17. *See* JOINT COMMISSION ON MENTAL HEALTH OF CHILDREN, SOCIAL CHANGE AND THE MENTAL HEALTH OF CHILDREN 99–100 (1973). *See also* ELLIS COSE, RAGE OF A PRIVILEGED CLASS (1994).

18. Kiev, *Psychiatric Disorders in Minority Groups, in* PSYCHOLOGY AND RACE 416, 420–24 (P. Watson ed., 1973).

19. J. MARTIN & C. FRANKLIN, *supra* at 43. *See* G. ALLPORT, *supra* at 159.

20. J. MARTIN & C. FRANKLIN, *supra* at 4.

21. *See* G. ALLPORT, *supra* at 170–86, 371–84, 407–8.

22. Allport, *The Bigot in Our Midst*, 40 COMMONWEAL 582 (1944), *reprinted in* ANATOMY OF RACIAL INTOLERANCE 161, 164 (G. deHuszar ed., 1946).

23. *See* G. ALLPORT, *supra* at 62, 252, 460–61, 467–72 (rejecting view of racist conduct as catharsis and arguing that racist attitudes themselves can be curtailed by law). *But see* R. WILLIAMS, THE REDUCTION OF INTERGROUP TENSIONS 41 (1947); Berkovitz, *The Case for Bottling Up Rage*, PSYCHOLOGY TODAY, July 1973, at 24; Magruder, *Mental and Emotional Disturbance in the Law of Torts*, 49 HARV. L. REV. 1033, 1053 (1936) ("[i]t would be unfortunate if the law closed all safety valves through which irascible tempers might legally blow off steam").

24. *See* Krogman, *An Anthropologist Looks at Race*, 7 INTERCULTURAL EDUC. NEWS 1 (1945), *reprinted in* ANATOMY OF RACIAL INTOLERANCE, *supra* at 20, 25; Mekeel, *Race Relations*, 27 MENTAL HYGIENE 177 (1945), *reprinted in* ANATOMY OF RACIAL INTOLERANCE, *supra* at 81, 87, 89 [hereinafter cited as Mekeel]; H. Powdermaker, *Prejudice in the World Today, in* PROBING OUR PREJUDICES (1944), *reprinted in* ANATOMY OF RACIAL INTOLERANCE, *supra* at 27; Redfield, *What We Do Know about Race*, 57 SCI. MONTHLY 193 (1943), *reprinted in* ANATOMY OF RACIAL INTOLERANCE, *supra* at 7, 11, 13 [hereinafter cited as Redfield]. *See generally* O. COX, *supra*; W. WILSON, Power, Racism, and Privilege (1973). *See also* DERRICK BELL, AND WE ARE NOT SAVED (1987).

25. *See* M. GOODMAN, *supra*.

26. *See id.* at 36–60. *See also* G. ALLPORT, *supra* at 289–301.

27. M. GOODMAN, *supra* at 55.

28. *Id.* at 56.

29. *Id.* at 58.

30. *Id.*

31. *See id.* at 60–73.

32. *See* F. WERTHAM, A SIGN FOR CAIN 89 (1966) (racial prejudice depersonalizes the victim, thereby rationalizing violence and inhumane treatment).

33. *See generally* Brown v. Board of Educ., 347 U.S. 483 (1954). *Brown* turned, clearly, on the stigmatizing effect—the indignity or affront of separate schools—because by hypothesis the schools were "equal." *See id.* at 492.

34. Wooley v. Maynard, 430 U.S. 705 (1977) (considerations of privacy and autonomy held to prevent New Hampshire from punishing citizens for putting tape over state motto, "Live Free or Die," on license plates).

35. *See* W. PROSSER, HANDBOOK OF THE LAW OF TORTS, 10, at 36 & n.85 (4th ed. 1971).

36. *See id.* 10, at 36 & n.78.

37. M. DEUTSCH, I. KATZ, & A. JENSEN, SOCIAL CLASS, RACE AND PSYCHOLOGICAL DEVELOPMENT 175 (1968).

38. *Id.*

39. M. GOODMAN, *supra* at 246.

40. K. KENISTON, ALL OUR CHILDREN 33 (1977).

41. G. ALLPORT, *supra* at 139.

42. *See generally* A. HIGGINBOTHAM, IN THE MATTER OF COLOR (1978).

43. *Id.* at 20.

44. *Id.*

45. G. ALLPORT, *supra at 472.*

46. R. WILLIAMS, *supra* at 73.

47. G. ALLPORT, *supra* at 470.

48. *Id.*

49. *Id.* at 439. *See also* G. Allport, *Prejudice: A Problem in Psychological and Social Causation* 4, Supp. Ser. No. 4, J. SOC. ISSUES (1950) (examination of prejudice as a mode of mental functioning).

50. H. Triandis, *The Impact of Social Change on Attitudes, in* ATTITUDES, CONFLICT AND SOCIAL CHANGES 132 (1972) (quoted in KATZ, *Preface,* TOWARD THE ELIMINATION OF RACISM 8 (P. Katz ed., 1976)).

51. G. MYRDAL, AN AMERICAN DILEMMA 20 (1944) (fallacy of theory that law cannot change custom).

52. 424 S.W.2d 627 (Tex. 1967).

53. *See* W. PROSSER, *supra* 9, at 34 (integrity of person includes "all those things which are in contact or connected with it").

54. RESTATEMENT (SECOND) OF TORTS § 46 (1965). Some states have adopted the RESTATEMENT view. *See, e.g.,* Grimsby v. Samson, 85 Wash. 2d 52, 60, 530 P.2d 291, 296 (1975).

55. Alcorn v. Anbro Eng'g, Inc., 2 Cal. 3d 493, 498, 468 P.2d 216, 218, 86 Cal. Rptr. 88, 90 (1970).

56. 2 Cal. 3d 493, 468 P.2d 216, 86 Cal. Rptr. 88 (1970).

57. *Id.* at 496–97, 468 P.2d at 217, 86 Cal. Rptr. at 89. The firm's secretary later "ratified" the act by firing the plaintiff. *Id.* at 497, 468 P.2d at 217, 86 Cal. Rptr. at 89.

58. 25 Cal. 3d 932, 603 P.2d 58, 160 Cal. Rptr. 141 (1979).

59. *Id.* at 941, 603 P.2d at 64, 160 Cal. Rptr. at 146.

60. 2 Cal. 3d at 499 & n.5, 468 P.2d at 219 & no.5, 86 Cal. Rptr. at 91 & n.5.

61. *Id.* at 947, 603 P.2d at 67, 160 Cal. Rptr. at 150.

62. 355 F. Supp. 206 (S.D. Fla. 1973).

63. 100 So. 2d 396 (Fla. 1958).

64. *Id.* at 396–97.

65. *Id.* at 396.

66. *Id.* at 398.

67. *Id.*

68. 355 F. Supp. at 209–10 & n.3.

69. 46 Ill. App. 3d 162, 360 N.E.2d 983 (1977).

70. 1 Kan. 2d 213, 563 P.2d 511 (1977).

71. 46 Ill. App. 3d at 167, 360 N.E.2d at 986 (citing Slocum v. Food Fair Stores of Florida, Inc., 100 So. 2d 396 (Fla. 1958)).

72. Restatement (Second) of Torts § 46 comment d (1965).

73. *See id.* illustration 4 (such an insult, made over the phone to a telephone operator, which causes severe emotional distress, is "not so outrageous or extreme" as to render the speaker liable).

74. 46 Ill. App. 3d at 165–66, 360 N.E.2d at 985. The court also held that the word "nigger" did not impute to the plaintiff an inability to perform the duties of his chosen profession, one of the categories of defamation per se in Illinois. 46 Ill. App. 3d at 166, 360 N.E.2d at 985.

75. 1 Kan. 2d at 214–15, 563 P.2d at 514.

76. *Id.* at 215, 563 P.2d at 514. *Cf.* W. PROSSER, *supra* 111, at 737 ("It must be confessed at the beginning that there is a great deal of the law of defamation which makes no sense."). *See also* Mitchell v. Tribune Co., 343 Ill. App. 446, 99 N.E.2d 397 (1951), *cert. denied*, 342 U.S. 919 (1952) (upholding dismissal of complaint alleging that newspaper called plaintiff "Chink" and "Negro" on ground that such did not constitute defamation per se and special damages were not alleged; plaintiff's race not indicated); Davis v. Meyer, 115 Neb. 251, 212 N.W. 435 (1927) (holding that calling plaintiff "half-breed Mexican" is not defamatory).

77. Jones v. R.L. Polk & Co., 190 Ala. 243, 67 So. 577 (1915); Natchez Times Publishing Co. v. Dunigan, 221 Miss. 320, 72 So. 2d 681 (1954); Bowen v.

Independent Publishing Co., 230 S.C. 509, 96 S.E.2d 564 (1957). *See also* Afro-American Publishing Co. v. Jaffe, 366 F.2d 649 (D.C. Cir. 1966) (held, white plaintiff defamed by black newspaper which described plaintiff as bigoted); Sharp v. Bussey, 137 Fla. 96, 187 So. 779 (1939) (upholding jury verdict, although limiting damages to $10,000, against defendant who told others that white plaintiff had danced with black women); Axton Fisher Tobacco Co. v. Evening Post Co., 169 Ky. 64, 183 S.W. 269 (1916) (held, allegation that newspaper falsely reported that plaintiff employed black foreman to supervise white female employees stated cause of action in libel).

78. W. Prosser, *supra* 111, at 737.

79. 42 U.S.C. § 1983 (1976 & Supp. III 1979).

80. 605 F.2d 330 (7th Cir. 1976).

81. *Id.* at 338.

82. *Id.*

83. 284 F. Supp. 933 (E.D. Pa. 1968).

84. *Id.* at 937 (quoting Screws v. United States, 325 U.S. 91, 111 (1945)). It is telling that the court considered the officer's gun, rather than his uniform or badge, or the fact that he was on duty, as "the symbol . . . of police authority."

85. *Id.*

86. *Ex parte* Hamilton, 376 U.S. 650 (1964) (per curiam), *rev'g* 275 Ala. 574, 156 So. 2d 926 (1963).

87. City of Minneapolis v. Richardson, 307 Minn. 80, 82–83, 239 N.W.2d 197, 200 (1976) (crowd of people observed police making arrest; police used dogs to disperse crowd; dog bit hand of man next to black youth, then leapt at black youth who struck it with rolled-up poster; black youth arrested, dragged face down to police car, called "nigger" by police). *See also* City of Minneapolis v. State, 310 N.W.2d 485, 487 (Minn. S.Ct. 1981) (Minnesota anti-discrimination statute prohibits police officer calling white person "nigger lover").

88. L.A. Times, Aug. 20, 1980, at I-1, col. 1. The guideline has been adopted by at least three dozen San Francisco agencies and school districts. Interview with Al Walker, Secretary, San Francisco Civil Service Commission, in San Francisco, Calif., Oct. 9, 1980. *See also* Thompson v. City of Minneapolis, 300 N.W.2d 763 (Minn. S. Ct. 1980) (upholding dismissal of city employee, under city civil service commission rule prohibiting language "wantonly offensive" to public, for making subsequently published racist remarks in presence of newspaper reporter).

89. No. 840149, King Co. (Wash.) Super. Ct. (July 31, 1978). *See* Seattle Times, Aug. 1, 1978, at A1, col. 1.

90. *See* Seattle Times, Aug. 1, 1978, at A11, col. 1.

91. 52 N.Y.2d 72, 417 N.E.2d 525, 436 N.Y.S.2d 231 (1980).

92. *Id.* at 76, 417 N.E.2d at 527, 436 N.Y.S.2d at 233.

93. *Id.* at 76–77, 417 N.E.2d at 528, 436 N.Y.S.2d at 233. *See also* Browning v.

Slenderella Sys., 54 Wash. 2d 440, 341 P.2d 859 (1959) (en banc) (reducing salon's refusal to serve a black woman constitutes discrimination); Anderson v. Pantages Theatre Co., 114 Wash. 24, 194 P. 813 (1921) (theater's refusal to admit black attorney to show for which he held tickets constitutes discrimination).

94. 388 F. Supp. 603 (S.D. Ohio 1975).

95. 42 U.S.C. § 2000e-2(a)(2) (1976).

96. ILL. CONST. art. I, 20. The provision was derived from the criminal libel statute held constitutional in Beauharnais v. Illinois, 342 U.S. 250 (1952).

97. W. PROSSER, *supra* 1, at 3–4. *See* Kujok v. Goldman, 150 N.Y. 176, 178, 44 N.E. 773, 775 (1896); C. FIFOOT, HISTORY AND SOURCES OF THE COMMON LAW ch. 4 (1949); Albertsworth, *Recognition of New Interests in the Law of Torts*, 10 CALIF. L. REV. 461 (1922). *But see* Zepeda v. Zepeda, 41 Ill. App. 2d 240, 190 N.E.2d 849, *cert. denied*, 379 U.S. 945 (1963) (drastic change should originate with legislature).

98. *See* Michelman, *Property, Utility and Fairness: Comments on the Ethical Foundation of "Just Compensation" Law*, 80 HARV. L. REV. 1165, 1192 (1967); Yudof, *Liability for Constitutional Torts and the Risk-Averse Public School Official*, 49 S. CAL. L. REV. 1322, 1380–81 (1976).

99. Magruder, *supra* at 1035.

100. *E.g.*, Vosburg v. Putney, 80 Wis. 523, 50 N.W. 403 (1891).

101. *See* Note, *Torts: An Analysis of Mental Distress as an Element of Damages and as a Basis of an Independent Cause of Action When Intentionally Caused*, 20 WASHBURN L.J. 106, 116–17 & n.105 (1980) (citing cases involving pregnant women, children, and sick people); RESTATEMENT (SECOND) OF TORTS § 46, comment f (1965) ("The extreme and outrageous character of the conduct may arise from the actor's knowledge that the other is peculiarly susceptible to emotional distress, by reason of some physical or mental condition or peculiarity").

102. 2 Cal. 3d at 498 n.4, 468 P.2d at 219 n.4, 86 Cal. Rptr. at 91 n.4.

103. 88 Wash. 2d at 742, 565 P.2d at 1177.

104. *See* Bloustein, *Privacy, Tort Law, and the Constitution: Is Warren and Brandeis' Tort Petty and Unconstitutional as Well?*, 46 TEX. L. REV. 611, 620 (1968).

105. *See, e.g.*, Chiucholo v. New England Wholesale Tailors, 84 N.H. 329, 334–35, 150 A. 540, 543 (1930); Samms v. Eccles, 11 Utah 2d 289, 293, 358 P.2d 344, 347 (Utah 1961); Prosser, *Intentional Infliction of Emotional Distress: A New Tort*, 37 MICH. L. REV. 874, 877 (1939).

106. *See* Redish, *The Content Distinction in First Amendment Analysis*, 34 STAN. L. REV. 113, 113 & n.3 (1981) (citing cases).

107. *See* Shiffrin, *Defamatory Non-Media Speech and First Amendment Methodology*, 25 U.C.L.A. L. REV. 915, 962 (1978) (arguing that Supreme Court follows a "general balancing approach" in First Amendment cases, in some cases applying general rules while in others engaging in ad hoc decision making).

108. 315 U.S. 568 (1942).

109. *Id.* at 572. Although *Chaplinsky* was a "fighting words" case, and thus its statement about words which inflict injury "by their very utterance" arguably should not be read as a constitutional mandate, this clause has been quoted with approval by the Court as recently as 1974. *See* Lewis v. City of New Orleans (Lewis II), 415 U.S. 130, 133 (1974) (quoting Gooding v. Wilson, 405 U.S. 518, 525 (1972)).

Apparently, the Court never has overturned a conviction for "fighting words" except on an overbreadth analysis. For convictions overturned on an overbreadth analysis, see *Lewis II, supra*; Plummer v. City of Columbus, 414 U.S. 2 (1973) (per curiam); Rosenfeld v. New Jersey, 408 U.S. 901 (1972); *Gooding v. Wilson, supra*; Terminiello v. Chicago, 337 U.S. 1 (1949). *See also* Erznoznik v. City of Jacksonville, 422 U.S. 205, 211, 215, n.13 (1975) (striking down, as content-based discrimination, ordinance prohibiting drive-in motion picture theaters from exhibiting films containing nudity where screen visible from street, but implying that a "narrowly drawn nondiscriminatory traffic regulation requiring screening of drive-in theatres from public view" would be constitutional).

110. Rowan v. United States Post Office Dep't, 397 U.S. 728 (1970); Breard v. Alexandria, 341 U.S. 622 (1951); Kovacs v. Cooper, 336 U.S. 77 (1949). *But see* Martin v. Struthers, 319 U.S. 141, 149 (1943) (striking down ordinance prohibiting summoning resident to door in order to distribute handbills; *Breard* Court claimed *Martin* held ordinance invalid "as applied to the free distribution of dodgers 'advertising a religious meeting,'" 341 U.S. at 642).

111. FCC v. Pacifica Found., 438 U.S. 726 (1978); Young v. American Mini Theatres, Inc., 427 U.S. 50 (1976) (plurality opinion); Lehman v. City of Shaker Heights, 418 U.S. 298 (1974). *But see Erznoznik v. City of Jacksonville, supra.*

112. 403 U.S. 15 (1971).

113. 72 YALE L.J. 877, 878–86 (1963).

114. Emerson, *Toward a General Theory of the First Amendment*, 72 YALE L.J. 877, 882 (1963).

115. *See* A. MEIKLEJOHN, FREE SPEECH AND ITS RELATION TO SELF-GOVERNMENT (1948); A. MEIKLEJOHN, POLITICAL FREEDOM (1960).

116. Kingsley Int'l Pictures Corp. v. Regents of the Univ. of New York, 360 U.S. 684 (1959). *See* Paris Adult Theatre I v. Slaton, 413 U.S. 49, 67 (1973) (regulation of obscenity is "distinct from a control of reason and the intellect. . . . The fantasies of a drug addict are his own and beyond the reach of government, but government regulation of drug sales is not prohibited by the Constitution").

117. 413 U.S. 49 (1973).

118. *Id.* at 58 (footnote omitted).

119. *Id.* at 59–60 (quoting Jacobellis v. Ohio, 378 U.S. 184, 199 (1964) (Warren, C.J., dissenting)). Laurence Tribe finds three reasons articulated in *Paris,*

although his third reason appears substantially the same as the second reason given in the text. *See* L. Tribe, American Constitutional Law § 12–16, at 666–67 (1978).

120. Emerson, *supra* at 883 (quoting The Declaration of Independence para. 2 (U.S. 1776)).

121. *Id.* at 884–85.

122. However, if the language was intended and understood as demeaning, minority plaintiffs could sue other members of the same or another minority group. *See generally* Mebane, *In Carolina: Growing Up Black in the '40s*, Time, March 2, 1981, at 6, 7 (excerpt from M. Mebane, Mary (1981)) (maltreatment of "black Black" by lighter-skinned blacks).

123. The cause of action outlined is intended primarily to protect members of racial minority groups traditionally victimized. However, in some situations racial insults may cause harm when directed at members of the majority. The best example of such a situation would be the insult "You dumb honkey" directed at a white child by a black teacher in a predominantly black school. The potential for psychological harm in such a situation is obvious. And although the basis for the tort, the legacy of slavery and race discrimination, might seem to limit the class of those who can bring such actions to members of traditionally victimized minorities, it is the use of race to make invidious distinctions that is the ultimate evil the tort is designed to combat.

Notes to Chapter 2

1. On the social construction of sex roles, see, *e.g.*, Catharine MacKinnon, Toward a Feminist Theory of the State (1989) [hereinafter Feminist Theory of State]; Catharine MacKinnon, Feminism Unmodified: Discourses on Life and Law (1987) [hereinafter Feminism Unmodified]; Catharine MacKinnon, Sexual Harassment of Working Women: A Case of Sex Discrimination (1979); Catharine MacKinnon, *Pornography as Sex Discrimination*, 4 Law & Ineq. J. 38 (1986); and Catharine MacKinnon, *Feminism, Marxism, Method, and the State: Toward Feminist Jurisprudence*, 8 Signs 635 (1983). For an account focusing on women's sexuality, see Judith Laws & Pepper Schwartz, Sexual Scripts: The Social Construction of Female Sexuality (1977). *See also* Carol Gilligan, In a Different Voice (1982) (differences between men and women on ethic of caring). On the special issues of black women, see bell hooks, Ain't I a Woman: Black Women and Feminism (1986). On the construction of the social world in general, see Peter L. Berger & Thomas Luckmann, The Social Construction of Reality (1966).

2. *E.g.*, Feminism Unmodified, *supra*; *see also* Andrea Dworkin & Catharine MacKinnon, Pornography and Civil Rights: A New Day for Wom-

Notes to Chapter 2 | 171

EN'S EQUALITY (1988) [hereinafter NEW DAY] (suggesting women begin to challenge these notions as contingent, harmful, and false).

3. *Health and Beauty*, GODEY'S LADY'S BOOK (August 1848), *reprinted in* IMAGES OF WOMEN IN POPULAR CULTURE 129 (Angela G. Dorenkamp et al. eds., 1985).

4. James Gordon Bennett, *Women's Rights Convention, in* 1 HISTORY OF WOMAN SUFFRAGE 805 (1881), *reprinted in* POPULAR CULTURE, *supra*, at 418.

5. Susan Brownmiller, *Confessions: "He Made Me Do It!," in* AGAINST OUR WILL: MEN, WOMEN AND RAPE 381, *reprinted in* POPULAR CULTURE, *supra*, at 152.

6. LOIS GOLD, SUCH GOOD FRIENDS (1970).

7. ERICA JONG, FEAR OF FLYING (1974).

8. JUNE SOCHEN, ENDURING VALUES: WOMEN IN POPULAR CULTURE 61–74 (1987).

9. *See* Cass Sunstein, *Neutrality in Constitutional Law (With Special Reference to Pornography, Abortion, and Surrogacy)*, 92 COLUM. L. REV. 1, 18–29 (1992) (discussing issue of harm).

10. *See* Catharine A. MacKinnon, *Pornography, Civil Rights, and Speech*, 20 HARV. C.R.-C.L. L. REV. 1, 1–2 n. 1 (1985) [hereinafter *Civil Rights and Speech*].

11. *See* Nan D. Hunter & Sylvia A. Law, *Brief Amici Curiae of Feminist Anti-Censorship Taskforce, et al., in* American Booksellers Association v. Hudnut, 21 U. MICH. J.L. REF. 69, 70, 89 (1988) (describing FACT organization).

12. *See* Regina v. Butler, 89 D.L.R.4th 449 (1992).

13. Cynthia Tucker, *Rape Does Hurt Somebody*, S.F. CHRON., April 6, 1992, at A16.

14. Nancy Gibbs, *When Is It Rape*, TIME, June 3, 1991, 48, at 54. Consider also what occurred when Japanese Prime Minister Kiichi Miyazawa commented that American workers struck him as lazy and unproductive and "may lack a work ethic," a charge that made national headlines. On questioning, it appeared that the basis of his observation lay in the finding of Kabun Moto, former Japanese minister of international trade and industry, that American workers worked essentially a three-day week, being consumed by their weekend plans on Friday and recovering from the weekend on Monday. Americans were outraged; to Americans this behavior seemed normal, whereas the Japanese pattern of behavior seemed inhuman and robotic. *See* David E. Sanger, *Japan Premier Joins Critics of Americans' Work Habits*, N.Y. TIMES, Feb. 4, 1992, at A1. *But see* Steven R. Weisman, *More Japanese Demanding Shorter Hours and Less Hectic Work*, N.Y. TIMES, Mar. 3, 1992, at A8 (commenting that Americans work fewer hours but more intensely).

15. Anthony D'Amato, *A New Political Truth: Exposure to Sexually Violent Materials Causes Sexual Violence*, 31 WM. & MARY L. REV. 575, 576–85 (1990).

16. LARRY BARON & MURRAY A. STRAUS, FOUR THEORIES OF RAPE IN AMERI-

CAN SOCIETY 95–124 (1989); Larry Baron & Murray A. Straus, *Four Theories of Rape*, 34 SOC. PROBS. 467, 468 (1987); D'Amato, *supra*, at 585 (discussing U.S. Attorney General's Commission on Pornography Final Report (July 1986)).

17. D'Amato, *supra* at 588–90; Hunter & Law, *supra* at 113, 115–17; Thelma McCormack, *Making Sense of the Research on Pornography, in* WOMEN AGAINST CENSORSHIP 183, 192 (Varda Burstyn ed., 1985).

18. *Civil Rights and Speech, supra* at 8, 16–18, 22, 27; Andrea Dworkin, *Pornography and Grief, in* TAKE BACK THE NIGHT: WOMEN ON PORNOGRAPHY 286–88 (Laura Lederer ed., 1980). On the construction of sexuality and women's role generally, see FEMINIST THEORY OF STATE, *supra*, at 126–54, 171–83.

19. *Civil Rights and Speech, supra* at 16–17, 53–55. On the teaching function of pornography, see Edward Dinnerstein & Leonard Berkowitz, *Victim Reactions in Aggressive Erotic Films as a Factor in Violence against Women*, 41 J. PERSONALITY & SOC. PSYCHOL. 710 (Oct. 1981); Doug McKenzie-Mohr & Marla P. Zanna, *Treating Women as Sexual Objects: Look to the (Gender Schematic) Male Who Has Viewed Pornography*, 16 PERSONALITY & SOC. PSYCHOL. 296 (June 1990); and Robin Morgan, *Theory and Practice: Pornography and Rape, in* TAKE BACK THE NIGHT 134, 139 (Laura Lederer ed., 1980) (arguing that pornography is the theory, rape the practice).

20. *See, e.g., Columbia Univ. Seminars on Media and Society: Safe Speech, Free Speech, and the University* (PBS television broadcast, June 1991) (American Civil Liberties Union president Nadine Strossen describing leering and whistling at women postulated in moderator's hypothetical as (a) inoffensive and (b) protected speech).

21. *E.g.*, Hunter & Law, *supra* at 113, 127–28 (dismissing incident as exceptional or idiosyncratic; "men are not attack dogs").

22. Hunter & Law, *supra* at 102–5 (ordinance reinforces "double standard" according to which women are prim, frail, and in need of protection), 130–31 (deprives women of choice to express their sexuality in this way).

23. SUSAN BROWNMILLER, AGAINST OUR WILL (1975); ANDREA DWORKIN, INTERCOURSE (1987) (both arguing that systematic sexual violence against women is tacitly permitted or encouraged by men, that much intercourse is not fully consensual on the woman's part and could therefore be seen as rape).

24. *E.g.*, DWORKIN, *supra*.

25. For additional development of this idea, see Richard Delgado, *Shadowboxing: An Essay on Power*, 77 CORNELL L. REV. 813 (1992).

26. *See* THOMAS S. KUHN, THE STRUCTURE OF SCIENTIFIC REVOLUTIONS (1970) (exploring process of change in paradigms, within which orthodox or "normal" science operates).

27. Consider, for example, the recent works in a neoconservative vein that question whether African American leftist activists are the only legitimate voices

of the black community. *E.g.*, STEPHEN CARTER, REFLECTIONS OF AN AFFIRMA-TIVE ACTION BABY (1991); DINESH D'SOUZA, ILLIBERAL EDUCATION (1991); Randall L. Kennedy, *Racial Critiques of Legal Academia*, 102 HARV. L. REV. 1745 (1989).

Notes to Chapter 3

1. *E.g.*, Nadine Strossen, *In the Defense of Freedom and Equality: The American Civil Liberties Union Past, Present and Future*, 29 HARV. C.R.-C.L. L. REV. 143 (1994).

2. On legal realism, see Elizabeth Mensch, *The History of Mainstream Legal Thought, in* THE POLITICS OF LAW: A PROGRESSIVE CRITIQUE 13, 21–24 (David Kairys ed., rev. ed. 1990); and Jack Balkin, *Some Realism about Pluralism: Legal Realist Approaches to the First Amendment*, 1990 DUKE L.J. 375.

3. *E.g.*, THOMAS I. EMERSON, THE SYSTEM OF FREEDOM OF Expression (1970); Thomas I. Emerson, *Toward a General Theory of the First Amendment*, 72 YALE L.J. 877, 878–86 (1963) (setting out functions of the First Amendment— viz., search for truth; promotion of social change; self-fulfillment of the speaker; etc.).

4. *E.g.*, Stanley Ingber, *The Marketplace of Ideas: A Legitimizing Myth*, 1984 DUKE L.J. 1; Cass R. Sunstein, *Free Speech Now*, 59 U. CHI. L. REV. 255 (1992).

5. On critical race theory in general, see Richard Delgado & Jean Stefancic, *Critical Race Theory: An Annotated Bibliography*, 79 VA. L. REV. 461 (1993); on the feminist critique of pornography, see, *e.g.*, ANDREA DWORKIN & CATHARINE MACKINNON, PORNOGRAPHY AND CIVIL RIGHTS: A NEW DAY FOR WOMEN'S EQUALITY (1988).

6. For an example of vituperative writing by a mainstream columnist, see Jonathan Yardley, *The Code Word: Alarming*, WASH. POST, Aug. 16, 1993, at G-2 (describing two anti-hate speech writers as engaged in "euphemism," "evasion," "pop psychology," "lunacy," "zealot(ry)," "totalitarianism," "phrenology," "New-speak," "Doublethink," and more).

7. *See* STEVEN H. SHIFFRIN, THE FIRST AMENDMENT, DEMOCRACY, AND ROMANCE 86–109, 140–69 (1990) (reevaluating these claims).

8. *See* Ingber, *supra* at 77–85.

9. On the way pornography constructs the social reality of women as sexual-ized, see generally DWORKIN & MACKINNON, *supra*; chapter 2, this volume.

10. On these "aberrations" and exceptions to free speech (which number in the dozens), see chapter 4, this volume.

11. *See* chapter 6, this volume.

12. *See* STANLEY FISH, THERE'S NO SUCH THING AS FREE SPEECH, AND IT'S A GOOD THING, TOO (1994).

13. *See, e.g.*, RICHARD DELGADO ET AL., WORDS THAT WOUND (1993); Kent Greenawalt, *Insults and Epithets: Are They Protected Speech?* 42 RUTGERS L. REV. 287 (1990).

14. WORDS THAT WOUND, *supra*.

15. Charles R. Lawrence III, *If He Hollers Let Him Go: Regulating Racist Speech on Campus*, 1990 DUKE L.J. 431.

16. *See* Mari J. Matsuda, *Public Response to Racist Speech: Considering the Victim's Story*, 87 MICH. L. REV. 2320 (1989).

17. *See* Yardley, *supra*; NAT HENTOFF, FREE SPEECH FOR ME — BUT NOT FOR THEE (1992).

18. *See* HENTOFF, *supra*.

19. *Id.*; Nat Hentoff, *Censuring the Censors of Free Speech*, CHI. TRIB., Sept. 2, 1993, at 27; Nadine Strossen, *Legal Scholars Who Would Limit Free Speech*, CHRON. HIGHER ED., July 7, 1993, at 1, 1–3.

20. Chapter 6, this volume.

21. *See* Strossen, *In the Defense, supra*, at 155–56. On the judiciary's somewhat tortured effort to come to grips with hate speech and hate crime, compare R.A.V. v. City of St. Paul, 112 S. Ct. 2538 (1992) (tolerating cross burning), with Wisconsin v. Mitchell, 113 S. Ct. 2194 (1993) (permitting sentence enhancement for racially motivated crimes) and two recent Canadian Supreme Court decisions, Regina v. Butler, 89 D.L.R. 4th 449 (1992) (upholding an antipornography law in face of objection that it limited speech, protected by the Canadian charter), and Regina v. Keegstra, [1990] 3 S.C.R. 697 (upholding a federal hate-speech law in face of similar objection).

Notes to Chapter 4

1. *E.g.*, Brown, *Racism and Race Relations in the University*, 76 VA. L. REV. 295, 316 (1990) (underreporting likely); Gibbs, *Bigots in the Ivory Tower, An Alarming Rise in Hatred Roils U.S. Campuses*, TIME, May 7, 1990, at 104; Lawrence, *The Debate over Placing Limits on Racist Speech Must Not Ignore the Damage It Does to Its Victims*, CHRON. HIGHER EDUC., Oct. 25, 1989, at B1, col. 1 (rate increasing); Tatel, *Clear, Narrow Policies on Offensive Speech May Not Run Afoul of the First Amendment*, CHRON. HIGHER EDUC., Feb. 7, 1990, at B1 (rate increasing); *see also When Is a Joke Not a Joke? Shouts and Swastikas are Getting the Last Laugh*, NEWSWEEK, May 23, 1988, at 79 (same); Leatherman, *More Anti-Semitism is Being Reported on Campuses, but Educators Disagree on How to Respond to It*, CHRON. HIGHER EDUC., Feb. 7, 1990, at 1, col. 3 (anti-Semitism increasing); Chung, *Racial Hate Victims Talk to State Panel*, SAN FRANCISCO CHRON., Oct. 7, 1989, at C11, col. 4 (hate crimes, harassment against Asians increasing in California schools). *But see* Leo, *Racism on American College Campuses*, U.S. NEWS & WORLD

Rep., Jan. 8, 1990, at 53 (reports exaggerated, "massively unconvincing," and "overblown"); Bernstein, *On Campus, How Free Should Speech Be?*, N.Y. Times, Sept. 10, 1989, at E5, col. 1 ("a handful of bigots").

For a further discussion of the harms of racist speech, see chapter 1 and this chapter, *infra*. For a discussion of the effects on black college students of racial tension and harassment, see Fleming, *Stress and Satisfaction in College Years of Black Students*, J. Negro Educ. 307 (1985). For a discussion of the resurgence of racism and anti-semitism in Europe, see *Racism Revived*, The Economist, May 19, 1990, at 14; *see also* Sherman, *Hate Crime Statutes Abound*, Nat'l L.J., May 21, 1990, at 3, col. 1 (U.S. states enacting anti-hate laws to deal with resurging racism).

2. U.S. Const. amend. I ("Congress shall make no law . . . abridging the freedom of speech"); Gitlow v. New York, 268 U.S. 652, 666 (1925) (applying free-speech guaranty to the states); *see* Hentoff, *Voodoo Constitutional Law*, Village Voice, Aug. 29, 1989, at 20, col. 1 (campus anti-racism rules "mug" the First Amendment, a step toward recreating spirit of Nazism and the Third Reich).

3. *E.g.*, New York Times v. Sullivan, 376 U.S. 254 (1964); United States v. Carolene Prods. Co., 304 U.S. 144, 152–53 n.4 (1938). The free-speech aspect of campus anti-racism rules is discussed *infra*.

4. In other words, there must be no way of protecting minorities that encroaches less on freedom of speech. Lewis v. City of New Orleans, 425 U.S. 130 (1974); Broadrick v. Oklahoma, 413 U.S. 601, 611 (1973); NAACP v. Button, 371 U.S. 415, 433 (1963) (state action limiting speech must be narrowly tailored to accomplish objective).

5. *See* Z. Chafee, Free Speech in the United States 223–25 (1941) (fear of official censorship a central concern of framers); *see also* Shunny, Brown Alumni Monthly, Nov. 1989, at 6 (punishing racists can backfire—it just encourages them and makes them martyrs) (letter to editor); Will, *Academic Liberal's Brand of Censorship*, San Francisco Chron., Nov. 7, 1989, at A22, col. 5.

6. *E.g.*, Will, *In Praise of Censure*, Time, July 31, 1989, at 71–72; O'Neil, *Colleges Should Seek Educational Alternatives to Rules That Override the Historic Guarantees of Free Speech*, Chron. Higher Educ., Oct. 18, 1989, at B1, col. 1 ("the exception we make today . . . may return to haunt us"); Taylor, *"Fighting Words" Laws Should Focus on Intent, Not Control*, The Recorder, Jan. 3, 1990, at 6, col. 1.

7. U.S. Const. amends. XIII & XIV (prohibiting slavery, and requiring equal protection of the laws); *see also* U.S. Const. amend. XV (requiring equal access to the vote).

8. This concern underlay enactment of the Wisconsin rule. *See* Statement of Regent Erroll B. Davis, Jr., Diversity Conference, UW-Madison, Nov. 17, 1989, at 2 (on file with author).

9. *See* Brown v. Board of Educ., 347 U.S. 483 (1954) (equality high value in our constitutional system); Jones v. Alfred H. Mayer Co., 392 U.S. 409 (1968) (upholding Congress's power to enact rules protecting this value); *see also infra* (place of equality in American legal system).

10. For accounts of this struggle, see, *e.g.,* D. BELL, AND WE ARE NOT SAVED (1987); V. HARDING, THERE IS A RIVER (1981). It is worth observing that few black people wrote the First Amendment narrative; the First Amendment coexisted with slavery. By the same token, few First Amendment absolutists have taken central roles in the struggle for black justice. Indeed, blacks have made their greatest gains when they acted in defiance of constitutional rules and understandings of the limits of free speech and assembly. Lawrence, When Racism Dresses in Speech's Clothing: Reconciling the First and Fourteenth Amendments (unpublished address at ACLU biennial meeting, Madison, Wis., June 15, 1989, on file with author); *see infra* this chapter (reconciling the two narratives).

11. For exposition of this view, see Matsuda, *Public Response to Racist Speech: Considering the Victim's Story,* 87 MICH. L. REV. 2320, 2356–80 (1989).

12. This upsurge has been paralleled by a similar increase in the society at large. *See* Van Tassel, *Colleges Fighting Growth in Prejudice,* N.Y. TIMES, Mar. 27, 1988, § 12NJ, at 4, col. 5 (incidents of racial prejudice increasing throughout country).

A sampling of campuses where such events have taken place includes: University of Connecticut (Asian students spat on and subject to racial slurs while riding to student dance, Hamilton, *U. Conn. Panel Is to Study Racial Abuse,* N.Y. TIMES, Nov. 13, 1988, 12CN, at 1, col. 5); University of Pennsylvania (fraternity sponsored rush party featuring black strippers who performed while audience shouted epithets, *Penn Fraternities Suspended,* N.Y. TIMES, Mar. 5, 1988, § 1, at 7, col. 1); Brown University (racial and homophobic graffiti and flyers, Berger, *Deep Divisions Persist in New Generation at College,* N.Y. TIMES, May 22, 1989, at A1, col. 1); University of Mississippi (arson destroyed all-black fraternity house, *Fraternity Row Integrated at Ole Miss,* N.Y. TIMES, Oct. 16, 1988, § 1, at 20, col. 1); Temple University (students formed a White Student Union, Wilson, *New White Student Unions on Some Campuses are Sparking Outrage and Worry,* CHRON. HIGHER EDUC., Apr. 18, 1990, at 1, col. 2); Fairleigh Dickinson University (racial brawls and fighting, Van Tassel, *supra*); Southern Connecticut (same, *Panel Seeks Penalties for Campus Racism,* N.Y. TIMES, June 25, 1989, § 12CN, at 10, col. 5); Rutgers University (vandalism, Van Tassel, *supra; see* CHRON. HIGHER EDUC., Sept. 6, 1989, at A2, col. 3); Yale (same, Hentoff, *Free Speech on the Campus,* 53 THE PROGRESSIVE 12 (May 1989)); Smith College (same, Van Tassel, *supra*); University of Michigan (slurs and caricatures, Lord, *The Greek Rites of Exclusion,* 245 NATION 10–12 (1987)); Hastings College (same, Shapiro, *Racist Caricatures Anger Students,* THE RECORDER, Feb. 10, 1989, § 1, at 1, col. 2); Arizona State University (same,

Berger, *Deep Racial Divisions Persist in New Generation at College*, N.Y. TIMES, May 22, 1989, at A1, col. 1); Wisconsin (same, *see infra* this chapter); Hamilton College (same, Carmody, *College Erred in Suspensions, A Court Rules*, N.Y. TIMES, Aug. 2, 1987, § 1, at 49, col. 1); and Oberlin College (same).

13. Gold, *Dartmouth President Faults Right-Wing Student Journal*, N.Y. TIMES, Mar. 29, 1988, at A16, col. 4.

14. Jones reportedly spilled beer on Sodl; Sodl reportedly responded by rubbing Jones's head and making a sarcastic remark about his hair. *Blacks at Columbia U. File Charges in Brawl*, N.Y. TIMES, Mar. 24, 1987, at B5, col. 5. Jones had a run-in with Sodl and his fraternity friends two weeks before this incident. *Columbia to Investigate a Reported Racial Brawl*, N.Y. TIMES, Mar. 23, 1987, at B2, col. 1.

15. *Columbia to Investigate a Reported Racial Brawl*, N.Y. TIMES, Mar. 23, 1987, at B2, col. 1.

16. *Id.*

17. *Blacks at Columbia U. File Charges in Brawl*, N.Y. TIMES, Mar. 24, 1987, at B5, col. 5.

18. Morgan, *50 Arrested in Anti-Racism Protest at Columbia*, N.Y. TIMES, Apr. 22, 1987, at B3, col. 1. The first protest included approximately 150 demonstrators. A new group, called Concerned Black Students of Columbia (CBSC), criticized the failure of the police and university to act quickly. *Blacks at Columbia U. File Charges in Brawl, supra.* The group and others staged a protest at police headquarters in Manhattan, where police responded by saying that it was the black complainants' own refusal to cooperate that was hampering the investigation. The complainants' attorney countered by accusing the police of acting in bad faith. *23 Seized in Protest on Columbia Clash*, N.Y. TIMES, Apr. 8, 1987, at B5, col. 1.

19. Carmody, *Columbia Report Cites Racial Unrest*, N.Y. TIMES, Apr. 23, 1987, at B2, col. 3 (reporting that an unidentified black man threw the first blow).

20. *Id.*

21. The attorney for the CBSC viewed the report as "an attempt to blame the victims ... for the fact that the university has not been able to do a proper investigation." *Id.* Other students described the school's disciplinary process as "a joke." *Id.*

22. Neuffer, *Columbia Begins Disciplinary Hearings on Protest*, N.Y. TIMES, May 27, 1987, at B3, col. 3.

23. Uhlig, *Columbia Panel Rejects Expelling Any Students in Protest on Racism*, N.Y. TIMES, Aug. 5, 1987, at B2, col.1. The warnings could be expunged from the students' records after one term of violation-free conduct. *Id.*

24. *White Columbia Student Is Ruled Bias Victim*, N.Y. TIMES, Jan. 13, 1988, at B1, col. 4. Krause had been suspended for one term but had received a stay. The jury awarded $1 in damages. *Id.*

25. Curtis, *College Campuses Reinforce Rules Barring Racism,* SAN FRANCISCO CHRON., Sept. 18, 1989, at A1, col. 1.

26. Curtis, *Racial, Ethnic, Sexual Slurs Banned on UC Campuses,* SAN FRANCISCO CHRON., Sept. 27, 1989, at A1, col. 3. Such words include terms widely regarded as disparaging of a person's "race, ethnicity, religion, sex, sexual orientation, disability and other personal characteristics." *Id.*

27. Discrimination and Discriminatory Harassment by Students in the University Environment, University of Michigan (adopted April 14, 1988).

28. Doe v. University of Michigan, 721 F. Supp. 852, 866 (E.D. Mich. 1989).

29. Wilson, *Colleges' Anti-Harassment Policies Bring Controversy Over Free-Speech Issues,* CHRON. HIGHER EDUC., Oct. 4, 1989, at A1, col. 2. Institutions that have already adopted policies include Emory University, the Universities of Texas, Wisconsin, California, Connecticut, Michigan, North Carolina at Chapel Hill, and Pennsylvania, Brown University, Pennsylvania State University, Trinity College, Mt. Holyoke, and Tufts University. Institutions that were recently considering anti-harassment policies include Eastern Michigan, Colorado, and Arizona State. In early October 1989, Tufts's administrators rescinded its policy, which had identified specific areas of campus where "demeaning" speech was restricted, believing that the policy would probably fail a court challenge. Ingalls, *Tufts Rescinds Controversial Policy Limiting Free Speech in Certain Areas,* CHRON. HIGHER EDUC., Oct. 11, 1989, at A3, col. 1.

Most rules are patterned after the "fighting words" exception of Chaplinsky v. New Hampshire, 315 U.S. 568 (1946), or the tort of severe emotional distress. Mt. Holyoke, a private college, has adopted a standard prohibiting—"unwelcome slurs, jokes, graphic written materials as well as all other verbal or physical action related to an individual's personal background or attributes," Mt. Holyoke College Statement on Human Rights (Oct. 1989) (on file with authors)—that appears to track no recognized exception to the First Amendment. Most policies contain detailed procedures for resolving complaints as well as substantive standards. Many university schemes emphasize informal resolution. If this approach fails or the grievant chooses not to pursue informal procedures, the university may institute formal proceedings. Most university rules provide for punishment, such as a reprimand, community service, or suspension, if there exists "clear and convincing evidence"; *see, e.g.,* University of Michigan policy, or if there exists a "reasonable basis for believing" that a violation has occurred. *See, e.g.,* Mt. Holyoke College policy. Most policies give the accused the right to appeal an adverse decision. *See, e.g.,* University of Wisconsin policy, this chapter. A few of these policies have been struck down on various grounds, including overbreadth. *See* this chapter, *infra,* and chapter 6.

30. Finn, *The Campus: "An Island of Repression in a Sea of Freedom,"* COMMENTARY 17, 18 (1989). Finn, professor of education and public policy at Vanderbilt

University, states that academic freedom is the only difference that separates our universities from those in totalitarian countries. *Id.*; *see also* Hentoff, *supra* ("If students are to be 'protected' from bad ideas, how are they to learn to identify and cope with them?"); Washburn, *Liberalism versus Free Speech*, 40 NAT'L REV. 39, 41 (1988) (free inquiry is the bedrock upon which a liberal education is built).

31. Kors, *It's Speech, Not Sex, the Dean Bans Now*, WALL ST. J., Oct. 12, 1989, at 1, at 16, col. 3. Kors is a professor of history at the University of Pennsylvania.

32. Minow, "Looking Ahead to the 1990's: Constitutional Law and American Colleges and Universities," Keynote Address to the National Association of Colleges and Universities Attorneys Meeting (June 28, 1989).

33. Minow, *supra* (raising possibility that this view may lead to an overactive state).

34. Washburn, *supra*, at 39.

35. Washburn, for example, writes that if we want free expression to yield to the sensitivities of the individual, the entire nature of the university must change. *Id.* at 40.

36. Washburn, *supra*, at 39.

37. O'Neil, *supra*. O'Neil served as president and professor of law at University of Virginia.

38. Will, *supra*, at 71–72. Will uses the Christian crucifix as an example. He concludes that members of the left will bestir themselves when the Ku Klux Klan burn this symbol, while the right reacts when pop singer Madonna uses it in her provocative musical performances. *Id.*

39. Sowell, *Campuses Attempting to Mask Truth by Closing Mouths*, ROCKY MT. NEWS, Apr. 16, 1990, at B22, col. 1.

40. Wiener, *Racial Hatred on Campus*, THE NATION, Feb. 27, 1989, at 260, 262. Mr. Wiener is a professor of history at UC Irvine.

41. *See* Jones, *Article 4 of the International Convention of the Elimination of All Forms of Racial Discrimination and the First Amendment*, 23 HOW. L.J. 429, 436 (1980); Kretzmer, *Freedom of Speech and Racism*, 8 CARDOZO L. REV. 445 (1987); I. BROWNLIE, PRINCIPLES OF PUBLIC INTERNATIONAL LAW 598–601 (4th ed. 1990); J. INGLES, POSITIVE MEASURES DESIGNED TO ERADICATE ALL INCITEMENT TO, OR ACTS OF RACIAL DISCRIMINATION: IMPLEMENTATION OF ARTICLE 4 OF THE INTERNATIONAL CONVENTION ON THE ELIMINATION OF ALL FORMS OF RACIAL DISCRIMINATION (1986); McDougal, Lasswell & Chen, *The Protection of Respect and Human Rights: Freedom of Choice and World Public Order*, 24 AM. U.L. REV. 919, 1075 (1975); Greenburg, *Race, Sex, and Religious Discrimination in International Law*, in T. MERON, HUMAN RIGHTS IN INTERNATIONAL LAW: LEGAL AND POLICY ISSUES 307, 309 (1984). For example, the Universal Declaration of Human Rights provides that persons are entitled to protection from

discrimination and its incitement (G.A. Res. 217, U.N. Doc. A/810, at 71 (1948)). The European Convention for the Protection of Human Rights and Fundamental Freedoms (Nov. 4, 1950, 213 U.N.T.S. 221) and the American Declaration of the Rights and Duties of Man (American Convention on Human Rights, OEA/ ser.K/XVI/1.1, doc.65 rev.3 (1970), *reprinted in* 9 Int'l Legal Materials 99 (1970) [hereinafter American Convention]) provide similar protections. The Convention on the Prevention and Punishment of the Crime of Genocide (Dec. 9, 1948, 78 U.N.T.S. 277, 280) requires states to prohibit "direct and public incitement" to commit that crime (*id.* at 280 (art. 3(c))). The International Covenant on Civil and Political Rights (G.A. Res. 2200, 21 U.N. GAOR Supp. (No. 16) at 49, U.N. Doc. A/6316 (1966)), which affirms freedom of expression, nevertheless states that "advocacy of national, racial or religious hatred that constitutes incitement to discrimination, hostility or violence shall be prohibited by law." *Id.* at 55 (art. 20, § 2).

42. International Convention on the Elimination of All Forms of Racial Discrimination, *opened for signature* Mar. 7, 1966, 660 U.N.T.S. 195 [hereinafter CERD]. CERD was signed but not ratified by the United States on September 28, 1966. *Id.* at 303.

43. N. Lerner, The U.N. Convention on the Elimination of All Forms of Racial Discrimination 155–56 (2d ed. 1980).

44. Dore, *United Nations Measures to Combat Racial Discrimination: Progress and Problems in Retrospect*, 10 Denver J. Int'l L. Pol'y 299, 299–300 (1981).

45. States [that are]

Parties condemn all propaganda and all organizations which are based on ideas or theories of superiority of one race or group of persons of one colour or ethnic origin, or which attempt to justify or promote racial hatred and discrimination in any form . . . :

(a) Shall declare an offense punishable by law all dissemination of ideas based on racial superiority or hatred, incitement to racial discrimination, as well as all acts of violence or incitement to such acts against any race or group of persons of another colour or ethnic origin. . . .

(b) Shall declare illegal and prohibit organizations . . . which promote and incite racial discrimination. . . .

(c) Shall not permit public authorities or public institutions, national or local, to promote or incite racial discrimination.

CERD, *supra*, at art. 4.

46. J. Ingles, *supra*, at 1. Although the United States is a member of several international organizations which have promulgated legislation denouncing racism, it has not ratified CERD. The United States supported the Convention with this reservation: "The Constitution of the United States contains provisions for

the protection of individual rights such as the right of free speech, and nothing in the Convention shall be deemed to require or to authorize legislation or other action by the United States of America incompatible with the provisions of the Constitution of the United States of America." CERD, *supra*.

47. Kretzmer, *supra*, at 500. A small minority of states formulated declarations and reservations regarding Article 4, and some have not carried out their obligation under that article to adopt the required legislation. Meron, *The Meaning and Reach of the International Convention on the Elimination of All Forms of Racial Discrimination*, 79 AM. J. INT. L. 283, 316 (1985). However, a large number of states have made efforts to implement all or part of their obligations under the Convention. N. LERNER, *supra*, at 166.

48. Race Relations Act, 1965, ch. 73, § 6(1) (amended in 1976 and 1986) [hereinafter 1965 Act].

49. Legal treatment of racial hatred in Great Britain began well before the modern period of treaties and statutes, with the case of R. v. Osborn, 25 Eng. Rep. 584 (K.B. 1732). Osborn accused "several Jews" of murdering a woman and her child because the father was a Christian. When some readers attacked and injured a group of Jews, the public prosecutor charged Osborn with seditious libel and incitement to commit breach of the peace. Although Osborn was convicted, later cases narrowed *Osborn* in various ways. Parliament responded by criminalizing hate speech in the Public Order Act of 1936, 1 Edw. 8 & 1 Geo. 6, ch. 6, 5; *see* McCrudden, *British Anti-Discrimination Law: An Introduction*, 2 DICK INT'L L. ANN. 65 (1983). With the rise of neo-Nazism, however, the statute proved inadequate.

50. 1965 Act, *supra*.

51. Public Order Act, 1986, ch. 64, §§ 17–18. Sections of the 1986 Act pertinent to racial hatred are:

§ 17 Meaning of "racial hatred":
In this part "racial hatred" means hatred against a group of persons in Great Britain defined by reference to colour, race, nationality (including citizenship) or ethnic or national origins.

§ 18 Use of words or behavior or display of written material:
(1) A person who uses threatening, abusive or insulting words or behavior, or displays any written material which is threatening, abusive or insulting, is guilty of an offense if—
　(a) he intends thereby to stir up racial hatred, or
　(b) having regard to all the circumstances racial hatred is likely to be stirred up thereby.
(2) An offense under this section may be committed in public or a private place, except that no offense is committed where the words or behavior are

used, or the written materials is displayed, by a person inside a dwelling and are not heard or seen except by other persons in that or another dwelling.

(3) A constable may arrest without warrant anyone he reasonably suspects is committing an offense under this section.

(4) In proceedings for an offense under this section it is a defence for the accused to prove that he was inside a dwelling and had no reason to believe that the words or behavior used, or the written material displayed, would be heard or seen by a person outside that or any other dwelling.

(5) A person who is not shown to have intended to stir up racial hatred is not guilty of an offense under this section if he did not intend his words or behavior, or the written material, to be, and was not aware that it might be, threatening, abusive or insulting.

(6) This section does not apply to words or behavior used, or written material displayed, solely for the purpose of being included in a programme broadcast or included in a cable programme service.

Id.

The Act was a compromise. Civil libertarians successfully insisted that provisions be incorporated to prevent the measure from becoming an unreasonable infringement on speech. Included were provisos that (1) prosecutions could only be carried out with the consent of the attorney general; (2) the statute would apply only to distribution of materials or words spoken in public; (3) only "threatening, abusive or insulting" speech would be covered; (4) intent must be shown; and (5) the racial group victimized must be one residing within Great Britain.

Under the revised statute, few prosecutions occurred. *R. v. Hancock* (unreported) indicated additional lacunae in the act. In *Hancock*, a white supremacist group distributed pamphlets proclaiming that nonwhites were genetically inferior and should be returned to their countries of origin. The wording was pseudoscientific and avoided language of threat or incitement, and the defendant was acquitted. *See* Longaker, *The Race Relations Act of 1965*, 11 RACE 125, 130–42 (1969). Britain responded by abolishing the element of intent from the Act, so that prosecution could be based on the objective likelihood of a speech-act's stirring up hatred. The Act was once again modified in 1986. The new Act permits a constable to arrest without a warrant "anyone he reasonably suspects is committing an offense under this section." Moreover, unlike earlier versions, the statute prohibits private as well as public behavior. The attorney general, however, must still consent to all prosecutions.

52. Bindman, *The Law and Racial Discrimination: Third Thoughts*, 3 BRIT. J. LAW & SOC'Y 110 (1976) (repeal would be seen as condoning racism and would be politically unwise); Matsuda, *supra*, at 234 (remaining controversy centers around proposals to lift some of the restrictions designed to protect freedom of

speech). *But see* Lasson, *Racism in Great Britain: Drawing the Line on Free Speech,* 7 B.C. 3RD WORLD L.J. 161, 170 (1987), at 171:

> Englishmen have a strong attachment to freedom of speech. The freedom was won . . . not just to enable people to say pleasant, fraternal and acceptable things . . . but to say distasteful, unacceptable, provocative, antagonistic things. Any criminal statute which is framed to circumscribe that freedom is likely to be given a bumpy ride, however desirable or even necessary the purpose may be.

Id. (quoting LONDON TIMES, Jan. 9, 1978, at 3, col. 2).

53. David Kretzmer, *supra* at 503–4, suggests three ways to interpret the British experience: (1) The British statute goes as far as possible in curbing free speech—a more effective one would unacceptably impair liberty. (2) The statute is imperfect, but serves to limit cruder forms of hateful speech and has some symbolic and educative value. (3) The law in its current version is inadequate, but having shown that speech may be limited without dire consequences, it may be expanded cautiously as social conditions dictate. In any event, the principal remaining question centers on whether to remove some of the law's restrictions at the risk of encroaching even further on free speech.

54. CAN. CONST. pt. 1, §§ 1–34 (1982) [hereinafter CHARTER].

55. *Id.*

56. Canadian Criminal Code, R.S.C. ch. C-46, 319.1, 319.2, 319.3(a)-(d) (1985) (amended by R.S.C. ch. C-42, § 319.2 (1988)).

57. *See* Hunter, *When Human Rights Become Wrongs,* 23 U.W. ONT. L. REV. 197 (1985). Under the Canadian Charter of Rights (Canadian Charter) and the United States Constitution, free expression cases are treated in much the same way. Sedler, *The Constitutional Protection of Freedom of Religion, Expression, and Association in Canada and the United States: A Comparative Analysis,* 20 CASE W. RES. J. INT'L L. 577, 593 (1988). The Canadian Charter guarantees fundamental freedoms of religion, expression, and association. These liberties are "subject . . . to such reasonable limits prescribed by law as can be demonstrably justified in a free and democratic society." CHARTER, § 1; *see* Regel, *Hate Propaganda: A Reason to Limit Freedom of Speech,* 49 SASKATCH. L. REV. 303, 305 (1984). To determine the constitutionality of laws limiting speech, a two-step test is used. Sedler, *supra,* at 479–80. The first step is to determine whether an individual right falls under the Charter. The second is to analyze whether the restriction is justified by an "interest of sufficient importance to warrant overriding a constitutional right," *id.* at 579–81 (quoting Regina v. Edward Brooks and Art, Ltd., 2 S.C.R. 713 (1986)), and whether the "means chosen to attain these objectives [are] appropriate or proportional to the ends." *Id.*

58. The first was the least controversial; it merely carries out Canada's respon-

sibilities to legislate the provisions of the United Nations Convention on Genocide. The second, public incitement of hatred, drew fire; one of the criticisms is that the reaction of the audience dictates whether or not an offense has occurred. The third and fourth provisions, willful promotion of hatred other than in a private conversation and spreading false news, have been rarely applied.

59. The Penal Code of the Federal Republic of Germany 220(a) (J. Darby trans., 1987).

60. *Id.* at § 131.

61. *Around the World; 11 Youths Sentenced in Italy for Anti-Semitic Acts*, N.Y. TIMES, Oct. 29, 1980, at A5, col. 1.

62. Instrument of Government, *reprinted in* vol. XVI, CONSTITUTIONS OF THE COUNTRIES OF THE WORLD (1985) [hereinafter Instrument of Government].

63. In interpreting this statute, the Norwegian Supreme Court balances section 135(a) with the right of freedom of speech. *Id.* Speech is protected but not absolute; the criminal law can sanction its exercise when it becomes abusive. *Reprinted in* initial report (CERD/C/R,25/Add.3) *amending* ch. 16 of the Penal Code. Finland ratified the Convention on July 14, 1970, and inserted Article 6 into its penal code. It states:

a) Anyone disseminating to the public statements and other information in which a section of the population is threatened, slandered or insulted on account of being of a certain race, colour, national or ethnic origin or confession of faith shall be sentenced for discrimination against that section of the people to imprisonment for two years at most or to pay a fine.

Id. at art. 6(a).

64. Racial Discrimination Act of 1975, *reprinted in* ACTS OF THE PARLIAMENT OF THE COMMONWEALTH 349 (1975).

65. *Id.* at 355.

66. New Zealand Race Relations Act of 1971, no. 150, *reprinted in* 4 N.Z. Stats. 3590 (1971). The 1977 amendments made wording changes and increased the fines. The amendments did not affect the substance of the law. 4 N.Z. Stats. at 3590 (1977).

67. These theories came into focus particularly after World War II as the world strove to understand the horror of the Holocaust. *See, e.g.*, B. BETTELHEIM & M. JANOWITZ, DYNAMICS OF PREJUDICE (1950); E. HARTLEY, PROBLEMS IN PREJUDICE (1948); Lawrence, *The Id, The Ego and Equal Protection: Reckoning with Unconscious Racism*, 39 STAN. L. REV. 317 (1986).

68. T. ADORNO, E. FRENKEL-BRUNSWICK, D. LEVINSON & R. SANFORD, THE AUTHORITARIAN PERSONALITY (1969).

69. J. KOVEL, WHITE RACISM — A PSYCHOHISTORY 231 (1984); Handlin, *Prejudice and Capitalist Exploitation, in* 6 COMMENTARY 79 (1948).

70. *E.g.*, BETTELHEIM & JANOWITZ, *supra* (ethnic prejudice increases in times of economic depression); Handlin, *supra*; J. KOVEL, *supra*, at 231; Delgado, *The Imperial Scholar*, 132 U. PA. L. REV. 561, 570–71 (1984).

71. I. KATZ, STIGMA — A SOCIAL PSYCHOLOGICAL ANALYSIS 121 (1981).

72. *Id.* at 221; C. KLUCKHOLM, NAVAHO WITCHCRAFT (1944). Compare these scapegoating theorists with those of the closely related "internal colonialism" school, *e.g.*, O. COX, CASTE, CLASS AND RACE: A STUDY IN SOCIAL DYNAMICS (1948); Cho, *Theories of Racial Inequality: From Assimilation to Internal Colonialism, reprinted in* RACE, CLASS, CULTURE IN AMERICA: CRITICAL PERSPECTIVES OF THIRD WORLD AMERICA 245 (L. Shinagawa ed., 1983), and those who advocate the "frustration-aggression" approach to understanding prejudice. *E.g.*, D. BETHLEHEM, A SOCIAL PSYCHOLOGY OF RACE 100–01 (1985); G. SIMPSON & J. YINGER, RACIAL AND CULTURAL MINORITIES: AN ANALYSIS OF PREJUDICE AND DISCRIMINATION 68 (4th ed. 1972).

73. G. ALLPORT, THE NATURE OF PREJUDICE 400–403, 482 (25th Anniversary ed. 1979).

74. G. ALLPORT, *supra*, at 79–80.

75. On the confrontation theory, see generally I. KATZ, *supra*, at 16, 109; Westie, *The American Dilemma: An Empirical Test*, 30 AM. SOC. REV. 527, 529 (1965).

76. G. ALLPORT, *supra*, at 470–71 (emphasis in original).

77. New York Times v. Sullivan, 376 U.S. 254, 270 (1964).

78. Abrams v. United States, 250 U.S. 616, 630 (1919).

79. 343 U.S. 250 (1952).

80. *Id.* at 257–58.

81. 376 U.S. 254 (1964) (libel of public figures requires showing of actual malice); *see also* Garrison v. Louisiana, 379 U.S. 64 (1964) (overturning libel judgment won by public official by analogizing case to seditious libel).

82. 112 S. Ct. 2538 (1992).

83. *See, e.g.*, L. TRIBE, AMERICAN CONSTITUTIONAL LAW 861 n.2 (1988) (citing Smith v. Collin, 439 U.S. 916, 919 (1978) (Blackmun, J., dissenting from denial of certiorari)).

84. These cases are collected and discussed in chapter 2.

85. Commentators have categorized these goals differently. The following are those proposed in T. EMERSON, THE SYSTEM OF FREEDOM OF EXPRESSION 3–6 (1970), and Emerson, *Toward a General Theory of the First Amendment*, 72 YALE L.J. 877, 878–86 (1963). For other treatments, see Blasi, *The Checking Value in First Amendment Theory*, 1977 AM. B. FOUND. RES. J. 521; Bork, *Neutral Principles and Some First Amendment Problems*, 47 IND. L.J. 1 (1971); Meiklejohn, *The First Amendment Is an Absolute*, 1961 SUP. CT. REV. 245; Redish, *The Value of Free Speech*, 130 U. PA. L. REV. 591 (1982).

86. *E.g.*, G. ALLPORT, *supra*, at 170–86, 371–84, 407–8.

87. K. GREENAWALT, SPEECH, CRIME AND THE USES OF LANGUAGE (1989). *See also* Greenawalt, *Insults and Epithets: Are They Protected Speech?* 42 RUTGERS L. REV. 287 (1990) (putting forth similar argument, drawn from his book).

88. Universities might decline to enact such rules even if it were constitutional to do so. *See* Address by Delgado, State Historical Society, Madison, Wis., Apr. 24, 1989.

> I believe that racist speech benefits powerful white-dominated institutions. The highly educated, refined persons who operate the University of Wisconsin, other universities, and major corporations would never, ever themselves utter a racial slur. That is the last thing they would do.
>
> Yet, they benefit, and on a subconscious level they know they benefit, from a certain amount of low-grade racism in the environment. If an occasional bigot or redneck calls one of us a nigger or spic one night late as we're on our way home from the library, that is all to the good. Please understand that I am not talking about the very heavy stuff—violence, beatings, bones in the nose. That brings out the TV cameras and the press and gives the university a black eye. I mean the daily, low-grade largely invisible stuff, the hassling, cruel remarks, and other things that would be covered by rules. This kind of behavior keeps nonwhite people on edge, a little off balance. We get these occasional reminders that we are different, and not really wanted. It prevents us from digging in too strongly, starting to think we could really belong here. It makes us a little introspective, a little unsure of ourselves; at the right low-grade level it prevents us from organizing on behalf of more important things. It assures that those of us of real spirit, real pride, just plain leave—all of which is quite a substantial benefit for the institution.

(Citing S. BROWNMILLER, AGAINST OUR WILL (1979) (rape is the crime of all men against all women; even men who would not consider assaulting a woman nevertheless benefit from *in terrorem* effect fear of rape inspires in women)).

89. *See* Delgado, *Derrick Bell and the Ideology of Racial Reform: Will We Ever Be Saved?* 97 YALE L.J. 923, 936 (1988) (summarizing these and other constraints).

90. *See* American Booksellers Ass'n, Inc. v. Hudnut, 771 F.2d 323 (7th Cir. 1985), *aff'd*, 475 U.S. 1001 (1986); C. MACKINNON, FEMINISM UNMODIFIED 175–95 (1987); MacKinnon, *Not a Moral Issue*, 2 YALE L. & POL. J. 321 (1984).

91. Interview with Michael Olivas, Professor of Law, U. Houston, Madison, WI (Feb. 4, 1990). Universities must also avoid applying regulations only in racially charged and highly polarized situations. *Id.* Olivas is Director, Institute of Higher Education Law & Governance, and author of a leading casebook on higher-education law.

92. Bob Jones Univ. v. United States, 461 U.S. 574 (1983) (government's "overriding interest in eradicating racial discrimination in education" outweighs institution's free exercise claim to a tax exemption); *see* Laycock, *Tax Exemption for Religiously Discriminatory Schools*, 60 Tex. L. Rev. 759 (1987).

93. University of Pennsylvania v. EEOC, 110 S. Ct. 577 (1990) (action brought on behalf of an Asian woman denied tenure, in part, because her writings focused on Asian issues).

94. In general, we need the First Amendment to protect minorities from tyranny by the majority. But with racist insults and epithets, the majority uses speech to construct a stigma-picture of the minority. Arguably, the cautions that ordinarily operate in favor of protecting speech do not apply here.

Of course, it may be pointed out that some of the framers and theoreticians of the Constitution and First Amendment favored slavery and the oppression of colored peoples. See T. Hobbes, Leviathan, pt. II, ch. 221 (Of the Liberty of Subjects); D. Boumgold, Hobbes' Political Theory 93–97 (1988); J. Locke, Two Treatises of Government, 2d Treatise, §§ 17, 24, 85; R. Gant, John Locke's Liberalism 67 (1987). Yet later in our history we committed ourselves — through the Thirteenth, Fourteenth, and Fifteenth Amendments — to an anti-subordination principle. *See* text *supra*. Generally, empowered persons will favor competition and the marketplace of ideas, while those lacking a strong voice will view the universalizing, quasi-objective values of the marketplace of ideas with mistrust and will prefer the more contextualized perspectives afforded by equal protection analysis. Our dilemma is that we wish to promote both values at the same time. One cannot, however, "balance" incommensurables; creation of a new category of speech-act for behavior by which a more powerful group creates a stigma-picture of a weaker one seems to be the only solution.

95. *See* K. Greenawalt, *supra*.

96. H. Kalven, The Negro and the First Amendment (1965).

Notes to Chapter 5

1. *See, e.g.,* Derrick Bell & Preeta Bansal, *The Republican Revival and Racial Politics*, 97 Yale L.J. 1609 (1988); Richard Delgado, *Zero-Based Racial Politics and an Infinity-Based Response: Will Endless Talking Cure America's Racial Ills?*, 80 Geo. L.J. 1879 (1992); Robert Justine Lipkin, *Kibitzers, Fuzzies and Apes without Tails: Pragmatism and the Art of Conversation in Legal Theory*, 66 Tul. L. Rev. 69 (1991).

2. *See* Laurence Tribe, *The Curvature of Constitutional Space: What Lawyers Can Learn from Modern Physics*, 103 Harv. L. Rev. 1 (1989) (drawing further analogies between modern and modernist legal thought and relativity physics).

3. We have identified the following: Alternative Museum, New York City, Prisoners of Image: Ethnic and Gender Stereotypes, curated by Robbin Hender-

son and Geno Rodriquez (1989); The Balch Institute for Ethnic Studies, Philadelphia, Ethnic Images in Advertising (1984), Ethnic Images in Comics (1986), Ethnic Images in World War I Posters (1988), Ethnic Images in Toys and Games (1990); Berkeley Art Center, Berkeley, Ethnic Notions: Black Images in the White Mind, The Janette Faulkner Collection of Stereotypes and Caricature of Afro-Americans (1982); Galeria de la Raza, San Francisco, Cactus Hearts/Barbed Wire Dreams: Media, Myths, and Mexicans, curated by Yolanda Lopez (1988) (telephone interviews with Phyllis Bischof, Librarian for African and African American Collections, U.C. Calif. at Berkeley; Jan Faulkner, Collector and Clinical Professor, Psychiatry, U.C.S.F.; Robbin Henderson, Director, Berkeley Art Center (Feb. 1992)). *See also* Jessie Smith, Images of Blacks in American Culture: Reference Guide to Information Sources 289 (1988) (listing collections of Black Americana).

4. "Ethnic Notions." Interview with Jan Faulkner, *supra.*

5. Robert Hughes, *Two Centuries of Stereotypes*, TIME, Jan. 29, 1990, at 82 (describing opening of exhibit at Corcoran Gallery).

6. *Ethnic Notions* (P.B.S. 1986) (on file with authors). By the same filmmaker, see also *Color Adjustment*, TV documentary on racial images of the last forty years on prime-time television.

7. *Cf.* ROBERT JAY LIFTON, THE NAZI DOCTORS (1986) (pointing out that German administrators and physicians who carried out atrocities were highly educated); I-III ELIE WIESEL, AGAINST SILENCE (1985) (same).

8. *See* Richard Delgado & Jean Stefancic, *Norms and Narratives: Can Judges Avoid Serious Moral Error?* 69 TEX. L. REV. 1929 (1991) (judges rarely see beyond current moral paradigm). Of course, it is possible that consciousness will not progress, but regress or remain at the same level—i.e., we may *never* condemn David Duke or the Willie Horton commercial. David Duke is an ex-white supremist who campaigned for state and national office in the late 1980s and early 1990s. The Willie Horton commercial featured a black recidivist; its purpose was to imply that Democrats are soft on crime.

9. The term, as well as the fallacy it names, are our own inventions.

10. For the earliest known discussion of this fallacy, see JOHN RUSKIN, 3 MODERN PAINTINGS 152 (1885); *see also* W. K. Wimsatt, Jr., & M. C. Beardsley, *The Affective Fallacy*, 57 SEWANEE REV. 31 (1949) (further discussion of literary fallacies).

11. JOSEPHINE MILES, PATHETIC FALLACY IN THE NINETEENTH CENTURY 10–56 (1965) (giving examples, from prominent poets, of nature weeping, smiling, groaning, all in sympathy with humans); *see also infra* (setting out our view that both fallacies are rooted in *hubris*).

12. Some of the works we found particularly helpful are the following: ARTHUR G. PETTIT, IMAGES OF THE MEXICAN AMERICAN IN FICTION AND FILM (1980); CATHERINE SILK & JOHN SILK, RACISM AND ANTI-RACISM IN AMERICAN

Popular Culture (1990); Raymond W. Stedman, Shadows of the Indian: Stereotypes in American Culture (1982); E. Wong, On Visual Media Racism: Asians in the American Motion Picture (1978); From Different Shores: Perspectives on Race and Ethnicity in America (Ronald Takaki ed., 1987) [hereinafter Different Shores]; Split Image: African Americans in the Mass Media (Jannette L. Dates & William Barlow eds., 1990) [hereinafter Split Image].

For additional works, see bibliographies in Silk & Silk, *supra* (dealing with African Americans). *See also* Edward W. Said, Orientalism (1985) (dealing with Asian Americans).

For examples of sexist images concerning women, see Tama Starr, The "Natural Inferiority" of Women: Outrageous Pronouncements by Misguided Males (1991). For a discussion of other minority groups and their role in U.S. civil rights history, see Stetson Kennedy, Jim Crow Guide: The Way It Was 26–46 (1990).

13. *See* Split Image, *supra*, at 6. On black characters and types generally in U.S. literature, see Sterling Brown, The Negro in American Fiction (2d ed. 1972) (detailing recurring caricatures, such as the contented slave, wretched freedman, tragic mulatto, brute Negro, entertaining clown, etc.); John L. Grigsby, *Judas, Jesus, Job or 'Jes a Happy Ole Nigga: Or, Will the Real Uncle Tom Please Step Forward?*, 1986 Pubs. Miss. Phil. Ass'n 51.

14. Split Image, *supra*, at 5–6.

15. *See* Split Image, *supra*, at 7.

16. The dandified image (the "Coon") showed the folly of the North's policy concerning freedom, while that of the happy Southern slave reassured whites that blacks were happiest in "their natural condition." *See* Split Image, *supra*, at 7. The dandified urban "coon" image, played by white actors, reappeared in the 1920s and continued until the 1950s in the phenomenally popular radio serial "Amos 'n' Andy." *See* Melvin Ely, The Adventures of Amos 'N' Andy: A Social History of an American Phenomenon (1991).

17. *See* The Classic Slaves Narratives (H. Gates ed., 1987); Split Image, *supra*, at 10.

18. *See id.* at 8. William L. Van Deburg, Slavery and Race in American Popular Culture 35–36 (1984) (arguing that Uncle Tom's character was but a slight improvement over previous stereotypes).

19. Silk & Silk, *supra*, at 139; Split Image, *supra*, at 11; Van Deburg, *supra*, at 43.

20. *See* Split Image, *supra*, at 11. This obsession with sexual matters dates back to Puritan times in Massachusetts, and has surfaced in similar stereotyping of the four major racial groups in the United States. *See* Stedman, *supra*, at 81; Van Deburg, *supra*, at 122–25 (on recurring image of the Negro as beast).

21. SILK & SILK, *supra*, at 49.

22. *Id.* at 50; *see* Russell Merritt, *D. W. Griffith's The Birth of a Nation: Going After Little Sister, in* CLOSE VIEWINGS: AN ANTHOLOGY OF NEW FILM CRITICISM 215 (1990).

23. THE LEOPARD'S SPOTS (1902).

24. SILK & SILK, *supra*, at 127. Wilson's comment probably was intended as praise, for he added: "[o]ne of my regrets is that it is so horribly true." *Id.*

25. *Id.* at 31–32.

26. *Id.* at 45; SPLIT IMAGE, *supra*, at 11–12; VAN DEBURG, *supra*, at 100–102. On the status of the Negro at that time, see RAYMOND W. LOGAN, THE NEGRO IN AMERICAN LIFE AND THOUGHT: THE NADIR, 1877–1901 (1954).

27. SILK & SILK, *supra*, at 46.

28. 163 U.S. 543 (1896).

29. SILK & SILK, *supra*, at 63; VAN DEBURG, *supra*, at 120–21, 202–3.

30. *See The Congo, in* THE NEW POETRY 291 (H. Monroe ed., 1932).

31. Derrick A. Bell, Jr., Brown v. Board of Education *and the Interest-Convergence Dilemma*, 93 HARV. L. REV. 518, 524 (1980); Mary Dudziak, *Desegregation as a Cold War Imperative*, 41 STAN. L. REV. 61, 71–73 (1989).

32. *See Color Adjustment, supra* (describing last 40 years of media depiction and noting, among other things, the resemblance between current shows featuring sanitized, myth-making Rhodes scholars, super-Negroes, and previous images); *see also* SPLIT IMAGE, *supra*, at 254–80 (same); George Zinkhan et al., *Changes in Stereotypes: Blacks and Whites in Magazine Advertisements*, 63 JOURNALISM Q. 568 (Autumn 1986).

33. STEDMAN, *supra*, at 253 (noting descriptions that explorers Christopher Columbus and Amerigo Vespucci gave). For further writings on Columbus and his early impressions, see THE FOUR VOYAGES OF COLUMBUS (J. M. Cohen trans. & ed., 1969).

34. DEE BROWN, BURY MY HEART AT WOUNDED KNEE 2–5 (1972); FAIRFAX DOWNEY, INDIAN WARS OF THE U.S. ARMY (1776–1865) (1963); ROBERT A. WILLIAMS, THE AMERICAN INDIAN IN WESTERN LEGAL THOUGHT (1990).

35. DANIEL DEFOE, ROBINSON CRUSOE (Michael Shinagel ed., W. W. Norton & Co. 1975) (1719).

36. WILLIAM SHAKESPEARE, THE TEMPEST (Stephen Orgel ed., Oxford University Press 1987) (1611).

37. JAMES FENIMORE COOPER, THE LAST OF THE MOHICANS (William Chorvot ed., Houghton Mifflin 1958) (1826).

38. STEDMAN, *supra*, at 50–51; *see* JENNI CALDER, THERE MUST BE A LONE RANGER (1974).

39. STEDMAN, *supra*, at 75; *see* M. ROWLANDSON, THE SOVEREIGNTY & GOODNESS OF GOD, TOGETHER WITH THE FAITHFULNESS OF HIS PROMISES

Displayed: Being a Narrative of the Captivity and Restoration of Mrs. Mary Rowlandson (1682).

40. Stephen Osborne, *Indian-Hating in American Literature 1682–1859*, 50(10) Diss. Abstr. Int'l 3228A (1990); Stedman, *supra*, at 77–78 (historian Richard Drinnon has referred to this literature as "violence pornography").

41. Stedman, *supra*, at 78.

42. *Id.* at 121.

43. *Id.* at 123. For a treatment of the cannibal concept, see Michael Harner & Alfred Meyer, Cannibal (1979); Marvin Harris, Cannibals and Kings: The Origins of Cultures (1977).

44. Stedman, *supra*, at 125.

45. *Id.* at 126. Vine Deloria, Jr., wrote, "[w]e were never slaves. We gave up land instead of life and labor. Because the Negro labored, he was considered a draft animal. Because the Indian occupied large areas of land, he was considered a wild animal." Vine Deloria, Jr., Custer Died for Your Sins 7–8 (1969).

46. On Indians in films, see jon tuska, The Filming of the West (1976); John E. O'Connor, Hollywood: Stereotypes of Native Americans in Film (1980).

47. Similarly, stereotypes in adult fiction are replicated in juvenile literature. *See* "I" Is Not for Indian: The Portrayal of Native Americans in Books for Young People (Naomi Caldwell-Wood & Lisa A. Mitten comps., 1991); Magda Lewis, *Are Indians Nicer Now?*, *What Children Learn from Books about Native North Americans*, in How Much Truth Do We Tell the Children? The Politics of Children's Literature 135 (Betty Bacon ed., 1988).

48. Stedman, *supra*, at 209, 218–20.

49. *Id.* at 62.

50. *Id.* at 62–63; *see* William Penn's Own Account of the Lenni Lenapi or Delaware Indians (A. Myers ed., 1970).

51. *See* Alexander Saxton, The Indispensable Enemy: Labor and the Anti-chinese Movement in California 19–45 (1971); Wong, *supra*, at ii–v.

52. Saxton, *supra*, at 19–45; Wong, *supra*, at xi–xvii.

53. R. Westen, Racism in U.S. Imperialism: The Influence of Racial Assumptions on American Foreign Policy, 1893–1946 (1972) (reviewing history of immigration quotas and policies); Wong, *supra*, at xx. For a general treatment of anti-Asian sentiment, see stuart creighton miller, The Unwelcome Immigrant: The American Image of the Chinese 1785–1882 (1969).

54. Donald Hata, "Undesirables," Early Immigrants and the Anti-japanese Movement in San Francisco, 1892–1893 (1979); Miller, *supra*; Wong, *supra*, at xi–xvii.

55. *See* Chae Chan Ping v. United States, 130 U.S. 581 (1889); *see also* Shin S. Tsai, The Chinese Experience in America 56–81 (1986).

56. TAKAKI, *supra*; WONG, *supra*, at 3, 108.

57. WONG, *supra*, at 34–38, 55–103.

58. WONG, *supra*, at 74 (much in the manner that Hollywood created the "generic Indian" with either whites or Indians of any convenient tribe assigned to play the part).

59. *Id.* at 88–92.

60. *Id.* at 93.

61. *See* RICHARD GRIFFITH & ARTHUR MAYER, THE MOVIES 108 (1970). *Compare* WONG, *supra*, at 102–3, *with* SPLIT IMAGE, *supra* (discussing white actors in blackface portraying blacks in minstrel shows).

62. For two Supreme Court cases upholding curfews placed on Japanese Americans, see Hirabayashi v. United States, 320 U.S. 81 (1943), and Korematsu v. United States, 323 U.S. 214 (1944).

63. B. HOSOKAWA, NISEI: THE QUIET AMERICANS 348 (1969); *see* MAISIE CONRAT & RICHARD CONRAT, EXECUTIVE ORDER 9066: THE INTERNMENT OF 110,000 JAPANESE AMERICANS (1972).

64. HOSOKAWA, *supra*, at 292–301.

65. PETTIT, *supra* (cataloging and describing the evolution of these and related images). For treatments of Mexicans in popular and high literature, see C. ROBINSON, WITH THE EARS OF STRANGERS: THE MEXICAN IN AMERICAN LITERATURE (1963); C. ROBINSON, *Mexico and the Hispanic Southwest, in* AMERICAN LITERATURE (1970); Carl Allsup, *Who Done It? The Theft of Mexican American History,* 17 J. POPULAR CULTURE, Winter 1983, at 150.

66. If the Mexican is quiet, the observer will think, "Oh, he is one of that kind"; if ebullient and outgoing, will assimilate him or her to the other type, and so on.

67. PETTIT, *supra*, at 32–40. These images naturally tended to justify U.S. expansion. *See generally* RODOLFO ACUNA, OCCUPIED AMERICA: A HISTORY OF THE CHICANO (1981).

68. PETTIT, *supra*, at xiv-xvii; *see* Juan Garcia, *Americanization and the Mexican Immigrant, in* DIFFERENT SHORES, *supra* at 69, 69–70.

69. PETTIT, *supra*, at 22–25; *see also* CECIL ROBINSON, WITH THE EARS OF STRANGERS: THE MEXICAN IN AMERICAN LITERATURE (1963) (tracing this and other Latin stereotypes).

70. *See* PETTIT, *supra*, at 84–85.

71. *See id.* at 85–104; *see also* I & II ALBERT JOHANNSEN, THE HOUSE OF BEADLE AND ADAMS AND ITS DIME AND NICKLE NOVELS: THE STORY OF A VANISHED LITERATURE (1950).

72. *See* PETTIT, *supra*, at 131; for a filmography, see *id.* at 264–69.

73. *Id.* at 237–45.

74. In Plessy v. Ferguson, 163 U.S. 537, 550–51 (1896), the Court failed to see any difference between requiring blacks to sit in a separate railroad car and a

similar imposition on whites. For Taney, if blacks found that requirement demeaning, it was only because they chose to put that construction on it; the cars were equal. *See also* Herbert Wechsler, *Toward Neutral Principles of Constitutional Law*, 73 HARV. L. REV. 1 (1959) (making similar criticism of *Brown v. Board of Education:* whites forced to associate with blacks were mistreated just as seriously as blacks denied the right to associate with whites—both were denied freedom of action).

In the campus-speech controversy, some argue that the right of a racist to hurl an ethnic insult must be balanced against the right of a person of color not to receive it. Who is to say which right (to speak—or not to be spoken to) is superior? Denying one right strengthens the other, but only at the expense of the first.

75. On the view that the cost of racial remedies is always placed on blacks or low-income whites, see Derrick Bell, Bakke, *Minority Admissions, and the Usual Price of Racial Remedies*, 67 CAL. L. REV. 3 (1979).

76. On the reigning marketplace conception of free speech, see Abrams v. United States, 250 U.S. 616, 630 (1919) (Holmes, J., dissenting); ALEXANDER MEIKLEJOHN, FREE SPEECH AND ITS RELATION TO SELF-GOVERNMENT (1948); JOHN MILTON, AREOPAGITICA (Michael Davis ed., 1965) (classic early statement). *See also* Stanley Ingber, *The Marketplace of Ideas: A Legitimating Myth*, 1984 DUKE L.J. 1 ("market" shown to favor entrenched structure and ideology).

77. *Id.*; *see* MILNER BALL, LYING DOWN TOGETHER: LAW, METAPHOR AND THEOLOGY 135 (1985); 1 & 2 PAUL RICOEUR, TIME AND NARRATIVE (1984–85). For modernist/ postmodern expositions of this view, see, *e.g.*, PETER L. BERGER & THOMAS LUCKMAN, SOCIAL CONSTRUCTION OF REALITY (1967); NELSON GOODMAN, WAYS OF WORLDMAKING (1978).

78. *See Color Adjustment, supra* (noting that socially progressive TV shows from modern era—*e.g., East Side-West Side, Frank's Place, The Nat King Cole Show*--had brief runs, while *Amos 'N Andy* had a long run on both radio and TV). *Cf.* WAYNE C. BOOTH, THE COMPANY WE KEEP: AN ETHICS OF FICTION 40 (1988) (minds we use in judging and interpreting stories have been formed, in large part, by those very stories).

79. *E.g.*, SILK & SILK, *supra*, at 31–32, 45 (occasional writer or artist able somehow to work against weight of dominant narrative).

80. *E.g.*, CHARLES CHESNUTT, THE CONJURE WOMAN (1898); ZORA NEALE HURSTON, THEIR EYES WERE WATCHING GOD (1937).

81. Paul Gray & Bruce W. Nelan, *The Power of a Well-Told Tale*, TIME, Oct. 14, 1991, at 91.

82. For an earlier exposition of this view, see Richard Delgado, *Critical Legal Studies and the Realities of Race—Does the Fundamental Contradiction have a Corollary?*, 23 HARV. C.R.-C.L. L. REV. 407, 407–8 (1988).

83. City of Richmond v. J. A. Croson Co., 488 U.S. 469, 499–506 (1988); Thomas Ross, *The Richmond Narratives*, 68 TEX. L. REV. 381 (1989) (criticizing *Croson* Court for refusing to see racism in governmental history that to others spoke loudly).

84. *See* Darryl Brown, *Racism and Race Relations in the University*, 76 VA. L. REV. 295 (1990) (suggesting that we construct ideas of race and racism to make transgressions all but invisible); Lawrence, *The Id, the Ego and Equal Protection: Reckoning with Unconscious Racism*, 39 STAN. L. REV. 317 (1987) (stating that operation of unconscious masks racial acts).

85. The Willie Horton commercial depicted a black criminal recidivist. It aired as part of the 1988 presidential campaign as an attempt to portray the Democrats as soft on crime.

86. Charles Lawrence, *If He Hollers, Let Him Go*, 1990 DUKE L.J. 431, 466–67 (pointing out that courts construed First Amendment law narrowly, so as to uphold convictions of peaceful civil rights protestors; citing cases).

87. On "triumphalism"—the view that conquerors always construct history so that they appear to have won fairly through superior thought and culture rather than by force of arms, see Richard Delgado, *Norms and Normal Science: Toward a Critique of Normativity in Legal Thought*, 139 U. PA. L. REV. 933 (1991); Martin, *College Curriculum Scrutinized in "Politically Correct" Spotlight*, DENVER POST, Jan. 25, 1992; *cf.* MILTON, *supra*. For the view that many Enlightenment figures were genteel or not-so-genteel cultural supremacists, see BELL, *supra*, at 26–51 (pointing out that the document's Framers calculatedly sold out the interests of African-Americans in establishing a union of free propertied white males).

88. *See* Buckley v. Valeo, 424 U.S. 1, 17–19 (1976).

89. This "economic determinist" view is associated with Derrick Bell, and earlier with Charles Beard.

90. The American Civil Liberties Union, for example, follows a policy of challenging virtually every campus speech code as soon as it is enacted. *See, e.g.*, Doe v. University of Mich., 721 F. Supp. 852 (E.D. Mich. 1989); U.W.M. Post, Inc. v. Regents, Univ. of Wis., 774 F. Supp. 1163 (E.D. Wis. 1991).

91. Derrick Bell, *Racial Realism*, 24 CONN. L. REV. 1 (1992).

92. *E.g.*, RICHARD RODRIGUEZ, HUNGER OF MEMORY (1982); *see also* STEVEN CARTER, CONFESSIONS OF AN AFFIRMATIVE ACTION BABY (1991); THOMAS SOWELL, CIVIL RIGHTS: RHETORIC OR REALITY? (1984); SHELBY STEELE, THE CONTENT OF OUR CHARACTER: A NEW VISION OF RACE IN AMERICA (1990).

Notes to Chapter 6

*An earlier version of this chapter was written with the assistance of David Yun.

1. By paternalism, we mean a justification for curtailing someone's liberty

that invokes the well-being of the person concerned and requires him or her to do or refrain from doing something for his or her own good.

Could it be argued that the opposite position, namely advocacy of hate speech regulation, is also paternalistic, in that it implies that minorities need or want protection, when many may not? No. The impetus for such regulation comes mainly from minority attorneys and scholars. *See, e.g.,* Charles R. Lawrence III, *If He Hollers Let Him Go: Regulating Racist Speech on Campus,* 1990 Duke L.J. 431; Mari Matsuda, *Public Response to Racist Speech: Considering the Victim's Story,* 87 Mich. L. Rev. 2320 (1989). An argument emanating from the protected group cannot be paternalistic (although it could be misguided on other grounds). A gay who found gay-bashing inoffensive, or a Mexican who enjoyed being called "spic" or "wetback" has an easy recourse—not to file a complaint.

2. *See, e.g.,* Nat Hentoff, Free Speech for Me — But Not for Thee: How the American Left and Right Relentlessly Censor Each Other 18–41 (1992) [hereinafter Hentoff, Speech]; Marjorie Heins, *Banning Words: A Comment on "Words That Wound,"* 18 Harv. C.R.-C.L. L. Rev. 585, 592 n.39 (1983) [hereinafter Heins, *Banning*] ("Tolerating ugly, vicious speech is a small but necessary price to pay for the freedom to advocate social change and justice."); Nadine Strossen, *Regulating Hate Speech on Campus: A Modest Proposal?,* 1990 Dduke L.J. 484, 562–69 [hereinafter Strossen, *Regulating*] (arguing free speech protects minority groups and promotes social change toward racial equality). In the context of gender, see Nadine Strossen, *A Feminist Critique of "The" Feminist Critique of Pornography,* 79 Va. L. Rev. 1099, 1167–71 (1993) [hereinafter Strossen, *Critique*] (opposing anti-pornography rules in the interests of women). These are not the only arguments that are made against regulating hate speech, of course. *See* chapter 7. They are, however, an important set of arguments, because (1) they are prominently and frequently repeated; (2) they are insidious—those who make them can pretend to be serving minorities' best interest.

3. *See, e.g.,* Strossen, *Regulating, supra.*

4. The National Institute Against Prejudice and Violence estimates that twenty to twenty-five percent of minority students are victimized at least once during their college years. Deb Riechmann, *Colleges Tackle Increase in Racism on Campuses,* L.A. Times, Apr. 30, 1989, pt. I, at 36.

5. Michael Greve, Executive Director, Center for Individual Rights, Washington D.C., address at Michigan State University (Oct. 22, 1992).

6. For a recent discussion of the international dimensions of hate speech and hate crimes, see generally Striking a Balance: Hate Speech, Freedom of Expression and Non-discrimination (Sandra Coliver ed., 1992) [hereinafter Striking a Balance]. See also chapter 8.

7. University of Texas, General Information: Institutional Rules of Student Services and Activities 174 app. C (1990–91).

8. Diane Curtis, *Racial, Ethnic, Sexual Slurs Banned on U.C. Campuses*, S.F. CHRON., Sept. 27, 1989, at A1.

9. 721 F. Supp. 852 (E.D. Mich. 1989).

10. *Id.* at 856.

11. *Id.* at 864, 866 (citing Broadrick v. Oklahoma, 413 U.S. 601 (1973) (upholding state statute prohibiting state employee's receipt of political contributions and membership in political organizations because the act was "clear and precise")).

12. 774 F. Supp. 1163 (E.D. Wis. 1991).

13. 112 S. Ct. 2538 (1992).

14. *Id.* at 2541.

15. 113 S. Ct. 2194 (1993).

16. *Id.* at 2200. *See also* Barclay v. Florida, 463 U.S. 939, 947, 949 (1983) (holding the Constitution does not prohibit sentencing judge from considering racial hatred where it bears a rational nonarbitrary relationship to statutory aggravating factors). *But see* Dawson v. Delaware, 112 S. Ct. 1093, 1096–99 (1992) (holding that admission of defendant's membership in a white supremacist prison gang into evidence at sentencing hearing where this evidence was not relevant to any of the issues in the proceeding violated First Amendment rights).

17. 3 S.C.R. 697 (Can. 1990).

18. 89 D.L.R. 4th 449 (Can. 1992).

19. *See* chapter 1; Rhonda G. Hartman, *Revitalizing Group Defamation as a Remedy for Hate Speech on Campus*, 71 OR. L. REV. 855 (1992); Jean C. Love, *Discriminatory Speech and the Tort of Intentional Infliction of Emotional Distress*, 47 WASH. & LEE L. REV. 23 (1990); Shawna H. Yen, *Redressing the Victim of Racist Speech after R.A.V. v. St. Paul: A Proposal to Permit Recovery in Tort*, 26 COLUM. J.L. & SOC. PROBS. 589 (1993).

20. *See, e.g.*, HENTOFF, SPEECH, *supra*, at 134 (quoting Yale University president Benno Schmidt); *cf.* Strossen, *Critique*, *supra*, at 1140–41 (making a similar argument in the context of rules against pornography and their effect on women).

21. *See* GORDON W. ALLPORT, THE NATURE OF PREJUDICE 467–73 (1954) (rejecting view that racist conduct serves as catharsis and arguing that laws and norms against discrimination change behavior for the better); text *infra* (social science laboratory and field evidence). The mechanism by which racist speech and acts encourage further racist speech and acts probably consists of a combination of habituation (our tendency to repeat an action that is enjoyable and brings no penalty); cognitive dissonance ("he must deserve it—look how badly I treated him before"); and social construction of reality (the images we disseminate of and toward minorities create a world in which they are always one-down). *See also* Richard Delgado, *Rodrigo's Chronicle*, 101 YALE L.J. 1357, 1374 (1992) (on a fourth mechanism, perseveration, as a response to frustration and stress).

22. *See* Leonard Berkovitz, Aggression — Its Causes, Consequences and Control (1993); Mari Matsuda, *Victim's Story, supra* at 2329–31 (noting that racial violence is often preceded by racist propaganda or slurs); Leonard Berkowitz, *The Case for Bottling Up Rage*, Psychol. Today, July 1973, at 24.

23. Rick & Gail Luttman, Chickens in Your Backyard: A Beginner's Guide 121 (1976):

> Bored chicks often start by picking each other's toes (or even their own). Older birds may start picking at the base of the tail or near the vent. Should a bird get caught in a fence or otherwise trapped, the other chickens may mercilessly pick it until it is plucked bare and eaten alive. An injury of any sort provides an occasion for picking to start. The chickens may finish off one unfortunate bird and nonchalantly go on to eat others.

24. The experiment was first done by a third-grade school teacher from Riceville, Iowa, on April 5, 1968, in response to the death of Martin Luther King, Jr. *See* William Peters, A Class Divided: Then and Now (1971). The teacher, Jane Elliott, set out to teach her students what it would feel like to be discriminated against and made to feel inferior. On the day of the exercise, "Discrimination Day," she divided the class into two groups, one consisting of blue-eyed children, the other of brown-eyed ones. For that day, the brown-eyed group would be treated as superior to the blue-eyed ones: better, cleaner, more civilized, and smarter. They were also given extra privileges, including additional recess time and use of the playground equipment, and granted an opportunity to go to lunch first. Moreover, they could drink directly and at will from the fountain. The behavioral effects of this staged demonstration were striking: the young brown-eyed children immediately sat up straighter in their chairs than their blue-eyed classmates, who behaved listlessly and raised their hands less often. Within a short time the brown-eyed students seemed actually to believe they were superior. The next day, the teacher repeated the experiment but reversed the roles; this time the previously inferior blue-eyed children displayed greater alertness and self-confidence. Even more significantly, the students' performance on tests of spelling, math, and reading changed on the day of the exercise, exactly in accord with the behavioral changes. The exercise was subsequently repeated in several settings, including correctional facilities, with the same results. *Id.*; *see also PBS Frontline: A Class Divided* (PBS television broadcast, May 11, 1970; rebroadcast 1985).

25. Craig Haney et al., *Interpersonal Dynamics in a Simulated Prison*, 1 Int'l J. Criminol. & Penology 69, 80–81 (1973) (reporting the guards began to haze, browbeat, and even physically mistreat the prisoners).

26. Diane Sculley, Understanding Sexual Violence 100–117 (1990).

27. Stanley Milgram, Obedience to Authority (1974) (reporting results

of experiment in which one subject administered an electric shock to another when the latter missed a question asked by an authority figure).

28. *See, e.g.*, HENTOFF, SPEECH, *supra*, at 169 (quoting Eleanor Holmes Norton); Strossen, *Critique, supra*, at 1143–46; Strossen, *Regulating, supra*, at 512.

29. Nadine Strossen, ACLU National President, address to the Judicial Conference, Tenth Circuit Court of Appeals, Durango, Colo. (July 1992); *see also* Henry Louis Gates, *Let Them Talk*, NEW REPUB., Sept. 20 & 27, 1993, at 37, 44 (attributing same view to Strossen in the context of enforcement of University of Michigan speech code).

30. *See, e.g., Race Bias Prompted Most Hate Crimes: FBI's First National Statistics Show Blacks as Main Target*, S.F. CHRON., Jan. 5, 1993, at A2 [hereinafter Race Bias] (reporting national statistics); Thom Shanker, *Hate-Crime Numbers Rise*, DENVER POST, June 29, 1994, at 2–A. *But see* Eugene H. Czajkoski, *Criminalizing Hate: An Empirical Assessment*, FED. PROBATION, Sept. 1992, at 36, 38 (reporting Florida statistics, inconsistent with national figures, which showed 43 percent of hate crimes were committed by blacks against whites, while 39 percent were committed by whites against blacks).

31. *See* Riechmann, *supra*.

32. *See* STRIKING A BALANCE, *supra*, at 109, 221, 223, 240, 259, 307 (describing efforts of various countries to control hate speech).

33. Strossen, *Regulating, supra*, at 567.

34. *See, e.g.*, Strossen, *Critique, supra*, at 1166–71 (noting that curtailing speech might have some costs for feminists); Anthony Lewis, address at the University of California Extension, Sacramento, Cal. (Feb. 1992).

35. *See, e.g.*, Charles Lawrence, *If He Hollers, supra*, at 466–67 ("Our petitions often go unanswered until they disrupt business as usual and require the self-interested attention of those persons in power. Paradoxically, the disruption that renders this speech effective usually causes it to be considered undeserving of first amendment protection"). We are not arguing that speech and remonstrance are ineffective tools for the reformer; rather, we believe that our legal system and its definition of free speech often stand in the way of effective protest and communication.

36. *See* STANLEY FISH, IS THERE A TEXT IN THIS CLASS? (1980) (arguing that members of different "interpretive communities" will perceive the same message very differently).

37. *See, e.g.*, HENTOFF, SPEECH, *supra*, at 100–102, 111, 159, 167; Strossen, *Regulating, supra*, at 562 (urging government officials, private individuals and groups, and civil libertarians to speak out against racism); Jon Wiener, *Racial Hatred on Campus*, THE NATION, Feb. 27, 1989, at 260, 262 (advocating that university leaders also speak out).

38. *See* HENTOFF, SPEECH, *supra*, at 167.

39. *See* Linmark Associates v. Township of Willingboro, 431 U.S. 85, 97 (1977) (citing Whitney v. California, 274 U.S. 357, 377 (1927) (Brandeis, J., concurring)); *see also* LAURENCE TRIBE, AMERICAN CONSTITUTIONAL LAW § 12–8, at 837 (2d ed. 1988) (noting that First Amendment protection should apply to speech when dialogue is possible, that is when "talk leaves room for reply").

40. Benno Schmidt, President, Yale University, Remarks at *Campus Speech*, panel discussion at Yale Law School (Oct. 1, 1991).

41. *See, e.g.*, Sally McGrath, *Student Denies Insulting Black during Scuffle*, BOULDER (CO) DAILY CAMERA, Aug. 28, 1993, at B-1; Manning Marable, *No Longer as Simple as Black and White*, BOULDER (CO) DAILY CAMERA, Aug. 12, 1993, at B-3 (describing Florida prosecution of assailants who murdered a black person who talked back following a racial slur).

42. *See* Marable, *supra*.

43. Some might suggest that the student should "talk back" by publishing these remarks rather than saying them directly to the hate-speaker, but that approach is unlikely to be any more successful. First, it provides little comfort or protection for the student at the very moment when his psyche, and perhaps his body, are in danger. Second, remarks on a printed page are no more likely to affect the bigoted speaker than they would if spoken directly to him.

44. *See* R.A.V. v. City of St. Paul, 112 S. Ct. 2538, 2543–49 (1992).

45. Need for a rule can be documented through hearings on the extent of the problem of campus racism and by showing that other approaches such as counseling, lectures, and special seminars have failed to control it.

46. On fighting words, see Chaplinsky v. New Hampshire, 315 U.S. 568, 569, 572 (1942) (upholding conviction of Jehovah's Witness who called city marshall a "God damned racketeer" and a "damned Fascist" on the ground that words which "by their very utterance inflict injury or tend to incite an immediate breach of the peace" are not protected by the First Amendment). The fighting words doctrine was later recharacterized by the Court to encompass "those personally abusive epithets which, when addressed to the ordinary citizen, are, as a matter of common knowledge, inherently likely to provoke violent reaction." Cohen v. California, 403 U.S. 15, 20 (1971). *See also* Rodney A. Smolla, *Rethinking First Amendment Assumptions about Racist and Sexist Speech*, 47 WASH. & LEE L. REV. 171, 198 (1990) ("Nearly everyone seems to concede that a verbal attack directed at a particular individual in the sort of face-to-face confrontation that presents a clear and present danger of a violent physical reaction may be penalized").

47. *See* Title VII, 42 U.S.C.A. 2000e-2(a) (1988); Meritor Savings Bank v. Vinson, 477 U.S. 57, 67 (1986). For a campus hate speech rule drafted in language that parallels workplace harassment regulation, see text *infra*.

48. *See, e.g.*, MICHAEL OLIVAS, THE LAW AND HIGHER EDUCATION 599–601 (1989); *see also* Mary Becker, *Conservative Free Speech and the Uneasy Case for*

Judicial Review, 64 U. COLO. L. REV. 975, 1040 (1993) (arguing that the university has compelling interest in providing atmosphere that is conducive to learning).

49. *See* Wisconsin v. Mitchell, 113 S. Ct. 2194 (1992); *see also* Barclay v. Florida, 463 U.S. 939 (1983) (allowing sentencing judge in capital trial to consider racist motivation of criminal when deciding whether to impose the death penalty). This second provision would apply to all campus offenses, such as stealing books and tampering with student records—not just hate speech.

50. The institution's interests are noninterference with the ability of a member of the community to carry out his or her work and studies, and maintenance of the peace. *See* Becker, *supra*, at 1040.

51. The first provision would be race-neutral, prohibiting only "serious, face-to-face insults calculated to interfere with a student's or worker's ability to carry out recognized campus functions, such as studying, working, and attending class" (or words to that effect). For a different approach based on the fighting-words exception, see text *supra*.

52. *See* RESTATEMENT (SECOND) OF TORTS § 46, cmt. f (1965) (exploiting a known susceptibility); chapter 3, *supra* (commenting on this provision).

53. Racial remarks are one of the most pervasive means by which discriminatory attitudes are imparted. They ritually inscribe and reinscribe racial hierarchy, reminding both the speaker and the victim where each stands in a society in which color matters. *See, e.g.,* ALLPORT, *supra*, at 77–78. The racial epithet communicates the message that racial distinctions demarcate those with worth, merit, status, and personhood from those without. Kenneth Clark, black psychologist and past president of the American Psychological Association, writes: "Human beings . . . whose daily experience tells them that almost nowhere in society are they respected and granted the ordinary dignity and courtesy accorded to others will, as a matter of course, begin to doubt their own worth." KENNETH CLARK, DARK GHETTO 63–64 (1965).

The psychological responses to racial tags and stigmatization include feelings of humiliation, anger, stress, self-hatred, and demoralization. ALLPORT, *supra*, at 142–61; MARY ELLEN GOODMAN, RACE AWARENESS IN YOUNG CHILDREN 55–58, 60 (rev. ed. 1964); GEORGE E. SIMPSON & J. MILTON YINGER, RACIAL AND CULTURAL MINORITIES: AN ANALYSIS OF PREJUDICE AND DISCRIMINATION 157–58 (4th ed. 1972); Ruben Martinez & Richard Dukes, *Ethnic and Gender Differences in Self-Esteem*, 22 YOUTH & SOC'Y 318, 332 (1991). The insult spoken is eventually overheard; its message is transmitted to succeeding generations. GOODMAN, *supra*. Race hatred becomes internalized, affecting the victim's self-regard and even relations with his or her own group. *See generally id.*; KENNETH CLARK, PREJUDICE AND YOUR CHILD 51 (1963).

Although the emotional damage of a particular affront is variable, depending on the setting, the victim's age, and other factors, the racial insult is always a dignitary harm, a violation of the victim's right to be treated respectfully. *See*

ALLPORT, *supra*, at 49–51. It violates principles of equality of all as moral agents enshrined in the Declaration of Independence and the equality-protecting provisions of the U.S. Constitution, U.S. Const. amends. XIII-XV, as well as various federal legislative acts, such as the Civil Rights Act of 1964, Pub. L. No. 88–352, 78 Stat. 241 (1964), *codified as amended at* 28 U.S.C. 1447, 42 U.S.C. 1971, 1975a-1975d, 2000a to 2000h-6 (1980).

54. On the role that fear to censorship, especially prior restraint, plays in First Amendment jurisprudence, see, *e.g.*, Abrams v. United States, 250 U.S. 616, 626–30 (1919) (Holmes, J., dissenting); ZECHARIAH CHAFEE, FREE SPEECH IN THE UNITED STATES 223–25, 314, 497–501 (1941).

55. Dun & Bradstreet, Inc., v. Greenmoss Builders, Inc., 472 U.S. 749, 759–60 (1985) (in a private-speech case, "there is no threat to the free and robust debate of public issues; there is no potential interference with a meaningful dialogue of ideas concerning self-government") (quoting Harley-Davidson v. Markley, 279 Ore. 361, 366 (1977)).

56. *See* TRIBE, *supra*, at 861 (discussing libel as assault and therefore justifying government interference). Most of the fighting-words cases concerned police officers and other governmental figures. *See, e.g.*, Lewis v. New Orleans, 415 U.S. 130 (1974); Gooding v. Wilson, 405 U.S. 518 (1972); Cohen v. California, 403 U.S. 15 (1971); Chaplinsky v. New Hampshire, 315 U.S. 568 (1942).

57. *See generally* Kenneth Karst, *Equality as a Central Principle in the First Amendment*, 43 U. CHI. L. REV. 20 (1975).

58. 112 S. Ct. 2538, 2548–49 (1992).

59. KENNETH J. DOVER, GREEK HOMOSEXUALITY 34 (1978).

60. See chapters 1, 2, and 5, this volume.

61. Just as some out-and-out racists seem to believe that they may do or say anything against members of minority groups with impunity, so some majoritarian commentators in the hate speech debate appear to believe that they may employ the most caustic language toward those on the other side, secure in the belief that those who defend the minority position will not respond. *See, e.g.*, Jonathan Yardley, *The Code Word: Alarming*, WASH. POST, Aug. 16, 1993, at B-2 (labeling the campus hate speech rules "a peculiar blend of totalitarianism and phrenology"; dismissing allegations of harm as "pop psychology"; characterizing the position of hate speech rule advocates as a case of evasion, euphemism, zealotry, newspeak, thought-police tactics, fascism, doublethink, ludicrous reasoning, and an "Orwellian nightmare").

62. 163 U.S. 537 (1896).

Notes to Chapter 7

*An earlier version of this chapter was written with the assistance of David Yun.

1. Isak Dinesen, Babette's Feast (Vintage Books, 1988).

2. By the term we mean those of centrist or moderately right-leaning persuasion who disavow liberalism or radical politics in search of change. *See generally* Gary Dorrien, The Neoconservative Mind: Politics, Culture and the War of Ideology (Temple U. 1993) (discussing the rise of the new conservatives). In this chapter, we focus on four authors—Donald Lively, Henry Louis Gates, Stephen Carter, and Dinesh D'Souza—who have written extensively about the hate speech controversy. Although we take issue with the general positions these authors take, we intend the term "neoconservative" in no disrespectful sense. Moreover, we write fully aware that social and political positions are not fixed or unitary, and that a person who is conservative or neoconservative on one issue may be progressive on another. *See* Richard Delgado, *Zero-Based Racial Politics: An Evaluation of Three Best-Case Arguments on Behalf of the Nonwhite Underclass*, 78 Georgetown L.J. 1929, 1931–45 (1990) (urging coalition with conservatives).

3. *See* Delgado, 78 Georgetown L.J. at 1932, 1940–45, 1947–48 (noting the incipient alliance between civil rights activists and progressive Republicans).

4. *See* chapter 3, this volume.

5. Donald E. Lively, *Reformist Myopia and the Imperative of Progress: Lessons for the Post-Brown Era*, 46 Vand. L. Rev. 865, 892 (1994).

6. *Id. See also id.* at 875, 880.

7. *See id.* at 892.

8. Dinesh D'Souza, Illiberal Education: The Politics of Race and Sex on Campus 140–55, 230–42 (Free 1991).

9. Stephen Carter, Reflections of an Affirmative Action Baby 177, 180–81 (Basic Books 1992).

10. Henry Louis Gates, Jr., *Let Them Talk: Why Civil Liberties Pose No Threat to Civil Rights*, New Republic 37, 43, 47–49 (Sept. 22 & 27, 1993) (reviewing Matsuda et al., *Words That Wound*.

11. *Id.* at 42–43.

12. On this form of racism, *see generally* Thomas F. Pettigrew, *New Patterns of Racism: Different Worlds of 1984 and 1964*, 37 Rutgers L. Rev. 673 (1985); Sheri Lynn Johnson, *Unconscious Racism and the Criminal Law*, 73 Cornell L. Rev. 1016 (1988); Charles R. Lawrence III, *The Id, The Ego, and Equal Protection: Reckoning with Unconscious Racism*, 39 Stan. L. Rev. 317 (1987).

13. Lively, 46 Vand. L. Rev. at 875–81.

14. *Id.* at 869, 884, 895–96.

15. Gates, New Republic at 44.

16. *Id.* at 42, 48–49.

17. Carter, Affirmative Action Baby at 180–81.

18. *See generally* Howard J. Ehrlich, *Campus Ethnoviolence: A Research Review*

(National Inst. Against Prejudice and Violence, 1992); National Inst. Against Prejudice and Violence, Community Response to Bias-Crimes and Ethnoviolent Incidents (1993) (discussing campuses that have adopted speech codes); Delgado, 85 NW. U. L. Rev. at 343–58 & n.121.

19. Carter, Affirmative Action Baby at 179.

20. D'Souza, Illiberal Education at 231–42 (suggesting that special programs and codes are necessary because affirmative action has failed or has been overly ambitious).

21. Vince Herron, Note, *Increasing the Speech: Diversity, Campus Speech Codes, and the Pursuit of Truth,* 67 S. Cal. L. Rev. 407, 424 (1994).

22. One may sometimes avoid, steel, or prepare oneself for the onslaught of the racist who is known, but not, of course, the one who is unknown.

23. *See* Gordon Allport, The Nature of Prejudice 62, 252, 460–61, 467–72 (Addison Wesley 1979) (suggesting that laws create and reinforce a common conscience and sense that racism and prejudice are wrong).

24. The costs include the physical and pecuniary burdens of holding hearings; the bureaucratization of university life; and the possibility that false or exaggerated charges may be filed. On the whole, these charges seem no greater than for other campus offenses, for example, cheating or plagiarism.

25. *See* D'Souza, Illiberal Education at 153 (cited in note 32) (pointing out John Stuart Mill's argument that even offensive speech serves the purpose of illustrating error); Carter, Affirmative Action Baby at 175 (stating that "on a university campus, perhaps more than any place else, unfettered debate is essential").

26. Carter, Affirmative Action Baby at 177.

27. Lively, 46 Vand. L. Rev. at 898.

28. D'Souza, Illiberal Education at 128, 239.

29. Gates, New Republic at 46–48.

30. *See* Ehrlich et al., *The Traumatic Impact of Ethnoviolence,* in The Price We Pay (L. Lederer & R. Delgado eds., 1996).

31. Gates, New Republic at 45.

32. Lively, 46 Vand. L. Rev. at 893–94.

33. D'Souza, Illiberal Education at 241.

34. Gates, New Republic at 38.

35. *Id.* at 37–38.

36. Lively, 46 Vand. L. Rev. at 879, 884, 897.

37. On the fear of governmental abuse and censorship, *see* Strossen, 1990 Duke L.J. at 489–92, 520–22, 533–38; Carter, Affirmative Action Baby at 176–78; Lively, 46 Vand. L. Rev. at 884; Gates, New Republic at 38.

38. On the fear of governmental censorship as animating much of First Amendment law, *see* Zachariah Chafee, Free Speech in the United States

19–21 (Harvard U. 1941). *See also* New York Times Co. v. Sullivan, 376 U.S. 254, 273 (1964).

39. *See* Charles R. Lawrence III, *If He Hollers, Let Him Go: Regulating Racist Speech on Campus*, 1990 DUKE L.J. 431, 452 (positing that racist speech is not intended to invite discussion, but is more like a slap in the face).

40. On the silencing argument, *see id.* at 452–56. For a general discussion of the topic, *see* Cass Sunstein, *Words, Conduct, Caste*, 60 U. CHI. L. REV. 795 (1993).

41. On the marketplace theory of the First Amendment, see Abrams v. United States, 250 U.S. 616, 624 (1919) (Holmes, J., dissenting). For a critique of that theory, *see generally* Stanley Ingber, *The Marketplace of Ideas: A Legitimizing Myth*, 1984 DUKE L.J. 1.

42. *See generally* Ehrlich et al., *The Traumatic Impact of Ethnoviolence, supra*; chapter 1, this volume.

43. *See generally* ELLIS COSE, THE RAGE OF A PRIVILEGED CLASS (HarperCollins 1993); Carter, Affirmative Action Baby.

44. It often is not. Hate speech is often uttered in many-on-one situations where a response is foolhardy. Indeed, many reported cases of hate crimes apparently began this way: a group of whites taunted a gay or black, who spoke back and was beaten or killed for his pains.

Notes to Chapter 8

1. STRIKING A BALANCE: HATE SPEECH, FREEDOM OF EXPRESSION AND NON-DISCRIMINATION (Sandra Coliver ed., 1992) [hereinafter STRIKING A BALANCE].

2. Kevin Boyle, *Overview of a Dilemma, in* STRIKING A BALANCE, *supra* at 1–8.

3. Paul Gordon, *Racist Violence: The Expression of Hatred in Europe, in* STRIKING A BALANCE, *supra* at 9–17.

4. *Id.* at 4.

5. *Id.* at 7.

6. Gordon, *supra* at 9–17.

7. STRIKING A BALANCE, *supra* at 75–312.

8. *Id.* at 315–46.

9. *Id.* at 222, 235–36, 237.

10. *Id.* at 242.

11. *Id.* at 195, 235.

12. *Id.* at 138, 221.

13. *Id.* at 223.

14. *Id.* at 194.

15. *Id.* at 240.

16. *See* STRIKING A BALANCE, *supra* at 106–29, 140–70, 201–7.

17. *Id.* at 155.

18. *Id.* at 168.

19. *Id.* at 234; *but see* Gilbert Marcus, *Racial Hostility: The South African Experience, in* STRIKING A BALANCE, *supra* at 208–22 (pointing out that in the old regime, hate-speech laws were used actively, but always against blacks).

20. STRIKING A BALANCE, *supra* at 122.

21. *Id.* at 259.

22. *Id.* at 123–24.

23. *Id.* at 130.

24. *Id.* at 140.

25. *Id.* at 148.

26. *Id.* at 159, 165.

27. STRIKING A BALANCE, *supra* at 9–17.

28. *Id.* at 171, 178–79.

29. *Id.* at 182.

30. *Id.* at 239.

31. *Id.* at 257.

32. STRIKING A BALANCE, *supra* at 15.

33. *Id.* at 159.

34. [1990] 3 S.C.R. 697 (Can.).

35. STRIKING A BALANCE, *supra* at 156.

36. *Id.* at 160, 163, 169.

37. *Id.* at 200.

38. *Id.* at 204.

39. *Id.* at 209.

40. STRIKING A BALANCE, *supra* at 262.

41. [1990] 3 S.C.R. 697, 745–49, 758, 811–12 (Can.).

42. STRIKING A BALANCE, *supra* at 156.

43. *Id.* at 245.

44. *Id.* at 135.

45. *Id.* at 191.

46. STRIKING A BALANCE, *supra* at 207.

47. *Id.* at 254–55.

48. *Id.* at 104.

49. Robert Post, *The Constitutional Concept of Public Discourse: Outrageous Opinion, Democratic Deliberation and* Hustler Magazine v. Falwell, 103 HARV. L. REV. 603, 645 (1990).

50. Frank Michelman, *Foreword: Traces of Self-Government*, 100 HARV. L. REV. 4, 27 n.86 (1986).

51. STRIKING A BALANCE, *supra* at 171–81.

52. *Id.* at 130–35; *see also id.* at 238–39.

53. Martin Redish & Gary Lippman, *Freedom of Expression and the Civic Republic Revival in Constitutional Theory: The Ominous Implications*, 79 CAL. L. REV. 267, 302–3 (1991); Nat Hentoff, *Free Speech on the Campus*, 53 THE PROGRESSIVE 12 (May 1989); *Voodoo Constitutional Law*, VILLAGE VOICE, Aug. 29, 1989, at 20.

Notes to Chapter 9

1. On the role of perspective in addressing racial harms, see, *e.g.*, Richard Delgado, *The Imperial Scholar: Reflections on a Review of Civil Rights Literature*, 132 U. PA. L. REV. 561, 568–69 (1984); Richard Delgado & Jean Stefancic, *Norms and Narratives: Can Judges Avoid Serious Moral Error?*, 69 TEX. L. REV. 1929, 1930 (1991) [hereinafter Delgado & Stefancic, *Norms and Narratives*] (criticizing judges' inability to understand the experiences of others); Charles Lawrence, *If He Hollers, Let Him Go: Regulating Racist Speech on Campus*, 1990 DUKE L.J. 431, 434–35 (explaining operation of perspective and experience in the hate-speech debate); Mari J. Matsuda, *Public Response to Racist Speech: Considering the Victim's Story*, 87 MICH. L. REV. 2320, 2335 (1989) (advocating narrow hate-speech exception to First Amendment).

2. Examples of the sort of categorical thinking we describe are legion. *Compare* R.A.V. v. City of St. Paul, 112 S. Ct. 2538 (1992) *and* Doe v. University of Mich., 721 F. Supp. 852 (E.D. Mich. 1989) (characterizing cases before them almost exclusively as First Amendment problems) *with* Loving v. Virginia, 388 U.S. 1 (1967) *and* Brown v. Board of Educ., 347 U.S. 483 (1954) (characterizing cases almost solely in protection-of-equality terms, even though they also contained regulatory and liberty components weighing in the other direction). All four of these cases contained both liberty and equality elements, and could have been characterized either way. By choosing the paradigm, the Court chose the outcome.

3. *See, e.g.*, Robert M. O'Neil, *Colleges Should Seek Educational Alternatives to Rules that Override the Historic Guarantees of Free Speech*, CHRON. HIGHER EDUC., Oct. 18, 1989, at B1, B3; Garry Wills, *In Praise of Censure*, TIME, July 31, 1989, at 71–72.

4. For commentators who fear that inroads into First Amendment doctrine will lead to censorship, see, *e.g.*, ZECHARIAH CHAFEE, JR., FREE SPEECH IN THE UNITED STATES 223–25 (1942) [hereinafter Chafee, FREE SPEECH]; George Will, *Academic Liberals' Brand of Censorship*, S.F. CHRON., Nov. 7, 1989, at A22.

5. On the harms of hate speech, see chapters 1, 2, this volume; Matsuda, *supra*.

6. U.S. Const. amend. XIII (forbidding slavery); U.S. Const. amend. XIV (providing for equal protection of the laws); U.S. Const. amend. XV (protecting right to vote). For an earlier discussion of this "equality paradigm," see Delgado, *Norms and Narratives, supra*, at 381–83.

7. The First Amendment paradigm includes suspicion of self-aggrandizing and illegitimate arrogation of power by a regulator of some sort. *See* CHAFEE, FREE SPEECH, *supra*, at 218–32, 314, 497–501. The defenders of minority rights fear the opposite—a deficiency of zeal or expertise in the arbiters of social equality.

8. *See generally* CHAFEE, FREE SPEECH, *supra*.

9. *See, e.g., id.* at 497–501; LIBERTY OF THE PRESS FROM ZENGER TO JEFFERSON (L. Levy ed., 1966).

10. *See* CHAFEE, FREE SPEECH, *supra*, at 497–501; Richard Delgado & David R. Millen, *God, Galileo and Government: Toward Constitutional Protection for Scientific Inquiry*, 53 WASH. L. REV. 349, 354–56 (1978); *see also* Dennis v. United States, 341 U.S. 494, 583 (1951) (Douglas, J., dissenting) (praising the Framers for redefining common-law treason to require an overt act).

11. *See generally* DERRICK BELL, RACE, RACISM AND AMERICAN LAW (2d ed. 1980) [hereinafter BELL, RACE, RACISM]; VINCENT HARDING, THERE IS A RIVER: THE BLACK STRUGGLE FOR FREEDOM IN AMERICA (1981).

12. For histories of these movements and heroes, see, *e.g.*, Plessy v. Ferguson, 163 U.S. 537, 552–64 (1896) (Harlan, J., dissenting); Harding, *supra*; JUAN WILLIAMS, EYES ON THE PRIZE: AMERICA'S CIVIL RIGHTS YEARS, 1954–1965 (1987).

13. On the ubiquitous balancing approach deployed in various areas of constitutional law, see LAURENCE H. TRIBE, AMERICAN CONSTITUTIONAL LAW 457, 789–94, 944–45, 977–87, 1037–39, 1251–55 (2d ed. 1988).

14. Stephen G. Gey, *The Unfortunate Revival of Civic Republicanism*, 141 U. PA. L. REV. 801, 888–89 (1993) (criticizing search for community values as inherently favoring status quo); Martin H. Redish & Gary Lippman, *Freedom of Expression and the Civic Republican Revival in Constitutional Theory: The Ominous Implications*, 79 CALIF. L. REV. 267, 294–97 (1991) (warning that deference to community values leads to censorship).

15. Nadine Strossen, *Regulating Hate Speech on Campus: A Modest Proposal?*, 1990 DUKE L.J. 484, 567–68 [hereinafter Strossen, *Regulating*].

16. Lawrence, *supra*, at 437.

17. *See id.* at 452–54 (explaining that historical association of racial epithets with violence against minorities often renders listener powerless to respond). One also recalls those parents who pretend to be "democratic" with their children: "Johnny, it's time we discussed your room."

18. On the difficulty of communication and dialogue when the subject of discussion concerns strongly held values rooted in radically different worldviews, see ALASDAIR MACINTYRE, AFTER VIRTUE 6–10 (2d ed. 1984).

19. For a lucid exposition of this concept, see generally STANLEY FISH, IS THERE A TEXT IN THIS CLASS? 14 (1980).

20. A group that enacted rules against self-criticism would resist evolution and orderly change. On this dialectic function of speech, see generally THOMAS I. EMERSON, THE SYSTEM OF FREEDOM OF EXPRESSION (1970).

21. That is, he or she is calibrating the two parts of the speech-community dyad so as to produce, in effect, a new dyad or interpretive community.

22. For example, "Should I approve this hate-speech rule which the adminis-tration of University X has enacted and the ACLU has challenged? My brother Judge Y thinks—, but the case law seems to hold—; moreover, there seem to be strong policy reasons in favor of—. Maybe I'll ask counsel what he or she thinks."

23. Thus, for example, the judge's understanding of such terms as "insult" (mild or serious?), "dignity," "fair," and "free," will affect, and almost predeter-mine, the outcome of a case implicating the boundaries of the interpretive com-munity. The judge's experiences with insult and invective, with black people, with historical episodes such as the Hollywood blacklist, and so on, will all play a role in that understanding.

24. See Richard Delgado, *Shadowboxing: An Essay on Power*, 77 CORNELL L. REV. 813, 817–19 (1992) [hereinafter Delgado, *Essay on Power*] (describing the ways in which cultural power encodes itself in the very meanings and pictures we use to communicate and understand social reality). In the analogous context of the role of patriarchy in modern society, see generally CATHARINE A. MACKINNON, FEMINISM UNMODIFIED: DISCOURSES ON LIFE AND LAW (1987) [hereinafter MACKINNON, FEMINISM UNMODIFIED]; CATHARINE A. MACKINNON, TOWARD A FEMINIST THEORY OF THE STATE (1989) [hereinafter MACKINNON, FEMINIST THEORY] (both detailing the way in which male power, or patriarchy, affects everything we do and see).

25. See Delgado & Stefancic, *Norms and Narratives, supra*, at 1956–57.

26. President's Message to Congress, CONG. GLOBE, 34th Cong., 3d Sess., app. 1, 1 (1857).

27. See ERVING GOFFMAN, STIGMA: NOTES ON THE MANAGEMENT OF SPOILED IDENTITY 2–8 (Touchstone 1986) (discussing generally the socially con-structed stigmatization of the ugly, deformed, and racially different, and detailing individual responses and adaptations to that construction).

28. That is, communication presupposes a common store of meanings, inten-tions, understandings, etc.

29. Delgado & Stefancic, *Norms and Narratives, supra*, at 1930, 1955 (arguing that judges are little better able than average people to escape current understand-ings of social reality).

30. *Id.* at 1934–52 (citing examples of judicial opinions written by eminent justices who misread how history would later judge these opinions).

31. See Delgado, *Essay on Power, supra*, at 818–19; *see generally* MICHEL FOU-CAULT, POWER/KNOWLEDGE (1980) (describing the way social discourse inscribes

and reinscribes power relations through what we decide to call "knowledge"); MacKinnon, Feminism Unmodified, *supra*; MacKinnon, Feminist Theory, *supra*.

32. *See, e.g.,* President's Message to Congress, *supra* (announcing that the State of the Union address is the product of impartial assessment of the country's interests, and denouncing abolitionism as an appeal to passion, prejudice, and hatred); Richard Delgado, *Rodrigo's Fourth Chronicle: Neutrality and Stasis in Anti-discrimination Law,* 45 Stan. L. Rev. 1133, 1139–47 (1993) (explaining how neutral principles of constitutional law disadvantage minority groups). We suspect that this observation is true beyond law—medical knowledge benefits doctors, military doctrine benefits generals, and so on. Generally, knowledge benefits those who control it.

33. *See* Bell, Race, Racism, *supra*, at 2–51 (providing historical illustrations of the themes of American racism).

34. *Id.* at 20–25; *see also* Derrick Bell, And We Are Not Saved: The Elusive Quest for Racial Justice 26–50 (1989) [hereinafter Bell, Not Saved] (discussing Constitutional Convention in light of fictional conversation with "Geneva").

35. On the way legal categories, headnotes, index numbers, and other research tools limit and confine legal thought and imagination, see generally Richard Delgado & Jean Stefancic, *Why Do We Tell the Same Stories? Law Reform, Critical Librarianship, and the Triple Helix Dilemma,* 42 Stan. L. Rev. 207 (1989) [hereinafter Delgado & Stefancic, *Triple Helix Dilemma*].

36. For statistics on recent Clinton appointees to the American judiciary, see Naftali Bendavid, *Diversity Marks Clinton Judiciary,* Recorder, Dec. 30, 1993, at 1 (giving net worths and law school alma maters of 27 recent Clinton federal judiciary nominees, seven of whom are worth more than one million dollars and only two of whom are worth less than $200,000); *see generally* 1 & 2 Almanac of the Federal Judiciary (1992).

37. Ass'n of Amer. Law Schools, Friday, January 8, 1993, AALS Plenary Session, 1993 A.A.L.S. Proc. 70.

38. *See Triple Helix Dilemma, supra,* at 213, 215–22; *see also Essay on Power, supra,* at 822–24.

39. On this legitimation function, see Alan D. Freeman, *Legitimizing Racial Discrimination through Antidiscrimination Law: A Critical Review of Supreme Court Doctrine,* 62 Minn. L. Rev. 1049, 1054–55 (1978).

40. *See* Derrick Bell, *Brown v. Board of Education and the Interest-Convergence Dilemma,* 93 Harv. L. Rev. 518, 524 (1980) [hereinafter Bell, *Interest-Convergence Dilemma*] (arguing that desegregation occurred only when it had become advantageous for elite whites).

41. Stanley Fish, Professor of Law and English, Duke University, address to

AALS Plenary Panel, San Francisco, California (Jan. 5, 1993). For a broader perspective on the general cultural canon in the United States, see generally Henry Louis Gates, Jr., LOOSE CANONS: NOTES ON THE CULTURE WARS (1992) (examining the impact of multiculturalism, nationalism, and the politics of identity on American society, education, and culture).

42. *See* Bell, *Interest-Convergence Dilemma, supra,* at 523–24.

43. Bell, *Interest-Convergence Dilemma, supra,* at 523; *see generally* Bell, RACE, RACISM, *supra* (economic determinist view of racial progress).

44. For example, it seems plausible that society began to take the rights of the mentally ill seriously when cures became possible and hospitalization costly, and that children's rights acquired urgency only when society began to need a reliable supply of healthy, well-educated workers for an industrial-technological economy.

45. For exposition of this hypothesis in connection with the "breakthrough" case of *Brown v. Board of Education,* see Bell, *Interest-Convergence Dilemma, supra,* at 524. For a more recent treatment confirming this hypothesis, see Mary L. Dudziak, *Desegregation as a Cold War Imperative,* 41 STAN. L. REV. 61, 62–63 (1988).

46. Beauharnais v. Illinois, 343 U.S. 250 (1952).

47. The most effective opponent of hate-speech regulation is the ACLU. *See, e.g.,* Marjorie Heins, *Banning Words: A Comment on "Words That Wound,"* 18 HARV. C.R.-C.L. L. REV. 585 (1983) (authored by an ACLU Staff Attorney); Strossen, *Regulating, supra,* at 489, 552–54.

48. *See* chapter 4 this volume (arguing that low-grade hassling benefits white-dominated institutions by keeping minorities on the defensive, preventing them from mobilizing around more costly reform measures, and assuring that students of color with spirit leave the institution).

49. For a comprehensive treatment of King's transformative rhetoric, see generally Anthony Cook, *Beyond Critical Legal Studies: The Reconstructive Theology of Dr. Martin Luther King, Jr.,* 103 HARV. L. REV. 985 (1990).

50. *Id.* at 1013, 1023–41 (analyzing King's theology and rhetoric); *see also* MARTIN LUTHER KING, JR., I HAVE A DREAM: WRITINGS AND SPEECHES THAT CHANGED THE WORLD (James Washington ed., 1992).

51. *See* WILLIAM L. SHIRER, THE RISE AND FALL OF THE THIRD REICH 231–76 (1960).

52. On the present-day use of the counterstory and its roots in trickster tales and picaresque humor, *see generally* Richard Delgado, *Storytelling for Oppositionists and Others: A Plea for Narrative,* 87 MICH. L. REV. 2411, 2411–15 (1989).

53. *Id.* at 2414. *See also* Kendall Thomas, *A House Divided against Itself: A Comment on "Mastery, Slavery, and Emancipation,"* 10 CARDOZO L. REV. 1481 (1989) (attempting to double-cross Hegel's construct of the Master/Slave relationship, inspired by African American trickster tales).

54. On the cultural-nationalist strain in recent race scholarship, see Gary Peller, *Race Consciousness*, 1990 Duke L.J. 758.

Notes to Chapter 10

* An earlier version of this chapter was written with the assistance of David Yun.

1. Fyodor Dostoyevski, The Brothers Karamazov 22 (Modern Lib. ed. 1950) (1880).

2. *Id.* at 26.

3. On free speech absolutism in general, or the ACLU position on hate speech and pornography in particular, see Alexander Meiklejohn, *The First Amendment Is an Absolute*, 1961 Sup. Ct. Rev. 245; Whitney v. California, 274 U.S. 357, 374–77 (1927) (Brandeis, J., concurring) (more speech, not suppression, is the solution for bad speech); Nadine Strossen, *In the Defense of Freedom and Equality*, 29 Harv. C.R.-C.L. L. Rev. 143 (1994); *Regulating Hate Speech on Campus: A Modest Proposal?*, 1990 Duke L. J. 484; Samuel Walker, Hate Speech: The History of an American Controversy (1994); Henry Louis Gates et al., Speaking of Race, Speaking of Sex: Hate Speech, Civil Rights, and Civil Liberties (1994) [hereinafter Speaking of Race]; Aryeh Neir, Defending My Enemy (1979).

4. On legal realism in general, see Felix Cohen, *Transcendental Nonsense and the Functional Approach*, 35 Colum. L. Rev. 809 (1935); Karl Llewellyn, *Some Realism about Realism . . . Responding to Dean Pound*, 44 Harv. L. Rev. 1222 (1931). Legal realism swept the law in the early years of this century, condemning to history the formalist view, attributed to Christopher Langdell and others, that law is a static, timeless science with one right answer for every question. *E.g.*, Roberto Unger, Knowledge and Politics 92–94 (1975) (on formalism and the view of law as a science). Realism holds that "the life of the law is experience," and that policy, wisdom, commonsense, and personal and class loyalties affect judicial outcomes as much as syllogistic logic, *e.g.*, Elizabeth Mensch, *The History of Mainstream Legal Thought*, in *The Politics of Law* 13, 21–24 (D. Kairys ed., rev. ed. 1990). *See also* chapter 3, this volume.

5. Wisconsin v. Mitchell, 113 S.Ct. 2194 (1993) (upholding penalty enhancement for bias-motivated crimes); Regina v. Keegstra, 3 S.C.R. 697 (Can. 1990) (upholding hate-speech legislation); Regina v. Butler, 89 D.L.R. 4th 449 (Can. 1992) (upholding antipornography measures). The Canadian free speech charter provisions are patterned after the U.S.'s First Amendment.

6. *See* chapters 6, 7, this volume.

7. For this reason, we will at times refer to the argument as the "periphery-center" one. At other times we will refer to it as the "single-valued jurisprudence"

or "totalistic" argument because it assumes only one supreme value, speech. See *infra*, analyzing and assessing several varieties of the argument.

8. *E.g.*, DEFENDING MY ENEMY, *supra*; SPEAKING OF RACE, *supra* (collection of essays on the need to defend Klansmen, cross-burners, Nazi marchers, and similar clients).

9. Most commentators who advance the argument simply assert some version of it (such as the slippery slope), without much support (for example, by showing why this particular slope is slippery). *E.g.*, DEFENDING MY ENEMY, *supra* (asserting that Jews need a strong First Amendment and thus that hate speech should flow freely). LEE BOLLINGER, THE TOLERANT SOCIETY (1986), comes closest to doing so. In a study of extremist (but not hate) speech, Bollinger identifies a number of mechanisms that might be supposed to connect the protection of extremist speech with protection of a central core of political speech [*e.g.*, 12–42, examining the idea that a *per se* rule protects against inadvertent encroachment on core speech functions; 43–75, evaluating claim that distrust of government argues against any form of regulation; 76–103, examining "fortress" model of First Amendment protection]. JOHN STUART MILL, ON LIBERTY (1882), puts forward the idea that speech must be broadly protected because what is thought error today may become tomorrow's truth [see text and *infra*, proposing that something similar may be taking place today regarding hate speech].

Other possibilities occur to us—that defending low-value, peripheral hate speech, a difficult exercise, keeps one fit and on one's toes (the overload principle); that defending peripheral speech will inculcate a general attitude of toleration among the citizenry so that all speech will flourish (the toleration argument, see Bollinger, *supra*); that, as in horticulture, attention to the periphery will cause the central core to be healthier (the pruning principle); that seeing others speak vigorously about *other* subjects will teach and encourage minorities to "talk back" to the hate speaker (the trickle-down theory) and thus the periphery will in time be no different from the core; and that speech is everywhere the same, and that therefore there is no core or periphery (the Platonic view of speech as essential, timeless, and devoid of contextual nuance or conditioning). Most of these hypothetical arguments for the principle of protecting the periphery have easy answers, and in any event except for the ones mentioned in the first paragraph of this note, are not put forward—to our knowledge, at any rate—by the argument's proponents.

10. SAMUEL WALKER, IN DEFENSE OF AMERICAN LIBERTIES: A HISTORY OF THE ACLU (1990).

11. SAMUEL WALKER, HATE SPEECH, *supra*, at 20, 165–67.

12. *Id.* at 20–21.

13. *Id.* at 160. For example, the ACLU defended the right of Father Terminiello, a suspended Catholic priest, to give a racist speech in Chicago. The United

States Supreme Court agreed with the ACLU in a landmark decision, Terminiello v. Chicago, 337 U.S. 1 (1949). Walker writes that the ACLU and other civil rights groups in the 1960s and 1970s were able to defend free speech rights of civil rights demonstrators by relying on *Terminiello. Id.* at 105–8.

14. SPEAKING OF RACE, *supra*, at 212.

15. Nadine Strossen, *A Feminist Critique of "The" Feminist Critique of Pornography*, 79 VA. L. REV. 1099, 1171 (1993).

16. SPEAKING OF RACE, *supra.*

17. *Id.*

18. *Id.* at 257–79.

19. *Id.*

20. Lee C. Bollinger, *The Skokie Legacy: Reflections on an "Easy Case" and Free Speech Theory*, 80 MICH. L. REV. 617, 629–31 (1982); LEE C. BOLLINGER, TOLERANT SOCIETY, *supra*; DEFENDING MY ENEMY, *supra* (making same general argument in case of Jews, who are in special need of an unfettered First Amendment).

21. LAURENCE H. TRIBE, AMERICAN CONSTITUTIONAL LAW, 12–8, at 838 n.17 (2d ed. 1988).

22. United States v. Schwimmer, 279 U.S. 644, 654–55 (1929).

23. Abrams v. United States, 250 U.S. 616, 630 (1919). *See* Schenk v. United States, 249 U.S. 47 (1919).

24. Brandenburg v. Ohio, 395 U.S. 444, 448 (1969). *See also* Community Party v. Subversive Activities Control Bd., 367 U.S. 1, 137 (1961) (Black, J., dissenting) ("freedoms of speech . . . must be accorded to the ideas we hate or sooner or later they will be denied to the ideas we cherish"); Cohen v. California, 403 U.S. 15, 22 (1971) ("even scurrilous speech must receive protection").

25. Collins v. Smith, 578 F.2d 1197 (7th Cir. 1978).

26. *See* Dennis v. United States, 341 U.S. 494 (1951).

27. On the infamous "Hollywood blacklist," and resulting exodus to Mexico and other countries by U.S. writers unable to obtain work, see JOHN COYLEY, REPORT ON BLACKLISTING (1956).

28. Mary L. Dudziak, *Josephine Baker, Racial Protest and the Cold War*, 81 J. AM. HIST. 543 (1994).

29. MARTIN B. DUBERMAN, PAUL ROBESON (1988); SHIRLEY GRAHAM, PAUL ROBESON: CITIZEN OF THE WORLD (1971).

30. GERALD HORNE, BLACK AND RED: W.E.B. DuBOIS AND THE AFRO-AMERICAN RESPONSE TO THE COLD WAR, 1944–1963 (1986).

31. On the recent right-wing barrage that has put liberals on the defensive, see Richard Delgado, *Stark Karst* (Book Review), 93 MICH. L. REV. (1995).

32. On the controversy over the National Endowment for the Arts, which has funded controversial artists like Mapplethorpe, see, *e.g.*, Robert Pear, *Chairwoman*

Comes "not to bury arts endowment but to praise it," DENVER POST, Jan. 27, 1995, at A4.

33. Mike Feinsilber, *A-bomb Exhibit to Shrink,* DENVER POST, Jan. 28, 1995, at A4, col. 2.

34. On the way in which hate speech can do this, see, *e.g.,* chapters 1, 4; Frank Michelman, *Response to Cass Sunstein, in* THE PRICE WE PAY: THE CASE AGAINST HATE SPEECH AND PORNOGRAPHY (Laura Lederer & Richard Delgado eds., Farrar, Straus, & Giroux 1996).

35. For our attempt to provide a number of possibilities, see text *supra.*

36. *See* Thomas Emerson, *Toward a General Theory of the First Amendment,* 72 YALE L.J. 877, 878–86 (1963) (setting out the underlying rationales of the First Amendment).

37. *E.g.,* Strossen, *Modest Proposal, supra* (terming the effect of hate speech a mere "anxiety" [at 492], "offensive" [at 497], "unpleasant" [at 499], or "harmful" [at 533]).

38. Rule utility justifies rules and principles by reason of the good (or evil) they produce; act utility judges the consequences of individual acts.

39. For example, "Nigger, get off this campus. Go back to Africa" conveys no new information, since the target obviously knows (1) he is African American, (2) his ancestors come from that continent, and (3) some individuals on campus hate him and wish he were not there.

40. *See, e.g.,* JEAN BAUDRILLARD, SIMULATIONS (1983) (on the real and the hyperreal in linguistic theory).

41. A principle of Kantian and Judeo-Christian ethics holds that human beings are valued not instrumentally—for what they can produce—but because of their value in themselves.

42. For example, privacy, property rights, the exercise of religion, the equal protection of the law, freedom from unreasonable searches and seizures, and from being enslaved.

43. *See, e.g.,* LAURENCE H. TRIBE, AMERICAN CONSTITUTIONAL LAW, *supra* at 861–86, 890–904, 931–34, 1046–47.

44. On these so-called exceptions, see chapter 4, this volume.

45. The term is our own. But it reflects the underlying values of neorepublicanism, the idea that deliberation by the citizenry lies at the heart of our system of law and politics. *See, e.g.,* Frank Michelman, *Law's Republic,* 97 YALE L.J. 1493 (1988); Cass Sunstein, *Beyond the Republican Revival,* 97 YALE L.J. 1539 (1988); Suzanna Sherry, *Civic Virtue and the Feminine Voice in Constitutional Adjudication,* 72 VA. L. REV. 543 (1986). Although a powerful political idea, neorepublicanism is not without its defects; see Richard Delgado, *Rodrigo's Fifth Chronicle: Civitas, Civil Wrongs, and the Politics of Denial,* 45 STAN. L. REV. 1581 (1993).

46. On the ubiquitous balancing test and its appearance in many areas of

constitutional law, see AMERICAN CONSTITUTIONAL LAW, *supra*, at 457, 789–94, 944–55, 987, 1037–39, 1251–55.

47. *See* DERRICK BELL, RACE, RACISM, AND AMERICAN LAW 26–30 (3d ed. 1993).

48. *Id.* at 30–36.

49. It was not necessary, in other words, to beat, threaten, or lynch every African American. Only an occasional such act was necessary, because every black knew of the system that supported or winked at such terroristic acts, and was thus constantly aware that he or she could easily become the next victim if he or she committed what the system considered a transgression.

50. On Americans' striking ignorance of Washington and national politics, see, *e.g.*, JAMES FISKLIN, DEMOCRACY AND DELIBERATION 57–64 (1991).

51. *Id.* at 63. *See also* PHYLLIS KANISE, MAKING LOCAL NEWS 110 (1990).

52. SUSAN FALUDI, BACKLASH (1990).

53. *E.g.*, Richard Delgado, *Rodrigo's Eighth Chronicle: Black Crime, White Fears: On the Social Construction of Threat*, 80 VA. L. REV. 503 (1994).

54. HARRY KALVEN, THE NEGRO AND THE FIRST AMENDMENT (1965) (arguing that civil rights gains would benefit all of society, including whites).

55. For example, Goss v. Lopez, 419 U.S. 565 (1975), strengthened due process rights in school disciplinary cases for all students, black or white; a host of cases assured the rights of peaceable assembly and protest [*e.g.*, RACE, RACISM, *supra*, at 424–43 (chapter 6, on rights of political protest)], and so on.

56. *See* R.A.V. v. City of St. Paul, Minnesota, 112 S. Ct. 2538, 2564–65 (1992) (Stevens, J., dissenting) (warning that the majority's opinion has turned First Amendment law on its head—fighting words that were once entirely unprotected are now entitled to greater protection than commercial, and possibly core political, speech).

57. *See* STEVE SHIFFRIN, THE FIRST AMENDMENT, DEMOCRACY, AND ROMANCE (1990) (First Amendment as romance). For a notable example of celebratory First Amendment jurisprudence, see ANTHONY LEWIS, MAKE NO LAW: THE SULLIVAN CASE AND THE FIRST AMENDMENT (1991).

Index

abolitionist movement, 140

abuse, racial. *See* racial insult(s)

Acacia fraternity, 53

ACLU, 41, 45, 53–54, 66, 95, 101, 107, 124, 138, 146, 149, 150, 151–52, 160, 161; in Michigan, 53; totalist argument, 158; in Wisconsin, 54

Adorno, Theodore, 60

African Americans, stereotypical treatment of, 71, 72–76

Agarwal v. Johnson, 13-14

aggression, and stigmatization, 100

Alcorn v. Anbro Engineering, Inc., 13, 21

Allport, Gordon, 61

Alyosha (Karamazov), 149

American-Arab Relations Committee, 124

American Civil Liberties Union. *See* ACLU

American Creed, 61

anti-Chinese legislation, 79

Anti-Defamation League of B'nai B'rith, 124

anti-discrimination imperative, 66

anti-Japanese: propaganda, 80; sentiment, 79

anti-Klan law, 50

anti-racism rules, campus. *See* hate speech regulations

anti-Semitism, 58, 151

apartheid, 125

Argentina, hate speech regulation in, 123

ARTICLE 19, 122, 124

Aryan supremacists, 161

Asian Americans: stereotypical treatment of, 78–80; anti-Asian films, 79

Association of American Law Schools, 143

asylum seekers, 127

Australia, hate speech regulation in, 58, 123, 128, 130

Austria, hate speech regulation in, 58, 127

"authoritarian personality," as source of racism, 60

Babette's Feast (film), 109

Balkin, Jack, 41

"bandido," as stereotype of Mexican Americans, 80

Battle at Elderbush Gulch, The (film), 77

BBC, 78

Beauharnais v. Illinois, 62–63

Beethoven, Ludwig van, 51

Bell, Derrick, 91, 147

"bellwether" argument, 114–15

"best friend" argument, 101–2

bigotry. *See* racism

Bill of Rights, speech community of, 142

Birth of a Nation, The (film), 29, 75

blackface minstrelsy, 73

blaming the victim, 120

blue eyes/brown eyes experiment, 100

Bob Jones University v. United States, 66

Bollinger, Lee, 152

Boyle, Kevin, 123

Bracero programs, 81

Bradshaw v. Swagerty, 15

Brandenburg v. Ohio, 153

Bricks without Straw (Tourgee), 75

Broken Arrow (film), 78

Brothers Karamazov, The (Dostoevsky), 149

Brown, William Wells, 73

Buffalo Bill series, 81

"buffoons," as stereotype of African Americans, 75

bullying, 100

Butler. See Regina v. Butler

Caliban, 77

campus anti-racism rules. *See* hate speech regulations

217